BRAZIL IN TRANSITION

POLITICS IN LATIN AMERICA
A HOOVER INSTITUTION SERIES

General Editor, **Robert Wesson**

Copublished with Hoover Institution Press,
Stanford University, Stanford, California

BRAZIL IN TRANSITION

Robert Wesson
David V. Fleischer

PRAEGER SPECIAL STUDIES • PRAEGER SCIENTIFIC

Library of Congress Cataloging in Publication Data

Wesson, Robert G.
  Brazil in transition.

  Bibliography: p.
  Includes index.
  1. Brazil—Politics and government—1954–
I. Fleischer, David V.   II. Title.
F2538.2.W47 1983   981'.06   82-16645
ISBN 0-03-063082-7
ISBN 0-03-063083-5 (pbk.)

*The Hoover Institution on War, Revolution and Peace,
founded at Stanford University in 1919 by the late President
Herbert Hoover, is an interdisciplinary research center for
advanced study on domestic and international affairs in the
twentieth century. The views expressed in its publications
are entirely those of the authors and do not necessarily
reflect the views of the staff, officers or Board of Overseers
of the Hoover Institution.*

Published in 1983 by Praeger Publishers
CBS Educational and Professional Publishing
a Division of CBS Inc.
521 Fifth Avenue, New York, New York 10175 U.S.A.

© 1983 by Praeger Publishers

3456789   052   987654321

Printed in the United States of America
on acid-free paper

Preface

This volume takes its place with the country studies that have already appeared in the Politics in Latin America Series of the Hoover Institution— works on Central America, Paraguay, Panama, Bolivia, Costa Rica, and Mexico. Like its predecessors, it aims to provide information on the background, institutions, problems, and policies of Brazil, in a form useful to all concerned with the affairs of our Latin American neighbors.

Brazil is a fascinating land, for its immensity, variety, and exoticism, from the promise of Amazonia to the flashing magic of Rio's carnival. It is intrinsically the most important country of Latin America, the industrial leader with more than one-third of the population of the entire region. Not least, it is something of a political trendsetter. At present it is engaged in a unique experiment in the gradual democratization of what was a few years ago an almost unqualified dictatorship. The outcome of this effort to qualify or unwind military government in a controlled and systematic way will be of huge importance not only for Brazil but also for Latin America and the Third World.

We express our appreciation to Ms. Margit Grigory for preparation of the manuscript and index. We are indebted to Professor Thomas Skidmore for reviewing parts and the whole of the manuscript.

Fleischer would like to thank his wife, Edyr, and their two children for their understanding and patience during the research and writing period in Albany, N.Y. The University of Brasília provided him research and sabbatical leave and the Brazilian National Research Council, a generous postdoctoral fellowship that made this project possible. The International Development Program at the State University of New York-Albany was the host institution during the elaboration of this book, and it made the research process functional and eased many burdens.

Fleischer's gratitude also goes to colleagues who read and commented on parts of his contribution to this book: Abdo Baaklini, Glaúcio Soares, Carlos Astiz, and Bolivar Lamounier. We are both indebted to the Hoover Institution for its support. The institutions and persons mentioned here, however, bear no responsibility for anything in this work.

This book is an equal collaboration, and both authors have gone over all parts. The order of names was decided by lottery.

Contents

Preface   v

Chapter One   THE AUTHORITARIAN-DEMOCRATIC
                 BACKGROUND   1
                 Independence   3
                 The Empire   4
                 The Old or First Republic   7
                 The Vargas Era   10
                 The Democratic Republic: 1945–64   14
                 Military Government: 1964   21
                 Notes   43

Chapter Two   BRAZIL AS A POLITICAL SOCIETY   47
                 Political-Electoral Styles   47
                 Political Participation   51
                 Political Socialization   52
                 Political Recruitment   54
                 Articulation and Interest Groups   56
                 Notes   71

Chapter Three   POLITICAL INSTITUTIONS   73
                 The Presidency   73
                 The Federal Bureaucracy   76
                 The Congress   79
                 The Judicial System   83
                 The Federal System   86
                 Notes   89

Chapter Four   POLITICAL PARTIES AND ELECTORAL
                 PROCESS   91
                 Historical Background   91
                 The Multiparty System: 1945–65   92
                 The Two-Party Experiment: 1966–79   103
                 The Restored Multiparty System   110
                 The 1982 Election   115

	Final Considerations	118
	Notes	120
Chapter Five	THE MILITARY	123
	Organization	123
	Political Role	128
	The Superior War College	132
	Security and Development	135
	Notes	138
Chapter Six	BRAZIL AND THE UNITED STATES	141
	Alliance	143
	Cooling Relations	145
	The United States and the Military Coup	149
	The Pro-United States Military Government	152
	Divergence	154
	Qualified Friendship	157
	Brazilian Foreign Policy	163
	Notes	165
Chapter Seven	CONCLUSION: THE BRAZILIAN CONDITION	167
	The Mixed Economy	167
	The Political Crux	174
	Notes	178
Bibliography		181
Index		187
About the Authors		199

1

The Authoritarian-
Democratic Background

Brazil, with half the area and population of South America, is set off from its Spanish-speaking neighbors not only by culture but by its distinctive history. For nearly half a millennium, Brazil has suffered less traumatic stress than any other major nation; it is possibly for this reason that its politics have long been more moderate than those of Spanish America.

It is probably true that, because of its exceptional continuity, Brazil is more the product of its past than most nations. Most of this past, from the Portuguese discovery (in 1500) to independence (de facto 1808, de jure 1822) was spent as a colony. In several ways, the Portuguese empire in the Americas differed from the contemporaneous Spanish empire. After Columbus's pioneering voyages the Spanish rapidly began to explore, conquer, and appropriate the vast territories of South and Central America, and they had basically completed this gigantic task by 1530. But Portugal did almost nothing to follow up the discovery of the Brazilian hump by a flotilla under Pedro Alvares Cabral in 1500. For Spain, power and riches came from the New World, where there were treasures to be looted and many millions of Indians to exploit and enserf. For Portugal, riches came from the Orient around Africa, following routes pioneered well before Columbus. The relatively few Indians of Brazil formed no great states and possessed no wealth. The land offered only a few jungle products, including logs called "brazilwood" that produced a red dye and gave the territory its name.

The first Portuguese town in Brazil was not established until 1532, and colonization did not begin in earnest until midcentury. An effort to set up captaincies for administrative purposes failed; but the population gradually increased, especially in the northern territories admirably suited for the cultivation of sugar. The Portuguese enslaved the Indians so far as possible; but when the Indians proved unsatisfactory and became scarce, Africans were imported in large numbers, especially from the Portuguese colony of Angola.

The three main racial components that have made up the unique Brazilian population were thus present early. The Portuguese were politically and economically dominant, but the separation between European-born and Brazilian-born was by no means so stark as the comparable division in Spanish America. Just as Portugal was less rigidly autocratic than Spain, the Brazilian upper classes were less stiffly reactionary than those of Spanish America. Few Portuguese women crossed the ocean, and settlers mixed freely with Indians and to a lesser extent with Negroes. The native population as such was largely exterminated; the raids of the *bandeirantes*, from about 1600 to 1750, amounted to large-scale Indian hunts. Yet the Indian contribution to the Brazilian stock and heritage should not be understated. Most of the *bandeirante* Indian-chasers were themselves part Indian,[1] and the Tupi language (close to the Guarani spoken in Paraguay) predominated in São Paulo and much of northern Brazil until the middle of the eighteenth century.[2] Until recent decades there was much interest in the study of Tupi, and it gave some 20,000 words to Brazilian Portuguese.

After surviving conflicts with the French and Dutch in the seventeenth century, colonial Brazil half-slumbered under a careless Portuguese administration for nearly two centuries. However, the discovery of gold in 1693 in what is now Minas Gerais ("General Mines") and of diamonds in the same area in 1727 caused the government in Lisbon to take a serious interest in its huge American estate. The administration was tightened, more controls were imposed, and the capital was transferred from Salvador, in the sugar country, to Rio de Janeiro, nearer the mines. Brazil was the world's leading producer of both gold and diamonds for a few decades. The Portuguese state was swamped with wealth comparable, relatively speaking, to the petrodollars of Saudi Arabia. Brazil prospered and saw rapid growth of population, both free and slave, and for the first time settlement spread significantly inland.

In the latter part of the eighteenth century, however, the deposits were thinned, revenues shrank, and discontent increased. Portuguese rule was always laxer than Spanish, but the colonials had ample reason to complain. The Brazilians were subject to extremely detailed regulation, down to the styles of clothing various classes should wear, and regulation was for the benefit of Portuguese interest. There were many legal monopolies, and nothing could be produced that Portuguese merchants might wish to sell in the colony. All manufacturing was forbidden. All trade with the outside world was to be by Portuguese ships and via Portugal. Brazil thus acquired a heritage of state intervention in the economy.

It also acquired a heritage of great social inequality. Under slavery, the traditional Iberian dislike for anything that could be called work, especially physical work, became a horror. A gentleman had to have a Negro carry any burden on the street, even a book. The upper classes would set out only in chairs slung from poles, somewhat like the sedans of oriental mandarins, accompanied by a squad of slaves. The ruling oligarchs were either officials, royal appointees, high clerics, or in larger numbers, the masters of huge plantations that amounted to feudal dominions. A Portuguese writer in 1799 justly blamed the woes of Brazil on slavery, backward agriculture, and latifundia.[3]

INDEPENDENCE

From the middle of the eighteenth century, the hold of Portugal on its enormous colony was becoming infirm. That small country, hurt rather than helped by the flow of unearned wealth, was sinking, like Spain, into the poverty that was to envelop it in modern times. On the other hand, Brazilian nationalism was blossoming, as Brazilians contemplated the beauty, riches, and abundance of their land and asked why the people, or most of the people, should be so poor—a question that has not been laid to rest to this day.

As controls became ineffective, the British were able to dominate foreign trade with the connivance of venal officials. With freedom of smuggling came freedom of thinking, and censorship was futile against the popularity of such writers as Rousseau, Voltaire, Adam Smith, Diderot, and Montesquieu. The American Revolution made a deep impression as the victory of fellow colonials over oppression. Likewise, the French Revolution, with its vibrant call for the Rights of Man, captivated Brazilians who had learned to admire French culture and thought. Republican thinking became widespread, even among the middle classes.

In 1789 a handful of fairly prominent men of the mining region of Minas Gerais formed a conspiracy in protest against taxation measures. They hoped to spark a rebellion in favor of a republic on the model of the United States. The plot was betrayed, and the leader, a dentist nicknamed *Tiradentes* ("Toothpuller"), was executed. (He eventually became the prime Brazilian national martyr-hero.) A little later, in 1798, a few middle-class men of Bahia formed a conspiracy for "liberty, equality, and fraternity," and various other subsequent movements showed the spread of republican talk.[4]

Brazilian independence might have been long delayed, however, if Napoleon had not invaded Iberia in 1807. Rather than surrender, the Portuguese court took flight. With British assistance, 60 ships carried not only the government but most of the Portuguese aristocracy, some 1,500 persons, to Brazil. Rio de Janeiro suddenly found itself converted from an administrative outpost to the capital of the far-spread Portuguese empire.

The influx brought new prosperity, and King João VI immediately opened the ports to the trade of all nations. For the first time, too, Brazil was governed as a unit; Portuguese America thus escaped the fractioning of Spanish America in and after the independence struggle. Upon the defeat of Napoleon in 1814, the government was free to return to Lisbon, but João had come to like his new residence, which in 1815 was raised to the status of kingdom. The Portuguese summoned João back, but he tarried until 1821, when he was faced with an ultimatum threatening the loss of his throne. On departing, he turned the Brazilian realm over to his son Pedro.

The Brazilians by this time had become accustomed to managing their own affairs, and nearly all of Spanish America had gained independence. Consequently, when the Portuguese government tried to recall Brazil to colonial subordination in 1822 and demanded that Pedro return to complete his education in Portugal, he was easily persuaded to proclaim independence. The new nation was declared an empire, to assert not merely equality with but superiority over the homeland. Thanks to the intercession of Britain, the Portuguese made no effort to reimpose their rule by force, and in 1825 recognized Brazil's independence. In compensation for its services, Britain received a favorable trade treaty, which, in the opinion of some, made Brazil an economic colony, almost a British protectorate, until the agreement expired in 1844.

THE EMPIRE

After independence, there were several regional revolts, and the imperial authority was not consistently firm until midcentury. Brazil, however, having become independent with no discontinuity of authority, suffered only a slight counterpart of the disorders that afflicted Spanish America in this period. Emperor Pedro I had a constituent assembly elected to adopt a constitution in 1823, but it turned out to be much too democratic. He quickly clashed with it, dissolved it, and had his own committee draw up a constitution to his liking. This became, after approval by municipal councils, the basic law of the empire until 1889, one of the most enduring constitutions in Latin American history.[5]

Pedro was immensely popular as the leader of independence, but he had an abrasive personality and preferred Portuguese to Brazilians. He was unjustly blamed in 1827 for the loss of southern lands that became Uruguay, and the French Revolution of 1830 exemplified the replacement of an inflexible monarch. Consequently, when Pedro insisted on an unpopular cabinet in 1831, he was compelled to abdicate in favor of his four-year-old son.

Pedro II, prematurely declared emperor at the age of 15, presided over the empire from 1841 until its demise in 1889. It was a constitutional monarchy, dominated, as Brazil has been until recent years, by a landholding aristocracy. There was an elected lower house of parliament and an appointed senate. The emperor, endowed with the power of "moderator," named ministers and could suspend laws. But freedoms of religion, of speech, and of the press were guaranteed by the constitution—Brazil has almost always, through many political vicissitudes, enjoyed a free press except under the Vargas dictatorship (1937–45) and during some years of the recent military government (1968–78).

The cabinet needed parliamentary backing, and Pedro allowed the parliament considerable authority but exercised his power to dissolve it. He balanced the Liberal and Conservative parties; cabinets lasted, on the average, little more than a year.[6] The parliament closely followed British precedents. However, those in office were quite free to manipulate elections, which served mostly to confirm post facto the emperor's choice of government. The political principle of the empire, which has prevailed most of the time since, was closely held authority tempered by personal liberty.

Progress was slow. The Portuguese colonial overlords had not favored education, and the Brazilian oligarchy did not see much need to promote it. Literacy at the beginning of the empire was 10 percent; at the end it was only 15 percent. Newspapers were permitted only after independence. Whereas Spanish America had several universities early in colonial times, Brazil had none until 1920, although several law and medical schools were established shortly after independence.

Brazilians slavishly imitated European styles, even to the use of British woolens in tropic heat; the language of the court was French. Society was patriarchic; the father ruled the family, and the monarch stood fatherlike over his people. There was much fondness for ranks and titles; eminent men were made "duke" or "baron" of this or that. Social position rested mostly on ownership of huge plantations; a holding of several square miles was considered small. Despite the immensity of the country and the small population of about five million, there was a severe shortage of land for small farmers along the coastal plain.

Like styles, the economy was foreign-dominated, and trade was in the hands of foreigners. It was taken for granted that Brazil exported raw products and imported manufactures. The colony had gone through cycles of prosperity based on various commodities—brazilwood, sugar, gold, and diamonds—and in the nineteenth century coffee was replacing sugar as the chief source of wealth.[7] A feature of the economy that has remained throughout most of subsequent Brazilian history was inflation, generated by the expansion of the money supply to cover recurrent deficits.

The cultured, intelligent, and well-intentioned Pedro II was one of the most capable rulers Latin America has known. But the monarchy was an anomaly in the otherwise republican hemisphere, the strength and prosperity of the democratic United States were impressive, and Europe was generally moving toward more representative government. Brazil was especially impressed by the fall of Napoleon III in France in 1870. Free speech and the lively press favored republicanism, which became increasingly popular after about 1868.

In 1870 a Republican Club issued a manifesto and inaugurated a campaign for an end to the empire. The positivist philosophy of Auguste Comte, looking to the scientific organization of society for rational progress, became widespread and merged into republican thinking. Pedro II seems to have had no royalist convictions, and he made no effort to repress subversive ideas or to sustain the dynasty.

Support for the monarchy was also eroded by more material causes. There was an economic slump, 1880–86, because of a fall in the price of coffee, which constituted two-thirds of exports. The free-thinking Pedro came into conflict with the Catholic hierarchy over the question of Freemasonry. Although the quarrel was settled and the church remained opposed to republicanism, it lost enthusiasm for the monarchy.

Pedro was also victim of his virtues in the slavery question. Plantation agriculture, especially in the sugar-producing northern regions, had been based on slavery from the beginning of the colonial period, and slaves were about half of the population of four million at the time of independence.[8] It was widely believed that slavery was indispensable to tropical agriculture, but there was an abolitionist movement from the beginning of the empire. The importation of slaves was forbidden under British pressure, theoretically from 1830, in practice from 1852, although the British were accused of wanting to stop the slave trade less for humanitarian reasons than to hurt Brazilian sugar production. Miscegenation was accepted, racial prejudice was not intense, and attitudes were often rather paternalistic. Many slaves were set free, or allowed to earn their freedom, and the freedmen were treated tolerantly; the proportion of slaves shrank during the empire from more than half to about 5 percent of a population grown to 14 million.

After the Paraguayan war (1865–70), there was an emotional anti-slavery drive, which the emperor joined. Several measures were passed for the gradual elimination of slavery, but they did not work fast enough to satisfy the country. The military authorities refused to cooperate in returning runaways, and in 1888 the parliament under Conservative leadership abolished slavery without compensation. Although slavery had clearly become uneconomic, its sudden end brought some dislocation until it could be replaced by a wage system (which left the Negroes economically no better off). The move was very popular, but the emperor received little credit, while the former slaveholders, who had been his most faithful supporters, saw no reason to continue to stand by the monarchy that had failed them.

Worst of all, Pedro found himself at odds with the military. Because Brazil did not have to fight for independence and engaged in only a few minor wars in its first decades, the military establishment was (unlike its counterparts in Spanish-speaking countries) small and politically weak through most of the period of the empire. The war with Paraguay, however, expanded it from 17,000 to more than 100,000, made military heroes, and gave the marshals and generals a sense of importance. They consequently began taking political positions, at least in defense of military interests, and they saw the emperor as insensitive to their sacrifices (some 40,000 were lost in the war) and needs. Pedro, the scholar and thinker, was not congenial to the military men, and instead of taking their advice, he sought to reduce their budget and to bring them more closely under control.

THE OLD OR FIRST REPUBLIC

The weakness and lack of legitimacy of the empire were such that minor discontents of the military sufficed to induce the highest officer, Marshal Deodoro da Fonseca, to surround the palace and announce the overthrow of the old order on November 15, 1889. There was no resistance, and Pedro went quietly into exile. The military took power, and they have retained at least residual authority over the state ever since. So far as civilian leaders have been formally in control, they have always had to defer to the armed forces and to attend to its needs.

In 1891 a constitution was drafted, rather closely patterned after that of the United States.[9] Brazil was made a federal republic with extensive autonomous powers for the states, which kept their own militias. There was an elected congress, and the president was chosen for a four-year nonrenewable term by popular vote, illiterates excluded. The motto of the republic was the positivist "Order and Progress," and its outlook was semiauthoritarian; a minority frankly desired a "scientific dictatorship" with republican trappings, perhaps something like the state instituted after 1964.

Marshal Deodoro became the first president, but he lacked political talents. Finding his ideas of a positivist order uncongenial to the Congress, he treated it roughly and dissolved it, only to have to resign himself. Deodoro was replaced by another marshal, Floriano Peixoto. The armed forces, however, were divided, and in 1893–95 there was a mutiny of naval forces allied with conservative and federalist groups of the southern states of Rio Grande do Sul and Santa Catarina. This schism enabled the Paulistas (of São Paulo) to assert themselves and to secure the election of a civilian president, Prudente de Morais, in 1894. Prudente was continually beset by military opposition, but he managed to finish his term. Thereafter to 1930, presidents were duly elected, and all except Marshal Hermes da Fonseca (1910–14) were civilians.

In this republican era, power lay basically with the landed gentry, commonly called "colonels" because of their positions in the national guard. Their political capital was the loyalty or docility of their peasants and dependents. They supported the state governor, who in return let them govern locally; the governors cooperated with the president, who let them manage their states.

The outgoing president had the largest voice in the selection of his successor, who usually won an overwhelming majority in managed elections, in which less than 2 percent of the population participated. A party victorious in an election would regularly disqualify opposition deputies. It became the practice to alternate the presidency between the two strongest and richest states, São Paulo and Minas Gerais. Parties were only statewide; no new national parties arose to replace the Liberals and Conservatives of the empire. The chief function of the state was to furnish jobs for needy members of the upper-middle and upper classes.

Despite narrowly oligarchic and corrupt government, Brazil prospered. Following the abolition of slavery, immigration flowed from Europe; the new arrivals, however, settled in the southern states only. Their numbers were never comparable to those going to the United States at the same time and were even less than the flow to Argentina, but they were largely responsible for the growth of industry. From the time of the founding of the republic, some Brazilians began dreaming of modernization and industrialization like that of the United States and Germany around this time, and a protective tariff was set in place to promote import substitution. For 30 years after 1898, however, the economy was based on coffee, while little was done for manufacturing. The government was dominated by the coffee barons, chiefly the planters of São Paulo. From the 1880s to the 1910s, spectacular riches came from the rubber boom, based on tapping trees of the Amazon jungle, but the boom was punctured by the competition of cheaper and better rubber from Oriental plantations, and it never greatly affected the economic center of Brazil.

During this period, when agriculture was the accepted vocation of Brazil, there was exceptional monetary stability because the producers wished to maintain the value of currency to purchase imported wares. President Manuel Campos Sales (1898–1902) cut expenditures, raised taxes, and balanced the budget in a fashion seldom possible in Brazilian history. The next several presidents continued policies of fiscal soundness, and the Brazilian currency was made convertible with fixed exchange rates, something now inconceivable. Trade prospered, and foreign firms became ever more conspicuous. Of 201 corporations authorized between 1899 and 1919, 160 were foreign, mostly British.[10] São Paulo in the 1910s furnished about half of Brazil's exports and a third of federal resources. The state of São Paulo consequently felt entitled to leadership, giving a junior role to Minas Gerais, with a larger population, and leaving other states far behind.

With coffee exports producing large amounts of foreign exchange, Brazil built up its navy to one of the world's largest, although ammunition had to be imported. In World War I, Brazil was from the first partial to the Allies. In 1917, after German submarines sank several Brazilian ships, Brazil entered the war. The hostilities at first disrupted foreign trade, but soon export surpluses began piling up, and industrial production, already growing steadily, doubled during the war years because of the inability of the warring powers to supply the market. The war years also saw the beginning of U.S. penetration of the Brazilian economy. The National City Bank established branches in Brazil in 1915, and other U.S. investments quickly followed. After the war, Americanization continued to replace Europeanization, bringing a more active spirit, fondness for technology, and a new passion for wealth through production.

Prosperity and optimism continued for a few years after the end of the war, but from 1922 tensions increased. Nationalists were beginning to raise a clamor for the nationalization of commerce and the retention of profits in the country. The growing cities, which could not be governed in the same simple way as the countryside, were becoming focuses of discontent. Most serious was civil-military conflict. There was a taste of it in 1910, when the conservatives turned to a military candidate to prevent the elevation to the presidency of a popular national figure, Rui Barbosa, who for the first time carried the campaign to the people in the name of antimilitarism. When Marshal Hermes da Fonseca was declared elected, the liberals felt grievously cheated.

In the 1920s military leaders, especially young lieutenants (*tenentes*), felt aggrieved by the unresponsiveness and selfishness of the governing oligarchy. In the positivist tradition, they believed it was up to the military to purify the nation, to provide honest government, and to promote modernization, after which democracy could become a reality. A candidate favored by the military was defeated in 1922 by the governor of Minas, Artur da Silva Bernardes. The senior officers accepted the defeat, but President Bernardes was troubled by a series of revolts from 1922 on. He instituted a state of siege and imposed press censorship when the *tenentes* rose again in 1924. The rebels were defeated after nearly three weeks of fighting in São Paulo and Parana. But some of them withdrew under the leadership of Captain Luis Carlos Prestes, who led the "Prestes Column" of about 1,500 men on an odyssey 14,000 miles back and forth across the interior[11] (and who afterwards became the permanent leader of the Brazilian Communist Party). By this time there was growing nostalgia for the empire as the good old times of order.

In 1926 Bernardes turned over the administration to a Paulista, Washington Luis Pereira de Souza, who lifted censorship and the state of siege. Coffee prices had recovered, and the country seemed more tranquil in restored prosperity. In 1929, however, commodity markets began the collapse leading to the great depression, which hit international trade with special violence. Coffee prices fell to a third or less of former levels partly because of overplanting during the golden years. Bankruptcies multiplied, and discontent mounted. In this condition, the election of 1930 was certain to be contested, and Washington Luis made the error of seeking to impose another Paulista as his successor.

The Old Republic was ready to collapse. After administering the country fairly well for a couple of decades, the political elite had failed entirely to absorb the new forces of the growing nation. The oligarchy, to the contrary, narrowed itself; the percentage of the population voting actually decreased, 1894 to 1926, from 2.5 percent to 2 percent, and leaders refused to consider such an elementary step toward democracy as the secret ballot. Their answer to the rising impatience of younger officers, the intellectuals, and the growing middle classes of the cities was immobility.

THE VARGAS ERA

The Old Republic was brought down by the ineptitude of President Washington Luis. In 1929 he defied the tradition of alternating the presidency and promoted his protégé, São Paulo governor Júlio Prestes, to become president in 1930. The indignant politicians of Minas, to strengthen their position, picked a young former governor from the southern state of Rio Grande do Sul, Getúlio Vargas, as the candidate of the anti-Paulista movement. They were joined in a "Liberal Alliance" by a multitude of persons, from army officers to Communists, who had become discontented with the narrow and decadent regime and saw in the quarrel of the two principal states an opportunity to break the grip of the oligarchy.

Vargas did not reach for his destiny as the leading figure of modern Brazilian history; greatness was pushed upon him. He was a politician of the old school who got his start through his father's station as a big rancher. He entered the state assembly, served as finance minister in the cabinet of Washington Luis, and was state governor 1928–30, all without displaying any reformist fervor. After becoming opposition candidate, he promised not to campaign outside his state and to accept the (preordained) victory of the official candidate. However, when he visited the main centers, the national mood was such that he was caught up in the general oppositionist enthusiasm. The Liberal Alliance, meanwhile, was pressing for land reform, and many military leaders, mostly former *tenentes*, were scheming for an armed uprising.

Júlio Prestes was duly declared elected by a large margin, and Vargas declined to challenge the results. Because of his diffidence, the preparations for military action seemed to have collapsed by June 1930. It happened, however, that the Liberal Alliance candidate for vice president, João Pessoa, governor of the northern state of Paraiba, was assassinated in September 1930 by a personal political enemy. The pro-Vargas forces were aroused to launch an attack, and the high military authorities gave them success by refusing to fight for Washington Luis against what seemed plainly to be a popular cause—the first time the Brazilian army deposed a civilian president.

The discontented faction of the oligarchy would have preferred merely to correct the results of the elections, but demand for basic change, especially on the part of the former *tenentes*, was so strong that the constitution was set aside and Vargas became personal ruler. He proceeded to carry out a purge of the old order, naming presidential representatives, "interventors," in place of elected governors and placing state militias under federal command, leaving the old local powers in place but subordinate to himself.

In 1932 the resentful Paulistas attempted to rebel, but other states, fearful of Paulista domination, stood by Vargas, as did the working classes of São Paulo. The Paulista government gave up after a three-month siege. There were no strong reprisals, and the federal government even assumed São Paulo's war debt, but the federal supremacy was definitely established, and the rural-dominated political system was at an end.

A constitutional assembly was elected in 1933 in response to the Paulista uprising, and in 1934 a democratic constitution was adopted. It provided for a secret ballot and suffrage for women, but it continued the limitation of the franchise to the literate, then about 20 percent of the adult population. Like the Mexican constitution, it consecrated the social functions of the state. A fraction (one-sixth) of deputies to the congress were to be elected by professional organizations, mostly employers, labor unions, and public servants, in a bow to fascist-corporate theory. Vargas was elected by the assembly to a four-year term as president without serious opposition in 1934, and legislative elections were held in 1935.

Politics was agitated by extremism, however, reflecting the confrontation of communists and fascists in Europe. There were radical leftist currents in Brazil from the beginning of the century, and a Comintern-affiliated Communist Party was founded in 1922.[12] It was of little importance until the depression, but its message of economic nationalism, expropriation of foreign corporations, and division of estates became attractive in hard times. Luis Carlos Prestes, the *tenente* who marched his column across the backlands and became a legendary Robin Hood figure, the "Knight of Hope," gave up on conventional politics, joined the Communist Party in May 1930, and went to the Soviet Union to live for several years. The party gained strength; in 1935 it had as many as 10,000 members,[13] much influence in the labor movement, and sympathizers in the armed forces.

In 1935 there were many strikes and riots, and Prestes and his fellows prepared for a revolution. In November an insurgency was begun by groups of soldiers and noncommissioned officers, entire regiments revolting in some places. Although the mutineers were mostly non-Communist, Prestes quickly joined the movement to turn it into a Communist revolution. There was no broad support among workers or the general public, however, and the uprising was repressed without difficulty. The result was a purge of the leftists, the banning of the Communist Party, and an allergy for communism in the armed forces that contributed to the military coup of 1964.

The fascists, or Integralistas, hoped the fiasco of the Communist uprising would bring them to power. The green-shirted Integralista Party of Plínio Salgado frankly imitated the successful parties of Mussolini and Hitler, with a uniformed corps, symbols, salutes, and opposition to communism, democracy, Masons, and Jews. It enjoyed the backing of Nazi Germany and of many members of the armed forces, especially naval officers—the popularity of its authoritarian ideas foreshadowed the "hard line" in the forces after 1964. Vargas sought the support of the Integralistas and borrowed from their doctrines, but he had no intention of admitting them to power. To the contrary, as the time approached for presidential elections in 1938, Vargas dramatically discovered a new Communist plot, the "Cohen Plan," forged by Olímpio Mourão Filho (who prematurely sparked the revolution of 1964). Vargas closed the congress by force without serious resistance and with the backing of the armed forces, and he decreed a new constitution, making himself dictator at the New State (*Estado Novo*). Plínio Salgado and his party, angry at being excluded, tried—almost successfully—to murder Vargas in May 1938 and were banned.

The constitution of 1937 was drawn up in advance by Francisco Campos, who was later responsible for the early constitutional documents ("Institutional Acts") of the 1964 military government. Campos was convinced of the need for a strong government to organize the nation. Under the constitution he drafted, the president had full legislative powers, even power to amend the constitution. It contained many social provisions, such as the promise of a minimum wage, but it made no provision for any kind of input from the people. The constitution, so far as it was one, was to take effect after a plebiscite, but Vargas never held one.[14]

The Vargas coup was generally viewed in the United States and Europe as fascist, and it seemed more or less such. Vargas was obviously inspired by the fascist tide in Europe. He ruled by decree, censored the press, repressed party politics, jailed his opponents (usually briefly), filled the airwaves with propaganda, and had his picture displayed in shops and offices. He exalted fascist virtues and proclaimed the decadence and death of democracy, at least until the elites taught the people how to be properly democratic. Yet he claimed that his state was not Nazi-fascist, and he was correct. He had no compulsory ideology beyond a vague nationalism, and he had no fascist-style mass party. His political style was not far from the traditional, as he upheld his own position by balancing various interests and factions and by satisfying pressing needs.

Vargas's policies were pragmatic and flexible and looked perceptively to new forces and new directions. He favored urban over rural interests, and industry over agriculture; his was a victory over the coffee interests, although he supported coffee prices at considerable cost to the treasury. He appealed especially to labor but remained attentive to public opinion and refrained from offending the old upper class.

One of Vargas's major achievements was promotion of industrialization with government planning, assistance, and, in some cases, participation. The depression seemed to show the need for self-sufficiency, and he began the program of import substitution that has remained the hallmark of Brazilian economic policy. Protective tariffs were raised to virtually exclude most imported consumer goods, and foreign access to Brazilian natural resources was restricted. In 1934 a National Petroleum Council was organized, forming the basis for the subsequent petroleum monopoly, Petrobras. Industrial plants tripled, 1930–40, and industrial production grew 11 percent annually, 1933–39.[15]

The promotion of industrialization was accompanied or preceded by the oganization of labor. Soon after coming to power, Vargas set up a ministry of labor, recognized the right of workers to organize, began government sponsorship of unions, and passed legislation (not fully effective) for a 48-hour workweek, minimum wages, paid vacations, medical benefits, educational facilities, job security, and pensions. Despite the cornucopia of benefits and the large growth in the number of unions, Vargas did not propose to give the workers political power. The minister of labor intervened in unions, managed their elections, and controlled their funds. One cost of the expansionist program was deficit financing; since 1931 inflation has been endemic in Brazil.

Although the Vargas New State was generally accepted because of doubts of the ability of representative government to meet the challenges of the times, it might well have encountered grave problems in a few years had there been no world war. But the prolonged world crisis of 1939–45 shielded it from serious opposition. The somewhat tardy decision to align Brazil with the United States was popular, as was the declaration of war against Germany, made after the sinking of many Brazilian ships, and the dispatch of an expeditionary force to Italy.

The war also helped Vargas's economic program. It became possible for the first time to export important quantities of Brazilian manufactures, and industry boomed. The first big state enterprise, the Vale do Rio Doce mining company, was established, and the old project of a steel plant at Volta Redonda was realized with U.S. assistance, all to the benefit of Vargas's prestige.

THE DEMOCRATIC REPUBLIC: 1945–64

While promoting national integration, industrialization, and the well-being of labor, Vargas presided over the rapid maturation of Brazil, the growth of old and new cities, the advancement of previously neglected education, and the expansion of transportation and communications, uniting the country and linking people, parties, and government. But Vargas's style of personal manipulation—he rarely held cabinet meetings—was increasingly inadequate. Moreover, the temper of the times changed. If a semifascist state was acceptable in the 1930s, it was no longer so when democratic powers were crushing fascism in Europe.

Vargas recognized that change was inevitable, and from 1942 he kept vaguely promising democracy after the war. Early in 1945 the press began defying censorship, and the authorities felt unable to take action.[16] When the expeditionary force came home, Vargas was rightly apprehensive; those who had fought for democracy in Italy were not prepared to tolerate dictatorship at home. Vargas bowed and scheduled elections for December. In preparation for the elections, the three parties that were to dominate the scene until the military coup were formed: the Brazilian Labor Party (PTB), to mobilize Vargas's working-class backing; the Social Democratic Party (PSD), to organize middle-class and rural support for Vargas; and the National Democratic Union (UDN), to unite the enemies of Vargas, many of whom looked back to the Old Republic.

As the election neared, Vargas indicated no successor but permitted large rallies of "Queremistas" to shout "We want Getúlio" ("*Queremos Getúlio*"), while friends of Vargas suggested that a constituent assembly should come before presidential elections. The suspicion grew that Vargas was maneuvering to remain in office, as he had in 1937, and when he named his brother to be police chief, a group of generals informed him that he was no longer in charge.

To the regret of many, Vargas yielded and withdrew to his ranch, and the chief justice of the Supreme Court became caretaker president. In the elections of December 1945, Vargas's former minister of war, Eurico Dutra, was chosen president. A congress was also elected, with authorization to draw up a new constitution. Among the members of the Senate was Getúlio Vargas, who was also elected deputy in several states.

The constitution adopted in 1946 was in several ways a reaction against the years of dictatorship.[17] It circumscribed the powers of the presidency and broadened those of the Congress, creating a potential for conflict between a president responsible to the voters in general and a congress subject to the still influential rural oligarchies of the overrepresented, smaller, and poorer states. The congress, elected by proportional representation, was hardly capable of positive policies but could effectively check the president. The states recovered autonomy, but less than they had known prior to 1930. The judiciary was also strengthened against the executive and authorized to declare laws unconstitutional; it was made the most independent in South America. Measures had been taken earlier to guarantee honest elections through a system of electoral courts, and elections have been reasonably clean since 1945.

Dutra was elected, with the unenthusiastic endorsement of Vargas, as candidate of the PTB and the PSD, but he followed his own conservative course. Dutra's main qualification had been lack of political ambition, and his administration was colorless, as he adhered to the constitution, invited the UDN to join his government, and favored private enterprise. He upheld freedom generally, except for banning the Communist Party (PCB).

Legalized because of the Soviet role in the war, the PCB in 1945 elected a senator and 14 deputies, and in elections for state legislatures in 1947, it polled 10 percent of the votes. The party had an estimated 200,000 members, controlled major unions, and showed enough agitational potential to alarm conservatives.[18] Prestes repeatedly made it clear that in case of conflict with the Soviet Union, Brazilian Communists should favor that country. The Supreme Court declared the party illegal on grounds of antidemocratic statutes, and Communists were removed from official positions, including elected ones. When the Soviet Union sneered at the action, Brazil broke diplomatic relations, with the approval of the United States in the deepening cold war. The status of the Communist Party was a chronic issue in subsequent years and an acute one in the last months of the democratic republic in 1964.

Dutra gave the people freedom to choose their next president in 1950, and their choice was the aging ex-dictator. Vargas had been speaking of himself as a victim of agents of imperialism, attributing his ouster in 1945 to interests desirous of keeping Brazil economically dependent, and he held himself as the most devoted servant of the people and "father of the poor." He promised more social benefits and industrialization, and the message was sufficiently convincing that Vargas received nearly half of the votes and half again as many as his nearest rival. His new lease on power was not successful, however. Vargas seems to have desired to be elected president mostly to confound his critics, and he had little in the way of positive program and was not much interested in a limited presidency. He was unable to do much in face of opposition in Congress and of the distrust of many of the military. His administration was marred by corruption, growing perhaps worse than ever before in Brazilian history. By 1953 he was regretting having left his ranch.

Vargas steered a moderately leftist course, however. In 1952 he decreed a limit to remittances by foreign corporations. In 1953 he established a petroleum monopoly, Petrobras, to exploit what were hopefully assumed to be the huge oil resources of Brazil. The nation, especially leftists and nationalists, applauded. This was a reversal of Dutra's position that U.S. companies should be invited to produce Brazilian oil. Vargas named as minister of labor João Goulart, a wealthy ranch owner and a neighbor of Vargas who was an even more opportunistic politician, prepared to work with Communists in the unions. Goulart early in 1954 tried to double minimum wages (inflation had picked up sharply after Vargas took office), but he was forced out by an indignant manifesto signed by many officers up to the rank of colonel, complaining that soldiers were paid less than laborers.

Sentiment was running against Vargas in the military, but his presidency was brought to an end by deeds not his. Vargas was annoyed by the steady beat of criticism from a leading journalist-politician, Carlos Lacerda, who was even more violent than he was eloquent. Air force officers formed a guard to protect Lacerda from an apparent danger of assassination. An attempt was made and bungled; in it, an air force major was killed. The air force investigated and found that leaders of Vargas's personal guard were implicated in the murder as well as in much corruption. It seemed to the military that honor demanded that Vargas resign or take leave; rather than withdraw a second time, he shot himself on August 24, 1954.

From the point of view of his place in history, Vargas did well, because he lifted himself from a failure, humiliated by criminal subordinates, to a martyr of the cause of the people. Crowds that had been hostile to him turned around to attack his enemies immediately after hearing the broadcast of his suicide note.[19] It was a somewhat confused and illogical message, but it was highly effective emotionally, blaming his and Brazil's troubles on selfish interests, foreign and domestic, and proclaiming the sacrifice of his life for his beloved people. It markedly raised the temperature of confrontation for years thereafter. The Communist Party (active although illegal) had been denouncing Vargas before his suicide, but afterward it identified its cause with that of the "father of the people." Vargas became a symbol of the masses and of populist politics.

Twice removing Vargas from power politicized the military and gave many officers the feeling that civilian politicians could not properly manage the nation. In the somewhat confused sequence of temporary presidencies after Vargas, the military continued to play a decisive part in the settlement of power, at one time setting aside the vice president, João Café Filho. Elections in 1955 gave victory to a moderate of the Vargas camp, the PSD-PTB candidate, Minas Gerais governor Juscelino Kubitschek. He won 36 percent of the votes in a divided field against Júarez Távora (UDN) and Ademar de Barros, who headed his own Progressive Social Party (PSP). Goulart, the radical-leaning former labor minister under Vargas, won the vice presidency (voting for the two offices being separate) with 40 percent. Many in the military, disliking Kubitschek and hating Goulart, wanted to annul the elections. But Minister of War Marshal Henrique Texeira Lott, with the backing of some of his fellow officers, ousted the acting president (Chamber President Carlos Luz, who had assumed office in the illness of Café Filho), forced the Congress to impeach both Luz and Café Filho, and assured the inauguration of Kubitschek on January 31, 1956.

In the administration of Kubitschek (1956–61), Brazilian democracy reached its zenith. He promised 50 years of progress in five, and he did not entirely fail. Thanks in part to the flood of foreign investment that he sought, the economy boomed; GNP grew 7 percent yearly, industrial production nearly 13 percent. The automobile industry became a monument to the Kubitschek government. Another and greater monument was the construction of the long-desired interior capital of Brasília. The cost of Brasília was excessive, however, and Kubitschek left a heritage of debt. The reserves built up during the war had long since been exhausted, and Kubitschek worsened the financial situation by breaking off negotiations with the International Monetary Fund on nationalistic grounds near the end of his administration.

Kubitschek became, with Dutra, one of the two presidents to finish his term under the constitution of 1946. The land was more prosperous than ever before, Brazilian culture was blooming, and national pride was high. At the end of this period, Brazilian democracy was crowned by the first election in Brazilian history to transfer power to the opposition. Jânio Quadros, the successful and popular governor of São Paulo, became the candidate of the conservative, anti-Varguista UDN. His victory, with nearly half the votes— the others being much divided—seemed the victory of new Brazil. Quadros won not as a candidate of a conventional party but as a striking personality, informal, independent, and dedicated to clean and efficient government. His principal opponent, more or less representative of the Vargas coalition, was a top military figure, Marshall Lott, minister of war under Kubitschek. Ironically, the Communists and radicals favored the marshal over the reformist ex-schoolteacher. João Goulart, running mate of Lott, again won the vice presidency, with 36 percent of the vote. It was a genuine democratic contest in which the people expressed their preference for the man who would sweep clean the halls of power.

Euphoria quickly subsided into disillusionment, however. Between his election in October and his inauguration in January, Quadros took a world tour, in the course of which he emphasized independence of foreign policy by visiting Cuba. He had no strategy for dealing with the hostile majority in Congress. Scornful of parties, even those nearest to being his own—the Christian Democratic Party (PDC) and the UDN—he made no effort to organize support either in the Congress or outside. He lost popularity by a sensible austerity program, raising the cost of living by devaluation and ending food subsidies. He antagonized labor by wage controls. He tried to cleanse the government and offended the politicians by checking patronage, the bureaucrats by attacking corruption. His friendly gestures toward Castro's Cuba troubled many in the military without winning the radicals. His numerous eccentricities made everyone wonder.

Congress passed no major bill proposed by Quadros. When he requested special powers to deal with the mounting economic problems, many thought he wanted to follow Vargas's path toward dictatorship. Carlos Lacerda, who had been one of Quadros's strongest backers, began bitterly denouncing him, and alleged that he was planning a coup. On August 23, 1961, without warning his own ministers, Quadros sent a resignation note to Congress.[20]

He submitted his resignation after seven months in office (a "miscarriage," said his detractors) primarily because he was convinced that it would not be accepted and that the people, or the armed forces, would insist that he was indispensable and would give him the full powers he believed were necessary, à la Charles de Gaulle. He was a bit unstable in any case, and he had used the threat of resignation to get his way in the past. He also reckoned that the military would certainly not accept the vice president, Goulart. But Quadros had cut himself off from almost everyone, had alienated the dominant sector of the military, and had no mass organization to come to his support. Quadros's resignation message imitated Vargas's suicide note, speaking of self-sacrifice and the persecution of the greedy interests, but withdrawal is less moving than death, and it had little effect—aside from the fact that it was more difficult for the people to demonstrate effectively in his favor since he was off in the new capital, populated mainly by bureaucrats. The Congress happily accepted his resignation, hardly anyone stirred, and the military kept the ex-president incommunicado to prevent his stirring up trouble.

The resignation of Quadros, however, was a big blow to Brazilian self-confidence, and it placed the democracy in question. As expected, most of the military leaders were resolved not to permit Goulart to become president because of his reputation for radicalism. Goulart, on a trade mission to China at the time, had expressed the desire to see Brazil converted into a "people's republic."[21] However, there was a general outcry, even among critics of Goulart, in favor of following the constitution, in a demonstration of the advance of constitutional democratic ideas since the dictatorship; and the military were reluctant to act contrary to general opinion. Moreover, the armed forces were divided, and the third army in Rio Grande do Sul, backed by Governor Leonel Brizola, Goulart's brother-in-law, seemed prepared to fight for the right of their fellow gaucho. The conservative generals consequently gave way and accepted a compromise whereby Goulart became president under a parliamentary system somewhat like that of the empire but with powers much inferior to those of the emperor.

The first part of Goulart's presidency was rather successful. He was moderate and fairly reassuring in statements and policies, and he largely disarmed the opposition. At the same time, he made it plain that he found the parliamentary system unworkable, as indeed it was, unless he were prepared to be something of a figurehead, as in traditional parliamentary governments. A plebiscite on restoration of presidential powers, part of the deal whereby Goulart became president, was advanced to January 1963—thanks to the pressure from military elements and contrary to the desires of the majority of Congress. The voters favored restoring the old presidency by five to one.

Thereafter Goulart's fortunes declined as though by tragic inevitability. The economic situation deteriorated, and inflation became ever more burdensome. The indicated remedy was an austerity program. For a time Goulart made moves in this direction, and his moderate ministers, led by Celso Furtado, drew up a three-year stabilization plan. Goulart even tried briefly to rein in the inflationary demands of the chief labor federation. But stabilization required patience, discipline, a sense of economic priorities, and a willingness to risk popular discontent for a long-term goal, none of which Goulart had. In giving up stabilization, he united the upper and middle classes against him without building solid support among the divided and distrustful leftists. The policies he adopted or proposed to please the left further hurt the economy, increased political tensions, and raised a threat to discipline in the armed forces, which closed the vicious circle. Goulart was an opportunist of no particular ideology, and he certainly did not want a genuine leftist revolution in which he, a large landowner, would lose personally. But he grossly overestimated the strength of the masses who cheered him, and failed to conciliate the middle classes.

Goulart advocated land reform with only nominal compensation, thereby alienating the conservative rural interests that were strongly represented in Congress. He had an eye on the Northeast, much agitated in the early 1960s by allegedly revolutionary "peasant leagues." These, however, were not in a position to help him very much; and for Goulart, as for Perón whom he admired, the "people" meant primarily the urban masses. In the previous decade, the cities had swollen and urban poverty had increased—or at least the awareness of it had—while the percentage of the population that was politically aware and voting rose steadily. Vargas and other populists, such as Ademar de Barros, long-time boss in São Paulo, showed the feasibility of earning power through offering the services of the government to the common people.

The "people" in effect, meant mostly the chief lower-class organizations, the trade unions. Vargas had patronized the formation of unions but had kept them closely managed. Kubitschek likewise held the reins of the unions and prevented radicals and Communists, generally speaking, from gaining positions of leadership. Goulart, however, was less capable of handling them, and soon after he took office, in September 1961, the Communists achieved a commanding position in principal unions and in the labor confederation. This was possible partly because of a 1960 law that gave labor leaders control of some patronage in the social security system; labor bosses thus acquired influence in the organizations set up originally as instruments of government control.

Goulart consequently found himself pushed along by the forces on which he principally relied and which he thought he should be able to manipulate. Early in 1963, radicals embarrassed him by demonstrations demanding that he jettison the stabilization program, and for a time the radicals were in command in the ministry of labor. Goulart hesitated and turned back, but when he saw his rivals gaining ascendancy in the unions, he took a more leftist position to meet the competition and began assisting the radical-nationalists and Communists in return for their support. He also shifted from a conciliatory policy toward the United States to the economic nationalism that had been growing since about 1950, making somewhat Marxist-sounding attacks on the foreign corporations and on the Brazilian oligarchy linked to them. As the economy slid, a populist politician could hardly fail to blame high prices and poverty on corporations, especially foreign.

Goulart's position was weakened by various moves of his friends in the latter part of 1963. One was a mutiny of sergeants in Brasília on September 12, protesting a Supreme Court ruling that they were not eligible for elective office. Only a few hundred men were involved, but their taking temporary control of key government installations was disturbing to the commissioned officers, who strongly objected to the politicization of their subordinates. Moreover, Goulart, who believed that the sergeants on his side might neutralize the generals opposed to him, refused to condemn the insurgency, thereby, in the officers' view, calling into question the basic hierarchy of the armed forces. A month later, Goulart further raised apprehensions by supporting an attempted general strike in São Paulo and Santos.

Goulart was meanwhile arousing hopes and fears by speaking of the need for "basic reforms." He urged Congress to pass various measures, such as land reform and votes for illiterates, but Congress was rather conservative despite a PTB-PSD majority, and it refused to act. Goulart did not try very hard to work with Congress, and he gave the impression of being more interested in getting the powers necessary to effect social change than in carrying out the reforms themselves. On October 3, at the insistence of his minister of war, Jair Dantas Ribeiro, he formally requested emergency powers, allegedly to combat violence and rightist subversion. But he found himself opposed not only by his regular political enemies but also by most of the radicals and labor leaders, who feared he might use his powers to their detriment. Goulart seemed to have hoped, without measuring the situation, to emulate the Vargas coup of 1937, but he lost prestige when he hastily withdrew the request.

As the economy spun downward in the first part of 1964, Goulart identified himself more completely with the radicals of the labor confederation. He put into effect a profits remittance law, passed long before but never applied, that pleased the nationalists by virtually cutting off foreign investment. His popularity seems to have shrunk along with the decline of production and with soaring prices; in March, the U.S. Embassy believed he was supported by 15–20 percent of the population.[22] But he probably would have been able to hold on for the remainder of his term, less than two years, if he had not permitted the radicals to lead him into a confrontation with the armed forces.

It would have been difficult to avoid, however. In an increasingly difficult situation, with inflation rampant and the economy going to pieces, the populist president had to take action. He could not abandon his supporters and take a course of stabilization; he could promise improvement only through redistribution and social change. But "basic reforms" meant more economic troubles, at least in the short run, and they required going outside the constitution, probably using violence, and neutralizing or securing the support of the military. This Goulart sought to achieve by mobilizing the masses in the armed forces, that is, the enlisted men, like the masses in the population. But the officers were sure to react violently.

MILITARY GOVERNMENT: 1964

The Goulart plan seems to have been to hold great mass meetings in the biggest cities to demonstrate the popular will and to overwhelm Congress by numbers, then to hold a plebiscite if Congress resisted, and probably to convoke a constituent assembly to write a new constitution. At the kickoff rally in Rio on March 13, 1964, Goulart was flanked by his brother-in-law, Leonel Brizola, ex-governor of Rio Grande do Sul and a federal deputy elected by a huge majority, a firebrand of the Left. Brizola, against a background of Communist placards, called for forceful action and proposed a new congress of the true people. Goulart ridiculed the Congress and the constitution, and proposed a plebiscite in which illiterates would participate. With Communist leaders at his side, he dramatically signed before the multitude decrees of doubtful legality, expropriating lands adjacent to federal highways, railroads and waterways, and private (Brazilian-owned) oil refineries. He promised more decrees concerning taxes and the extension of political rights to illiterates and enlisted men of the armed forces.

This created a general expectation of perhaps violent change. Two days later, Goulart presented a reform program to the Congress he had derided, and the labor confederation threatened a general strike if it were not passed forthwith. Stimulated by the president's support, nearly 100 marines occupied the building of the Communist-led metal workers' union on March 25 in support of some sailors who had been disciplined for illegal union activity in the navy. Goulart, aware that failure to punish the mutineers would alienate the military leaders, tried to avoid a decision, but he yielded, granted amnesty, and named a new naval minister and a new Marine Corps commander, both approved by the labor federation.

Goulart did not want an apolitical military but one prepared to serve his purposes. He had previously used military personnel in an attempted abduction of Carlos Lacerda, and he hoped to use the army to pressure Congress and to conduct a plebiscite.[23] For this purpose he had consistently advanced officers favorable to himself, so far as the rules permitted, despite inferior formal qualifications.[24] But he saw the sergeants as the key element, without whose concurrence the generals could not move. The noncoms tended, indeed, to be discontented, as their status and rewards hardly corresponded to the professional expertise expected of them. They were credited with having played a major role in thwarting the effort in August 1961 to keep Goulart from the presidency. The natural way for him to seek to ensure their support was by the same strategy he used with the workers, that is, to organize and politicize them. Thus he could not oppose their unionization, and Minister of Justice Abelardo Jurema, speaking to corporals and sergeants, called them "workers in uniform." Leftist propaganda was freely distributed in the ranks.[25]

Goulart seems to have believed (encouraged by yes-men) that he could mobilize the lower ranks without unduly antagonizing the officer corps; and, incredibly, he paid no attention to many warnings after March 13, 1964, of possible action against him. But the threat to military discipline was highly provocative not only to the generals worried by the specter of a "trade union republic" but even more to the junior officers, those most directly threatened by insubordination in the ranks.

A considerable sector of the officers corps had been opposed to Goulart for many years and had tried to block his accession. Some of them had been muttering about deposing him since shortly after he entered office. As he turned to the radical left in the latter part of 1963, anti-Goulart talk increased and developed into efforts to conspire for an eventual coup. Many of those involved had been passed over for promotion; Goulart's manipulation of advancements for political reasons caused considerable bitterness. In late January 1964, the prestigious head of the joint chiefs of staff, General Humberto Castelo Branco, who was known as a constitutionalist, joined the anti-Goulart movement and raised its standing among many officers with legalist views. But Castelo Branco was willing to move only with the support of the Congress and of state governors or after Goulart should act unconstitutionally or seem to be preparing to do so.

The events of March precipitated action. The generals were disturbed that Goulart required his military ministers to appear at the March 13 assembly, thus dragging the armed forces into a campaign abhorrent to most of them; at the same time, Goulart's attack on the constitution weakened his claim as constitutional president. The character of his program and the call for special powers, moreover, obviously implied his remaining in office beyond the elections scheduled for 1965; and it seemed clear that his radical allies were not prepared to risk electoral defeat.[26]

The anti-Goulart forces were encouraged by the huge anti-Goulart "March of the Family with God for Liberty," mostly of middle-class women, on March 19. It was widely known in army circles by this time that Castelo Branco and Marshal Artur da Costa e Silva were heading a movement to oust Goulart. Castelo Branco in effect publicized the movement by circulating a memorandum on March 20, warning of the threat of an assembly to change the constitution and of the power of Communist-dominated unions—a document that soon reached Goulart and that Castelo Branco eventually released to the press. Also in late March, the governors of the most important states—Ademar de Barros of São Paulo, Carlos Lacerda of Guanabara (Rio de Janeiro), and Magalhães Pinto of Minas Gerias—committed themselves to the overthrow. At the same time, more and more newspapers were calling for action against Goulart.

Goulart's amnesty for the naval mutineers, capped by his giving the labor federation a voice in the selection of the new naval minister, alienated many more officers. Army leaders saw the naval officers as having lost control of their men, and they did not want this to happen to themselves. The conspirators then felt able to project a coup for the first days of April. Goulart precipitated action sooner, however. Angered by attacks and desirous of showing his strength, Goulart overrode the advice of several aides and attended the meeting of some 5,000 sergeants in Rio on March 30. In the company of various radical leaders, he engaged in inflammatory rhetoric and denounced the upholders of military discipline.[27] Infuriated by hearing the speech on radio, an army commander in Minas Gerais, General Olímpio Mourão Filho, jumped the gun, set his forces of only about 2,500 men[28] rolling toward Rio, and issued a proclamation of the overthrow of the allegedly pro-Communist Goulart regime.

Many generals were still unprepared to move, and Castelo Branco tried to call off the insurrection until preparations could be completed, but it was too late. The issue was fairly well decided when the commander in São Paulo, General Amaury Kruel, adhered to the movement. For Kruel, a close personal friend and former aide whom Goulart had named to the post to replace an anti-Goulart general, it was a difficult decision. He repeatedly urged Goulart by telephone to separate himself from the radicals, but the populist president could not bring himself to turn his back on his passionate supporters.

The outcome was still unclear, however, because the troops in Rio de Janeiro, commanded by Goulart loyalists, were by far the strongest force. The coup or revolution became victorious when forces dispatched to oppose Mourão's column joined it. Goulart fled the same day, first to Brasília, then to Rio Grande do Sul, and to exile in Uruguay.

The generals had feared a prolonged struggle, but the Goulart government collapsed when punched. This was partly because Goulart was no fighter. He had few plans for coping with an uprising, and he never really tried to rally the supporters on whom he relied, giving them leadership and an example. Even if he had been more resolute, however, his position was fundamentally weak. His program seemed threatening to almost all elites and to politicians of all the traditional parties. Carried away by rhetoric and cheering, he made no effort to hold the support of moderate reformers. The radicals, on the other hand, had reason to distrust his shifting policies and obscure intentions, although he seems to have identified emotionally with the masses.[29] The generals saw him as favoring communism or at least carelessly opening the door to it; the chief theme of all the anti-Goulart manifestos was the need to save Brazil from communism. In the showdown, even Goulart's minister of war, General Jair Dantas Ribeiro, preferred to resign rather than cooperate with the radicals. Goulart's home state of Rio Grande do Sul also turned against him. Hardly anyone entered the lists on Goulart's side except the marines under the naval minister approved by the leftists, Admiral Cândido Aragão.[30]

There was thus accomplished, almost without bloodshed, a political change that its makers called not a coup but a revolution. It became a revolution in the sense of a profound alteration of the political order, because it was soon decided that the soldiers would not again march back to the barracks after removing the leadership repugnant to them but would stay on to oversee the national reconstruction. The military had been prepared for governing, as they saw it, by their training; and since the 1930s military men had played a large part in development schemes,[31] while middle and upper classes had been weakened, and civilian politicians in general had demonstrated their divisions—there were some 13 parties on the national scene—and incompetence. In effect, the military leaders and the Goulart group agreed that this type of constitutional government did not answer the needs of Brazil.

Moreover, the military leaders came from outside the traditional oligarchy and were loath to return to it power that it had lost because of its failures. They remembered that the armed forces had withdrawn after intervening in 1945, 1954, 1955, and 1961, only to see the old Vargas crowd come back; they were determined never to let it happen again.

There was at the same time a widespread feeling that it was necessary to have a military leader in charge. The civilians mistrusted one another, and the military, wanting to leave the old politics behind, trusted no civilian. When this decision had been made, however, it became necessary to protect military authority. This implied a narrowing over the next four years, as elements originally allied or neutral became doubtful or hostile toward the military oligarchy and were, so to speak, peeled away and discarded. It also implied a hardening of the regime in defense of its nonconstitutional power, until by 1970 it was an almost unlimited dictatorship. Thereafter, gaining assurance in its strength and having crushed all apparent opposition, it could govern more calmly and, after a few years, begin an opposite process of relaxation and accommodation.

Those who overthrew Goulart agreed only on their dislike for him, and they avoided talk of positive programs from fear of dividing their forces. Consequently, in the aftermath of their victory on April 1, the country faced great uncertainty as to leadership, institutions, and purposes. Some military radicals wanted to discard the Congress and state assemblies and to purge the courts. But most looked to a fairly quick reversion to civilian government.

The Congress was in session, and, following constitutional procedures, it immediately (in fact prematurely, before Goulart left the country) named the president of the Chamber of Deputies, Ranieri Mazzilli, acting president. He commanded no troops, however, and had virtually no authority. Marshal Artur da Costa e Silva, having been the senior commander in Rio (where the government was mostly conducted, despite formal transfer of the capital to Brasília), had assumed leadership of the revolutionary forces; he named himself commanding general and took over the Ministry of War. With the top officers of the navy and air force he formed a governing triumvirate, paying little attention to the civilians.

The first undertaking of the new rulers was to remove those held responsible for the old regime. To regularize the purge, the military leaders requested that the Congress pass an emergency powers act, but when the Congress hesitated to authorize the cancellation of mandates of its own members, the soldiers proceeded to authorize themselves. On April 9 they issued a constitutional document, called an Institutional Act, which became known as Institutional Act 1 (AI-1) when it had a series of successors. This document, drafted by Francisco Campos, author of the 1937 constitution of Vargas's New State, made the change of government much more than an inside coup and proclaimed proudly its inherent legitimacy: "A victorious revolution is invested with the right to exercise the constituent power . . . the revolution does not endeavor to be legitimized by Congress. . . ."

The act not only scorned the sanction of Congress but greatly reduced the power of that body, as the president (whom the Congress was to elect within 48 hours) was empowered to declare an emergency or martial law, to submit projects to Congress that became law if not rejected within 30 days, and to deprive persons (until June 15) of office and of political rights for 10 years. The constitution was made amendable by simple majority. Persons on active military duty were made eligible for the presidency, but the new president would only complete the term of Goulart to January 1966.

Castelo Branco

Costa e Silva seems to have wanted a weak civilian president, perhaps Mazzilli, whom he as commander of the armed forces could manage, thereby preparing a subsequent Costa e Silva presidency. However, Costa e Silva was not firmly enough in power to resist the general civilian desire for a military president rather than a civilian puppet. The preference of all the main parties (except Goulart's PTB) and of politicians still on the scene was General (later Marshal) Humberto Castelo Branco, who seemed to be the most "civilian," democratic-spirited, and politically neutral of high military leaders. General and ex-President Dutra might have been a logical choice, but he seemed too old at 80. Other leaders of the revolutionary movement, such as Mourão Filho, enjoyed less prestige and were more controversial. Governors of the principal states, all of whom laid hopes on the next presidential contest, sought and received from Castelo Branco assurances that he would preside over elections in due course; and Costa e Silva acceded to the candidacy of his fellow officer. Ex-presidents Quadros and Kubitschek also lent their support, and Castelo Branco was elected almost unanimously by the somewhat purged Congress on April 11, with a civilian vice president.

More than anyone else, Castelo Branco set the new direction of Brazil and became the architect of the new regime. Yet when chosen to be leader, he was almost unknown to the nation as a whole. The son of an army officer from the poor northern state of Ceará, he had passed brilliantly though the series of military schools and had received higher training in France and in the United States. In the 1920s and 1930s he was opposed to *tenentismo* and held to the conservative-constitutionalist side. He participated in the Brazilian Expeditionary Force (FEB) in 1944–45 as a member of the general staff. After the war he taught extensively at leading military schools, especially the newly established Superior War College (*Escola Superior de Guerra*, ESG). An adherent of the anti-Vargas UDN, he was much concerned with the problem of communism, especially to the force in the Northeast, which was his homeland and where he was stationed in the early 1960s. He was distressed by Goulart's opening to pro-communist parties and partisans,[32] and in July 1963 he was brought from Recife to be chief of staff in Rio in order to keep him from commanding troops. A stocky, unhandsome man, he was known for his intellectual gifts and military rectitude.

The first business of the new president was to complete the purge of the old regime, of those guilty or suspected of subversion, rather broadly defined, or corruption. The military men coming to power thought at first that the troubles of Brazil would be solved by eliminating undesirable characters, first by deprival of office and of political rights (to be elected or to carry on any political activity by speech or otherwise), secondly by criminal prosecution. Even before Castelo Branco became president, all leading politicians associated with Goulart were subjected to suspension of rights, "cassated" (*cassados*) as the Brazilians put it, as were some such as Quadros who had otherwise offended.

Soon after taking office, Castelo Branco removed 55 deputies from Congress, seven state governors, and some 4,500 bureaucrats; 122 officers were retired on political grounds. The trade unions were dissolved or purged, and many union leaders were arrested. The peasant leagues were disbanded. The universities were purged, and the National Union of Students was abolished. All manner of politicians sent in lists of rivals to be cassated.[33] Kubitschek was deprived of rights and went into exile, probably more because of his popularity than his sins, as the military government wanted no popular rivals. The cassation of popular figures reinforced the determination of the military to retain power for a long period, lest the persecuted politicians return to trouble their persecutors. Thousands of less notable persons suffered as much or more, as commissions of inquiry, with authority to hold prisoners 50 days without action, ferreted out real or supposed political wrongdoing and corruption.

Castelo Branco was no extremist, however, and worse abuse of authority came later. He wanted to "reimplant juridical order in Brazil," as he put it, and named an eminent lawyer and scholar, Milton Campos, to be minister of justice, to the displeasure of some of his fellow officers. He kept in place the Congress with some powers, the court system, and the old political parties (for the time being); the press remained practically free; and the 1946 constitution continued theoretically in effect. This moderation was in sharp contrast to the later military regimes in Chile, Uruguay, and Argentina. Castelo Branco stood against the "hard-line" (*linha dura*) sector, mostly composed of younger officers who had felt most threatened by Goulart's encouragement of insubordination and who were inclined to authoritarian, egalitarian-nationalistic programs and state-sponsored economic development, with little awareness of the need for political compromises.

After the initial purge, the most urgent task was to restore the economy, and the first year of the new regime saw a cascade of changes. The federal taxation system was modernized, and collection was improved, raising the percentage of taxes in the GNP from 18 percent in 1963 to 24 percent in 1966 and multiplying the number of persons paying direct taxes. The policy was adopted of indexing debts, taxes, savings, and so forth, in order to reduce the effects of inflation—a Brazilian invention that has spread around the globe. Inflation was slowly brought down, at the cost of a recession and hardship for the working class. The government tried to reassert control of unions under the laws and practices of the Vargas era.[34] The rule that workers could not be discharged after 10 years without very costly severance pay was abolished in favor of a guarantee fund based on employer contributions.

The profit remittance law of Goulart times was (against stiff resistance) relaxed, and foreign investment was welcomed and protected; foreigners were even permitted to participate in the development of some mineral resources. Castelo Branco scoffed at what he considered the false nationalism of those who would exclude or severely limit multinational corporations. He turned Brazilian foreign policy around from the pro-Cuban approach of Goulart to almost complete alignment with the United States in the global confrontation with communism. To clear relations with the United States, compensation was pushed through Congress for utility properties expropriated in Goulart days; they became the basis for the state electrical producer, Electrobras. The settlement outraged not only leftists but Carlos Lacerda and many hard-line officers. Roberto Campos, Castelo Branco's able adviser and minister of economics, tried to hold down wage increases, to free subsidized prices, and to promote exports for the sake of the balance of payments.

It seems to have been the intention of the government to keep wages constant as a percentage of GNP, but they declined in real terms until 1967 or 1968, while workers and businesses, especially small ones, were hurt by the credit squeeze of 1965. The policies of Castelo Branco were not all conservative, however. The government perceived the need for agrarian reform and tried both to use taxation to combat underutilization and to help landless families acquire properties. An agrarian law made possible the expropriation of land with payment by bonds, as Goulart had advocated, but the bonds, in contrast to Goulart's proposal, were indexed and so would have real value. Conservatives were indignant, but little was actually done contrary to the interests of large landholders, and the program was neglected after 1966.[35]

The military government undertook a stabilization policy that would not have been possible in democratic politics, and it shifted power from politicians and oligarchs to military men, bureaucrats, and technocrats. For example, reform of the social security system was delegated (not very successfully) to technocrats. Among Castelo Branco's closest collaborators, along with economist Roberto Campos, was Ernesto Geisel, head of the military Cabinet and president-to-be. Another was retired general Golbery do Couto e Silva, who had been chief of the National Security Council under Quadros and, after an interlude of combatting communism intellectually in Goulart times, returned to organize and head the National Information (intelligence) Service (SNI) under the military regime. He was adviser to presidents from 1964 (except 1967–74, when he was president of Dow Chemical's Brazilian subsidiary) and was one of the most influential figures until his resignation in 1981.

Relying on technical answers to problems, the military government publicized no programs and did not seek to mobilize popular support but worked quietly to implement policies.[36] Castelo Branco remained aloof, militarily indifferent to public opinion, disinclined because of his own temperament and in reaction to the demagoguery of the previous regime to act the politician and to try to sway opinion. In the spirit of military puritanism, it was not felt that there was any need for a mass party. There was not even much effort to consult with and secure the views of capitalists while trying to promote capitalist development. In order to give his economic program a chance, in July 1964 Castelo Branco somewhat reluctantly allowed the Congress to extend his term to March 15, 1967, at the same time declaring his own ineligibility for reelection.

Not surprisingly, as soon as the shock and euphoria passed, the Castelo Branco government faced mounting opposition from civilian politicians, especially aspirants to the presidency, such as Ademar de Barros of São Paulo, José de Magalhães Pinto of Minas Gerais, and Carlos Lacerda of Guanabara, all of whom saw themselves as meritorious participants in the revolution and who felt cheated as the military settled into power. Many who hoped for governorships or other high positions were also disappointed and went into opposition. Moreover, the necessity of successive policy choices narrowed the governing group, and there was no democratic reconciliation process. The military leadership, on the other hand, saw critics as subversives and as a danger to national unity and to the reconstruction program, and was not disposed to placate them. Ex-supporters became enemies; military leaders, unwilling to give up their revolution, resorted to harsh measures, repelling yet other layers.

The election of a mayor in São Paulo in January 1965, the first important popular vote since the revolution, was tranquil, however. In July 1965, a new electoral law somewhat restricted parties by banning coalitions under proportional representation, forbidding candidates to change party, and eliminating minor parties. Scheduled gubernatorial elections in 11 states were confirmed for October, a step seen as portending early full return to democracy. A controversy was stirred when the Supreme Court released Miguel Arraes, former governor of Pernambuco, who had been held for a year without being charged. Some military men were much exercised, and the president of the Supreme Court sent a telegram of protest to a leading hardliner, General Edson do Figueiredo. In the uproar, Castelo Branco had to intervene, and Arraes was sent into exile in a compromise. As a result, the radical military felt the Supreme Court had to be changed.

Much more tension arose from the gubernatorial elections of October, in which oppositionists or potential oppositionists won five of 11 contests. The hardliners were especially disturbed by the victories of PSD candidates and Kubitschek protégées Francisco Negrão de Lima in Guanabara and Israel Pinheiro in Minas Gerais. It looked as though the old politics might be coming back through the open electoral door. A group of captains called for the overthrow of Castelo Branco, who had promised to respect the results of the elections. The hardliners were arrested, but pressure for the annulment of mandates of the disliked victorious candidates became very strong, under the leadership of Gen. Afonso Augusto de Albuquerque Lima. The Vila Militar in Rio was readied for action. The hardliners, more nationalistic than Castelo Branco and not associated, generally speaking, with the FEB and ESG, were closer to Costa e Silva than to the president; Costa e Silva was consequently able to step in as intermediary and arrange a compromise. Under it, as the price for allowing the governors to take office, Castelo Branco took a series of restrictive measures.

The chief of these was a radical restructuring of the electoral system. Changes were proposed to Congress, but when the Congress refused to accept them, they were decreed as Institutional Act 2 on October 27, 1965. This Act dissolved the existing 13 parties; and subsequent enactments permitted only two parties (on the U.S. model), one the National Renovating Alliance (ARENA), to support the government, the other the Brazilian Democratic Movement (MDB), to act as the very loyal opposition.

The president was also given special powers until the end of his term on March 15, 1967, including legislation by decree and intervention in the states. Future presidents were to be indirectly elected. Civilians were made subject to military courts for offenses against the armed forces of the nation, and a new wave of cassations began. Meanwhile the Supreme Court had unanimously reelected its president despite his rebuke by Costa e Silva. The independence of the court was reduced by enlarging it from 11 to 15.

Because of the crisis, the course of democratization was much set back, to the evident regret of Castelo Branco. In yielding, however, Castelo Branco was able to consolidate his grip on the military, and General Albuquerque de Lima was sent away to a command post in Rio Grande do Sul; the hard line never recovered its strength. At the same time, although Castelo Branco probably preferred a civilian successor, he had to accept Costa e Silva.[37] In February 1966 this was confirmed by an agreement that Costa e Silva would be the candidate of the official party, ARENA, and would continue the basic policies of Castelo Branco.

Undemocratization was carried another step by Institutional Act 3 of February 1966, providing that state governors and vice governors were to be elected indirectly, by state legislatures, while mayors of cities affecting national security, that is, all those of importance, were to be named by the state governor. The only significant popular elections remaining were those for the weak national congress and state assemblies.

In July 1966 various state assembly representatives were cassated for criticizing the government, and the opposition MDB proposed that its entire membership in Congress resign in protest. Castelo Branco stopped this by threatening 10-year loss of political rights for any who did so. The last of the populist leaders on the scene, Ademar de Barros, was also cassated for having issued bonds contrary to the economic policy of the government. Lacerda, who had been nominated for the presidency by the UDN and who had broken with the government in October, was left as the outstanding leader in a nearly empty civilian field.

Opposition was not ended, however. Many Brazilian capitalists were severely critical of policies of the government that favored foreign, especially U.S., corporations, seeing an invasion of the Brazilian economy; fears of denationalization rose because Brazilian firms were often compelled by the financial stringency to sell out to stronger multinationals. Although there was a favorable balance of payments in 1966, a number of leading generals were critical of the government's failure to bring about more rapid economic recovery and of its dependence on foreign capital. On the other end of the political spectrum, in July the National Student Union was able, thanks to the cooperation of church authorities, to hold a clandestine congress in Belo Horizonte to oppose a reform of higher education that the government was trying to carry out with the assistance of the United States Agency for International Development (USAID).

The press was frequently critical and was subject to harassment, but as yet there was no systematic censorship. The government and opposition parties had equal radio and television time for the November 1966 congressional elections, but defamation and incitement to violence were prohibited. Candidates had to be officially approved, and parties tried to present men with unblemished records to pass the test. The official party, ARENA, won 277 seats in the Chamber of Deputies, compared with 132 for the MDB; but the government majority came mostly from the poorer rural and northern areas, while the MDB won in several of the most important states. Thanks to indirect elections, 17 of the 22 governorships were held by full supporters of the regime, many of them young technocrats who would certainly not have sought popular election; the other five were amenable to central direction.

Castelo Branco wound up his administration with a 10-year development plan to guide his successor and a new constitution to fix the new political system. This incorporated the institutional acts, centralized authority, and built economic management into the political structure. Passed by Congress at the beginning of 1967, it came into effect coincidentally with the presidency of Costa e Silva. Castelo Branco also shored up the state he was relinquishing with an administrative reorganization and a national security law to regularize the prosecution of what might be considered subversion. The economy, moreover, had been brought into order, with a balanced budget, by a stern and very unpopular austerity program. Finally, by insisting on his own ineligibility for reelection, Castelo Branco reaffirmed the old tradition of one-term presidencies as a rule valid for generals also. It has remained unchallenged.

Costa e Silva

Marshal Artur da Costa e Silva was a popular soldier of no special brilliance, and a former *tenente* who did not participate in the FEB and was never associated with the ESG. He came to the top somewhat by accident because he was the senior officer on duty in Rio when the movement erupted: he could hence occupy the ministry of war and make himself commander of the revolutionary forces. As commander, he signed Institutional Act 1. His plans were somewhat frustrated by the election of Castelo Branco, but the crisis of October 1965 assured him the presidency. He announced his candidacy in January 1966, making it impossible for any other officer to do so without imperiling the unity of the armed forces; and Castelo Branco, despite some irritation, had to acquiesce.

Costa e Silva spent three months campaigning as though he faced an opponent. In the Congress, however, he received 295 votes (255 deputies and 40 senators) against 180 (154 deputies and 26 senators) absent or abstaining, mostly in protest against this form of election. Castelo Branco had become widely disliked; Costa e Silva by contrast was good-natured and outgoing, and his entry to the presidency was greeted with relief. He stated that his aim was "to establish true democracy in Brazil."[38] He, like successive military presidents expressing this sentiment, was probably sincere, preferring to go down in history as having prepared for sound democratic civilian government. But circumstances and political forces led Costa e Silva, like Castelo Branco, to narrow the political process even more.

Costa e Silva retained none of Castelo Branco's ministers and named a cabinet dominated by 10 military men, with six technocrats and three civilian politicians. The most notable was Finance Minister Antônio Delfim Neto, in charge of economic policy. Although the leadership was new and represented a tendency within the military different from that of Castelo Branco, Costa e Silva broadly held to his commitment to continue the Castelo Branco economic policies. There were changes of emphasis, however. Costa e Silva made more effort to consult outside the government, listened more to businessmen and others, and even had an organization to sound public opinion.[39] The general approach was more nationalistic, although foreign capital continued to find itself welcome—and entered in growing quantities as the economic outlook improved. Emphasis was shifted from fighting inflation to promoting production. Land reform was placed on the back burner, although the government tried to collect land taxes. There was less concern for social justice. For the first months, however, the major fault of the new administration was that it did very little.

Partly because of lack of movement, tensions began rising on both sides, from the civilian sector that still did not fully accept the right of the military to rule and from the hardliners in the armed forces who wanted more revolutionary action to justify the revolution. The press ventured to criticize, and in June 1967 a new press law fixed severe penalties for attacking the president. The church, or at least its activist sector, was coming increasingly into conflict with the government, and some priests were arrested. Student disturbances increased from 1966, in protest against tuition, university rules, and dictatorship. In August 1967 another underground congress of the students' union was held in a Benedictine monastery near São Paulo; it condemned the government and U.S. imperialism and cemented an alliance among the organized students, the radical clergy, and the extreme left.

The death of Castelo Branco on July 18, 1967, in a plane crash gave Costa e Silva more freedom, but it also increased the isolation of the regime. A writer for Lacerda's newspaper published an abusive article about the deceased man, infuriating his former fellow officers. The journalist was banished to the privacy of the island of Fernando de Noronha, and Lacerda made his final break with the regime.

Toward the end of 1967, urban guerrillas formed the spearhead of the opposition of students, clerics, and labor leaders excluded from legal activity. The Congress was striving to reenlarge its powers and reassert control over expenditures; in November, it ventured to reject a presidential proposal on the rights of municipalities. Lacerda was flailing the government with increasing bitterness, but his effort to join forces in a "Broad Front" with those whom he had assaulted violently in the past, including Kubitschek and Goulart, was unconvincing and fruitless.

At the beginning of 1968, hopes were high for liberalization, direct elections, and return to civilian rule; and the Congress was seeking to question the military powers. Student disturbances in March cost several lives and hundreds of arrests, and the atmosphere was agitated by student unrest through most of the year. This was partly due to the example of student agitation in the United States, France, and elsewhere; but student grievances for the neglect of higher education coincided with the agitation of the church and the discontent of workers, whose wages had fallen, by the admission of Minister of Labor Jarbas Passarinho, by 15-30 percent.[40] In May 1968 there were successful wildcat strikes in the states of São Paulo and Minas Gerais. The government responded to student agitation with effective repression, however, and by October the students were leaving violent action to the terrorists.

Costa e Silva was trying in the latter part of 1968 to steer between civilian demands and pressure from the hardliners in a divided army. In September, however, an imprudent young federal deputy, emboldened by the unpopularity of the military government, brought a confrontation. Márcio Moreira Alves called for a boycott of ceremonies welcoming the president of Chile, spoke deprecatingly of the military government, and urged Brazilian girls not to date army officers; another deputy in effect seconded the motion. The military leadership, especially the younger officers, were enraged and demanded punishment. The leader of the government party, ARENA, claimed parliamentary immunity for the offenders. The Congress avoided a decision for several months, but when forced to vote, it rejected the demand to lift immunity by 216 to 141 (15 abstentions), with 94 ARENA members voting against the government.[41] Costa e Silva was under the same kind of pressure as Castelo Branco had been three years before. In officers' circles there had been talk of the need for sterner assertion of power in face of agitation in the streets; now, in anger at the Congress, the Vila Militar prepared to topple Costa e Silva.

In consequence, two days after Congress voted its defiance, Costa e Silva closed that body by force. The offending deputies were cassated along with 10 others, including the last strong representative of the old political order, Carlos Lacerda, who was subsequently arrested. State assemblies were closed. The press was placed under severe censorship. Most important, Costa e Silva decreed the Fifth Institutional Act (AI-5), giving the president virtually full dictatorial powers.

The new regime came to its completion in December 1968, and the following several years were of nearly unalloyed military government. The coup of 1965 had been supported at least by the Lacerdistas; that of 1968 was a purely military affair. Costa e Silva's chief problem thereafter was to maintain military unity, and most victims of cassation were military men. In April 1969 there was a purge of four senators, 95 deputies, and five Supreme Court judges; and many more persons were hit by repressions in a general antisubversive campaign in the following months. But Costa e Silva was still being pressed from both sides when he suffered a paralyzing, and soon after fatal, stroke at the end of August while he was working on a new and more liberal constitution.

Médici

Upon the incapacitation of Costa e Silva, the vice president and former UDN politician, Pedro Aleixo, constitutionally should have acceded to the office. But the military had no intention of permitting a civilian to assume the enormous powers of the presidency. (There was not a civilian vice president again until Aureliano Chaves in 1979.) The military ministers took charge as a junta to avert a major crisis or disruption of the unity of the armed forces, and they undertook to find a successor within the military. Each arm of the services was asked to propose three candidates after consultations with officers, and the nomination was made by the military ministers, the chiefs of staff of the three services, and the chief of staff of the armed forces.

By this time the ideological division between the Castelistas, associated with the ESG and inclined toward foreign capital and the United States, and the more nationalistic hard-line groups was blurred; and the selection of the new president could be made without bitter controversy. The choice fell on Emilio Garrastazu Médici, a somewhat lackluster general who had been chief of the SNI until taking command of the Third Army in 1969.

On being nominated, Médici said that Brazil needed "free universities, free parties, free trade unions, and a free church,"[42] and he, like his predecessors, seemed to believe in the desirability of democracy. He became a rather popular candidate, although Brazilians knew very little about him, and he had the advantage of a steadily improving economy, thanks to Castelo Branco and Roberto Campos. Médici insisted that Congress be recalled in order to sanction his presidency, and it convened after a recess of nearly a year on November 22, 1969, to elect him unanimously.

The order of the day was repression, however. Terrorism was increasing in 1969. The Communist Party rejected violence, but a variety of radical groups undertook urban, and later guerrilla, war in order to provoke a violent reaction. This, the leftists hoped, would arouse popular anger to make possible a revolution and seizure of power. There were shootings, hijackings, bank robberies, and a few kidnappings. The climax came in September, when U.S. Ambassador C. Burke Elbrick was seized. The junta paid the price demanded, the release of 15 political prisoners, in deference to the United States, despite the wish of some to threaten to shoot the prisoners instead. Several other diplomats were subsequently captured and held hostage.

In response, the government decreed banishment for dangerous persons and death or life imprisonment for subversion as it undertook energetically to crush the opposition. Hundreds were arrested in the last months of 1969, and torture became commonplace. The most important terrorist leader, Carlos Marighela, was shot in a police ambush in November 1969, thanks to information extracted by torture. The terrorist campaign was a failure; the people were more alienated by the terrorism than by the measures to repress it. By late 1970, the movement was practically at an end.

The government continued, however, to repress nonviolent opposition, and the accession of the Marxist Allende government in Chile seemed to the Brazilian military to prove the need for firmness. Many were deprived of political rights for speaking out, and dialogue practically ceased. Under the leadership especially of Evaristo Cardinal Arns of São Paulo and the Archbishop of Recife Dom Hélder Câmara, the church continued to criticize the government for its social policies and such matters as the mistreatment of Indians. Médici sought to lower the temperature of confrontation and to avoid the arrest of priests, but the controversy persisted. In response to criticisms of torture, Médici punished some police who had exceeded expectations. But repressions were severe. Censors sat in the offices of major newspapers, and they deleted anything conceivably offensive to the military state. Once a censor forbade publication of part of the law on censorship. On the other hand, the government made an effort to popularize itself through an advertising campaign, and it played on Brazil's winning the world soccer triple crown in July 1970.[43]

Strikes were prohibited, and the number in the chief industrial area, São Paulo, went down from 302 in 1965, to 12 in 1970 and none in 1971. Brazil acquired a reputation for thorough dictatorship. By modern standards, however, the number of victims was modest. The maximum number killed by government forces, or "disappeared," was 35 in 1971, declining to 9 in 1975 and zero thereafter.[44] This was only a fraction of a percent of the many thousands of casualties of repression in such countries as Argentina and Guatemala.

Under these circumstances, the political opposition was quite manageable. The government party, ARENA, won large majorities in municipal elections in November 1969, and in elections to state assemblies and Congress in November 1970—although invalid and blank ballots were numerous. In 1970, 1974 and 1978, there was only a single candidate for governor, who was suggested by the president and indirectly elected in nearly all states, with only one governorship (Guanabara, 1970) going to the opposition.

Médici's policies continued rather closely along the lines of Costa e Silva's. He was somewhat more assertive of Brazilian sovereignty and welcomed foreign capital only so far as it was deemed useful to Brazil; but in this he was only following the changing temper of the officers, some of whom criticized him for too much reliance on foreigners. Médici gave priority to construction of the trans-Amazon highway and to development of the Amazon basin, that perennial dream of the nationalists. Anticommunism was no longer so obligatory, and some in the military questioned the value of private property, favored state enterprises, and saw the military as the organization most capable of accelerating development.

Social policy was unchanged, and the share of the national income going to the poor, which had fallen considerably during the first years of military rule (the share of the poorest 40 percent going from 11 percent in 1960 to 9 percent in 1970),[45] continued slowly to decline. The collection of income taxes from the upper and middle classes continued to improve; whereas 600,000 paid in 1968, 5 million paid in 1971. However, the rich could afford to pay, and the poor improved their lot, although not their share, in the prosperity that saw 10 percent yearly growth up to 1974, when the Organization of Petroleum Exporting Countries (OPEC) price increase slammed the economy. It seems that almost 90 percent of the population, rich and poor alike, supported the Médici government.[46]

In March 1972 Médici forbade discussion of the succession until the second half of 1973 in order to forestall any candidacy that might prove embarrassing. Médici was then able to name, without audible opposition in or outside the military, Ernesto Geisel, former chief of military cabinet of Castelo Branco, director of Petrobras, and brother of Médici's War Minister Orlando Geisel. Geisel took office in March 1974.

Geisel

Despite his verbal adherence to democratic values, Médici presided over a rigid administration and left the state as authoritarian as he had found it upon taking office. Under Geisel, however, there was a definite turn toward relaxation, or redemocratization, called first "distension" or "decompression" and subsequently "opening" (*abertura*). Geisel, of stern German Lutheran background, was something of a technocrat as boss of Petrobras, one of Brazil's greatest enterprises. He was seen as a representative of the outlook of Castelo Branco.

Seeing the regime losing legitimacy as the economy slowed down in 1973–74, Geisel turned away from arbitrary arrests and torture. A turning point came after the deaths apparently by torture, of a respected São Paulo journalist, Vladimir Herzog, and of a labor leader, Fiel Filho, in late 1975/ early 1976 in the confines of the Second Army headquarters. This was in part a gesture of defiance of the president by the São Paulo military authorities. Geisel, however, was able to dismiss the commanding general, and thereafter torture of political prisoners was phased out (although the police claimed the right to continue to use strong methods of interrogation of common criminals). Geisel also eased censorship; censors were withdrawn from editorial offices, although papers were still held responsible. Eight months after his inauguration, Geisel supervised what were seen as fair and clean elections, in which the MDB won 16 of the 22 Senate seats at stake and 44 percent of the lower house, compared with only 28 percent in 1970.

Encouraged by its strong showing, the MDB began taking itself seriously as an opposition, and debates in Congress became livelier than at any time since 1968. Municipal elections in 1976 showed the opposition strong in the major cities and indicated possible opposition control of Congress. However, when the MDB balked at passing a judicial reform bill as presented in 1977, Geisel showed the limits of democratization. He recessed the Congress, enacted the reform by decree, and also decreed several electoral-political changes in what came to be called the "April Package." This reversal of democratization provided for the indirect election of half of the 44 Senate seats up for election in 1978, returned the basis of calculation of representation from the electorate to the population (to give more weight to the more backward states, in which the opposition was weaker), and maintained the indirect election of governors. The rules of the political game were thus altered to ensure ARENA majorities in the 1978 elections.[47]

Dissatisfaction continued more or less open, however, on the part of the advocates of change: the press, the bar, the church, and labor and student leaders. The country was growing up and demanding political breathing space. Characteristic was the expansion of higher education from 16,983 graduates in 1960 to 222,000 in 1976.[48]

Under Geisel, as under Médici, there was a division in the armed forces between those who wanted to hold power tight and to remake the country as they preferred and those who wanted to expand consultation and permit questioning. Toward the end of his term, as the succession began to occupy political minds, Geisel confronted menacing opposition from those who wanted fewer concessions to human and civil rights and who were displeased to see power possibly slipping from military hands. Representative of this tendency was Gen. Sílvio Frota, minister of war. From the beginning of 1977, he was acting like an independent candidate, visiting units, talking with politicians, taking positions different from those of the president, and making himself representative of the army in the government rather than vice versa. In October, when Geisel resolved to dismiss him, Frota tried to line up support to defy the president. But he failed to muster much backing; and Geisel was free to name his preference, João Baptista Figueiredo, chief of SNI.

The removal of Frota and a few of his friends left Geisel in the strongest position of Brazilian presidents since Vargas. In the last part of 1977, Geisel was trying to reduce the military share in politics, although he promised the High Command that constitutional changes would preserve the primacy of the armed forces in the state.[49] Médici had felt bound to consult his fellow generals in the choice of Geisel, but Geisel acted on his own in picking Figueiredo, who was not one of the most senior officers and certainly would not have been the choice of the High Command. Geisel did so partly to remove the choice of president from military politics.

As a gesture of independence, the opposition presented an alternative candidate, a retired general considered more liberal, Euler Bentes Monteiro. He received 266 votes against 355 for Figueiredo, in the first contested presidential election (albeit indirect) since 1964. In order to give Figueiredo more time to carry out a program of normalization, the presidential term was lengthened from five to six years. Moreover, Geisel gave a strong push to *abertura* by revoking Institutional Act 5 and a series of dictatorial powers as of January 1, 1979.

Figueiredo

Figueiredo seems to have been selected to carry on Geisel's policy of relaxation. Even before taking office, he promised amnesty for exiles, and he made the restoration of a freer and more democratic system the theme of his administration. The previously invisible intelligence chief took off his dark glasses and dour manners, joked and mixed with the people, acted the part of a folksy politician, and earned very high popularity in 1979 before deteriorating economic conditions deprived him and his policies of allure.

He proceeded to adapt the state to the new era. The students were permitted to reconstitute their national union in June 1979. In August 1979, almost 7,000 political leaders and followers, exiled for as long as 15 years, streamed back to Brazil from the United States, Europe, and Moscow. In November 1979, after much discussion, the two recognized parties, ARENA and MDB, were dissolved, and new or resurrected parties (except the Communist) were invited to enter the arena. This step to political freedom at the same time represented a political calculation, because the opposition MDB had been on the way to surpassing the progovernment party, and freedom to organize new parties would inevitably divide the opposition.

Censorship was ended for printed materials. Although the government quietly exerted pressure on the press, newsstands and bookstores soon blossomed with many radical and critical publications. It was considered rather scandalous when a package containing Marxist books sent from abroad was seized in April 1980; the official involved was reprimanded for acting contrary to policy.[50] Broadcast media remained under control, however, and the ordinary Brazilian did not read newspapers, much less books.

The progress of *abertura* through 1980 was uneven, with backward steps from time to time. Free labor unions and strikes were tolerated in 1979, but a big metal workers' strike in the São Paulo area in April 1980 was declared illegal, despite support for the workers by Cardinal Arns. Unions were intervened, and leaders were jailed for a time. As though for social balance, a special capital gains tax was imposed about the same time by equally authoritarian means.[51]

The elected representatives of the people showed a new boldness. The assembly in Rio Grande do Sul debated a tribute to the losers of 1964, and the Congress at times treated ministers roughly. In August 1980, a law on foreigners, passed through Congress by the provision for enactment of official proposals unless specifically rejected within 45 days, gave the government broad powers to expel foreigners deemed undesirable. This was aimed in large part at the numerous foreign priests who carried the message of "liberation theology" to the peasants and workers and at political exiles from other Latin American countries such as Chile.

Municipal elections, scheduled for November 1980, were delayed for two years against the wishes of the opposition parties. In September, three deputies were accused, under the National Security Law, of slandering the armed forces. In October, there was difficulty in securing from the Congress the requisite permission for Figueiredo to make a state visit to Chile, as the opposition refused to make a quorum until the last minute.[52] It was claimed that the "last political prisoner," a terrorist sentenced in 1972, was set free. In November, the Congress unanimously passed a law providing for direct elections of state governors and for an end to the indirectly elected third of the Senate, the so-called "bionic senators."[53]

Abertura represented an almost unprecedented program to relax authority, not to lose it but to improve its use. The process was consequently gradual and limited, subject to a delicate balance between pressures for fuller democracy and fears of loss of control. Stronger demands, as the parties pushed for ever new concessions, and radical speeches, as deputies tested the limits of official toleration, made the government hesitate or grip the reins more tightly. It was reluctant to consider surrendering some basic powers, such as the rule whereby proposals might become law unless acted on within a fixed short period (*decurso de prazo*) and the authority to issue decree-laws. The government was not disposed to allow deputies absolute immunity in the old style, and from time to time politician and journalist were prosecuted and occasionally imprisoned under the National Security Law for statements considered inadmissible. President Figueiredo and his ministers continued their commitment to democratization as a necessity for the country; however, Figueiredo wanted to move at his own initiative, not at that of the Congress, and concessions were to be made on the government's terms. The president made many such statements as, "Better a democracy in difficulties than a progressive dictatorship,"[54] but there was a perennial undercurrent of fear that the guns might be turned against the civilian institutions, that the hard-bitten military men might overrule Figueiredo and bring the charade of democratization to an end.

In this condition, a minor incident could mean a major crisis. For example, a bomb exploded in the car of two members of the army's security force, April 30, 1981, on the Riocenter conference and exposition grounds. It seemed fairly clear that army men were involved in planting the bomb, presumably to terrorize a leftist meeting celebrating May Day. Figueiredo probably would have liked to punish the guilty, and all political parties rushed to express support. But rightist violence had been practically immune to inquiry and prosecutions in the past, and it remained so. It was feared that Figueiredo would be removed if he really tried to check the security organs. The official investigation disclosed nothing, and it seemed to be agreed that there would be no inquiry into past abuses; in return, the forces would be more discreet.

Again there was nervousness that *abertura* might be reined in when its intellectual architect, General Golbery do Costa e Silva, resigned at age 70 in August 1981. Golbery, once a leader in the overthrow of Goulart, was leader among the Castelistas and especially enjoyed the confidence of Presidents Geisel and Figueiredo, sometimes being regarded as the most influential person in the country. It had been his business to check the *linha dura* and to promote liberalization within the armed forces. When he resigned, all the parties seemed to believe they had lost a champion, and there was general apprehension that he had been forced out by ascendant hardliners. However, Golbery's resignation may have owed most to age and weariness, and his replacement by another Figueiredo intimate, Gen. João Leitão de Abreu, seemed to change little.

Shortly afterward, in September 1981, the country congratulated itself when power was transferred smoothly to the civilian vice president, Aureliano Chávez, during Figueiredo's incapacitation because of a heart attack. It was recalled that upon Costa e Silva's stroke 12 years earlier, the civilian vice president had been set aside immediately; the ready acceptance of Chávez was a vote of confidence in *abertura* by the armed forces.

Perhaps encouraged by this acceptance, the Congress in October rejected the government's proposal for the use of *sublegenda* (a rule permitting votes for different candidates of a single party to be added together in favor of that party) in the upcoming elections. As in 1968, the government party divided; there was a major difference, however, in that it was the first time since 1964 that the Congress administered a major defeat to the government without being punished. However, the government submitted a new massive "November Package" of electoral reforms, prohibiting coalitions, requiring parties to field complete candidate slates for all offices, and obligating the voter to vote a straight-party ticket (*voto vinculado*) from city councilman to state governor. It was believed that this last measure would assist the government's cause because voters would first consider their choices for local political offices, creating a "bottom-up," reverse-coattails effect, and the government party controls the vast majority of municipal governments and mobilizational resources.

More important than electoral gimmicks was the condition of the economy. The prosperity of the Médici years brought acceptance to the regime despite its harshness; the softening of the economy since 1974, especially in the 1980s, made political change seem necessary—while also making it dangerous. The basic complaint was that the masses were poor, sometimes desperately poor, in a country everyone thought should be rich. This was the cause of discontent of intellectuals, labor leaders, politicians, and even many capitalists who felt freer to criticize since they no longer feared the radical left. The church, or a large proportion of the religious, was especially effective through "church base communities," a network of some 70,000 grassroots groups that reached the people as no other organization in Brazil could. And the church, having decided in the 1960s to stand with the masses, took a decidedly leftist, antigovernment position, almost equating private property with evil and the capitalism favored by the government with injustice and oppression.

In this situation, even members of the progovernment Democratic Social Party (PDS) hesitated to identify themselves too closely with the regime, and they tired of carrying the burden of unpopular measures without having the benefits of power. Early in 1981, the government had to hint that *abertura* was in danger in order to secure the election of its candidate, Nebrón Marchezán, to the presidency of the Chamber of Deputies. It was necessary to consult, not merely to decree measures; for example, the law on foreigners was several times modified to placate the church and other opposition forces. The outstanding labor leader, Luis Inácio da Silva ("Lula"), was sentenced to jail for activities in the big strike of May 1980, but he was freed on appeal. Labor leaders voted to set up a national confederation in August 1981, despite an official ban.

Nonetheless, the parties realized that democracy was a concession of the military, and they did not abuse the privilege. The elections of November 1982 were conducted reasonably honestly and they represented a major advance toward *abertura* and political normalization. Despite the requirement that voters write in names without the help of party labels, spoiled and blank ballots were few and participation was very high. Government and opposition divided honors. The former kept control of the electoral college (modified to overrepresent small states), a majority of governorships, and a plurality of the Chamber of Deputies. The latter won a majority of the popular vote and governorships in the important richer states representing a majority of the population. The president gained in prestige and continued to hold the whip hand, but the central authorities had increasingly to govern in concert with the nation, the cooperation of which was necessary to meet the difficult economic problems of Brazil.

NOTES

1. Rollie E. Poppino, *Brazil: The Land and People,* 2nd ed. (New York: Oxford University Press, 1973), p. 75.

2. José Honório Rodrigues, *The Brazilians: Their Character and Aspirations* (Austin: University of Texas Press, 1967), p. 100.

3. E. Bradford Burns, *A History of Brazil,* 2nd ed. (New York: Columbia University Press, 1980), pp. 79, 97.

4. Ibid., pp. 98-99.

5. Text in E. Bradford Burns, *A Documentary History: Brazil* (New York: Alfred A. Knopf, 1966), p. 211.

6. Rodrigues, *The Brazilians,* p. 107.

7. Poppino, *Brazil: The Land and People,* Chapter Four.

8. Andrew Marshall, *Brazil* (London: Thames and Hudson, 1966), p. 52.

9. Burns, *Documentary History,* p. 290.

10. Poppino, *Brazil: The Land and People,* p. 227.

11. Neill Macauley, *The Prestes Column: A Revolution in Brazil* (New York: New Viewpoints, 1974).

12. Cf. John W. Dulles, *Anarchists and Communists in Brazil, 1900-1935* (Austin: University of Texas Press, 1974).

13. Ibid., p. 521.

14. For Vargas's statement, see Burns, *Documentary History,* p. 346.

15. Burns, *History of Brazil,* p. 312; Stanley E. Hilton, *Brazil and the Great Powers, 1930-1939: The Politics of Trade Rivalry* (Austin: University of Texas Press, 1975), p. 27.

16. John W. Dulles, *Vargas of Brazil: A Political Biography* (Austin: University of Texas Press, 1967), p. 258.

17. Burns, *Documentary History,* p. 354.
18. Peter Flynn, *Brazil: A Political Analysis* (Boulder, Colo.: Westview Press, 1978), p. 139.
19. Burns, *Documentary History,* p. 368.
20. Ibid., p. 375.
21. Robert A. Hayes, "Military Class in Politics," in *Perspectives on Armed Politics in Brazil,* eds. Henry H. Keith and Robert A. Hayes (Tempe: Arizona State University Press, 1976), p. 163.
22. Phyllis R. Parker, *Brazil and the Quiet Intervention* (Austin: University of Texas Press, 1979), p. 66.
23. Alfred Stepan, *The Military in Politics: Changing Patterns in Brazil* (Princeton, N.J.: Princeton University Press, 1974), p. 69.
24. Ibid., pp. 165-66.
25. Luiz Vianna Filho, *O governo Castelo Branco* (Rio de Janeiro: José Olímpio, 1975), pp. 3-4.
26. Fernando Pedreira, *Brasil político, 1964-1975* (São Paulo: Difel, 1975), p. 50.
27. Abelardo Jurema, *Sexta-feira 13 de março: os últimos días do Governo João Goulart* (Rio de Janeiro: Edições o Cruzeiro, 1964), pp. 172-76.
28. John W. Dulles, *Unrest in Brazil: Political-Military Crisis, 1955-1964* (Austin: University of Texas Press, 1970), p. 304.
29. Jurema, *Sexta-feira 13 de março,* p. 137.
30. For detailed account, see *Visão,* March 11, 1974, pp. 8-32.
31. Georges-André Fiechter, *Brazil since 1964: Modernization under a Military Regime* (New York: Halsted Press, 1975), p. 35.
32. John W. Dulles, *Castelo Branco: The Making of a Brazilian President* (College Station, Texas: Texas A. & M. University Press, 1978), pp. 251-57.
33. Vianna Filho, *O governo,* p. 96.
34. James M. Malloy, *The Politics of Social Security in Brazil* (Pittsburgh, Pa.: University of Pittsburgh Press, 1979), p. 133.
35. Marta Cehelsky, *Land Reform in Brazil: The Management of Social Change* (Boulder, Colo.: Westview Press, 1979), pp. 111, 205, 223.
36. Pedreira, *Brasil político,* p. 34.
37. John W. Dulles, *President Castelo Branco: Brazilian Reformer* (College Station, Texas: Texas A. & M. University Press, 1980), p. 270.
38. Fiechter, *Brazil Since 1964,* p. 109.
39. Arturo Valle, *Estruturas políticas brasileiras* (Rio de Janeiro: Editora Laudes, 1970), p. 60.
40. Burns, *A History of Brazil,* p. 513.
41. Ronald M. Schneider, *The Political System of Brazil* (New York: Columbia University Press, 1971), p. 273.
42. Fiechter, *Brazil Since 1964,* p. 176.
43. Flynn, *Brazil,* p. 449.
44. Peter McDonough, *Power and Ideology in Brazil* (Princeton, N.J.: Princeton University Press, 1981), p. xviii.
45. Mário Henrique Simonsen, *Brasil 2000* (Rio de Janeiro, Ed. Bloch, 1972), p. 51.
46. Youssef Cohen, *Popular Support for Authoritarian Governments: Brazil under Medici* (Ann Arbor: University of Michigan Press, 1979), p. 84.
47. Riordan Roett, *Brazil: Politics in a Patrimonial Society* (New York: Praeger, 1978), pp. 79-80.
48. *Veja,* August 2, 1978, p. 62.

49. Walder de Goes, *O Brasil de General Geisel: Estudo do processo de tomada de decisão no regime militar-burocrático* (Rio de Janeiro: Nova Fronteira, 1978), p. 75.

50. *Veja,* August 25, 1979, p. 35.

51. *Visão,* July 21, 1980, p. 12.

52. *Latin American Regional Reports, Brazil,* October 17, 1980.

53. *New York Times*, November 14, 1980, p. A-5.

54. *Jornal do Brasil* (April 11, 1981), p. 1.

[handwritten annotations:] govt - dividido / oposición - unido - por ministros durante (gobierno)

[handwritten:] Tancredo Neves — Gob. de Minas Gerais - aspirante a la Presidencia 85. / San Paulo — Minas Gerais = 1889 - 1930 / Candidato de la oposición

2

[handwritten:] dirección indirecta — no el pueblo.

Brazil as a Political Society

[handwritten:] regimen = burocrático/autoritario / burocracia = fuerza política y grupo de interés.

POLITICAL-ELECTORAL STYLES

Following cleavages along both a rural-urban and a development continuum, three distinct styles of political interaction in Brazil can be distinguished: the traditional *coronelismo* in rural areas; clientelism; and mass political styles in medium and larger urban concentrations.

Coronelistic Style

[handwritten:] caudillo — el q' manda en los lugares rurales. en reboresión.

The term *coronel*, derived from the honorific guard appointment of "colonel" during the late nineteenth century, refers to a rural political leader or cacique at the municipal level. A *coronel's* economic and political powers are based on large landholdings, with domination of sharecroppers, tenants and laborers, a system varying somewhat across Brazil's diverse geographical regions.

Within a system of economic dependence of rural workers on their *patrão* or landowner, there are reciprocal arrangements of obligations and benefits, whereby the worker supplies labor and loyalty to the landowner in return for the latter's providing sustenance, support, and protection. The landlord, in most cases, commands the total political loyalty of his rural workers. At election time, the landlords and their *cabos eleitorais* (ward heelers, or canvassers) see to the rural workers' registration as voters and attempt to assure their voting for designated candidates by holding their registration cards until they are taken to the polls. Direct compensation in money and commodities may be forthcoming following the election.[1]

In most *municípios* that have retained this political style, two rival political factions, which may or may not be within the same political party, vie for control of the local government, each with its *coronel*, who has several large landowners in his coalition. The dominant *coronel* seeks to enhance and maintain his position through a bargain with incumbents in the state government. This is another type of reciprocal arrangement, whereby the local chief mobilizes the votes for candidates indicated by the state leaders in return for political patronage and prestige flowing from state governments to his *município*. This patronage takes the form of control over local appointments (especially in education, law enforcement, the judiciary, and tax collection), public works, and other appropriations. There may be a direct cash flow to the local *coronel* to assist in voter mobilization, in direct proportion to the number of votes actually cast for the right candidates.

These cash flows have been made less necessary during the 1970s in most areas by the Etelvino Lins Law, which provides funds for lodging, food, and transportation of voters from rural areas to the municipal seat of government to cast their ballots. These funds are administered by the electoral justice system and are disbursed by supposedly neutral local judges.

With increases in the number of landowners with small- and medium-sized properties and in the mechanization of agriculture, fewer voters are controlled by the coronelistic system of rural *municípios*. Many former rural workers and their families have either migrated to larger cities, found work in the urban center of the *município,* or live on its fringes working as rural day laborers (*boia frias*). In the latter two categories, workers have found alternatives to direct and total economic dependence on a single landowner and to the accompanying coronelistic voter mobilization. This has led to a change of political styles and, in many cases, to the gradual decadence of the *coronel* or to his political demise.

Clientelistic Style

Clientelism involves a noneconomic dependency between the politician and his mobilizers, on one hand, and the voters, on the other. When the recent rural-urban migrant takes up a salaried job in the urban setting, the employer's obligations to the employee end with the payment of at least the legal minimum wage plus social security and labor legislation contributions. The urban employer in most cases does not provide such protection as shelter, garden plots, children's education, or medical/burial assistance, nor does he command the social and political loyalty of the employee, as did the rural landowner. Lacking these traditional ties of vertical solidarity, urban residents seek substitutes in clientelistic networks with a different kind of *patrão.*

Political and social solidarity of urban workers (and even of the lower middle class) and their families are exchanged for favors and assistance in "making it" within the difficult urban environment, in regard, for example, to providing jobs and education for extended-family members, to furnishing medical-dental-pharmaceutical-legal assistance, and to cutting the bureaucratic "red tape" by intermediation with local agencies. Many urban professions lend themselves readily to the clientelistic style of politics: doctors, dentists, lawyers, pharmacists, and even public servants, who have large clienteles at their disposal and who shrewdly expand this base to a potentially "critical mass" necessary for election to public office.

In some transitional *municípios,* politicians with a clientelistic base may ally themselves with one of the local *coronéis*, who may be a blood relative, to form an electoral majority. Such arrangements have proven to be unstable over time, and the more urban-based politician decides to "go it alone," forsaking the support of the decadent rural chief.

Like the *coronel*, the clientelistic politician tries to control state patronage flowing to his *município*, but he concentrates on expanding social service state agencies and public employment in his city. This enhances his political prestige while enlarging his manipulative resources. When rival clientelistic groups compete in this manner, the city may become "overpopulated" with state and federal government agencies and regional offices, so that the service sector of the economy outnumbers the industrial and agricultural sectors combined. The rival efforts of the Andrada (UDN) and Bias Fortes (PSD) families in the city of Barbacena, Minas Gerais, provide the best example of the effects of such competition.[2]

The clientelistic style of politics ranges from that found in small urban centers of less developed *municípios*, involving the direct clienteles of a few liberal professionals, to large urban machines with networks of full-time political and social services, complete with communication media such as newspapers and radio stations. An example of the latter is the Chagas Freitas political machine in Rio de Janeiro, which has been active since the early 1950s. Chagas, a longtime federal deputy and political heir to the Ademar de Barros's apparatus in Rio, was twice indirectly elected governor of Rio de Janeiro by the MDB opposition party, in 1970 and 1978.[3]

Mass Politics/Populism

This is based on a mass appeal to the voter by the politician through political rallies or the mass media, with little or no reinforcement by individual social or political services. This appeal for voter loyalty is based on the alienation and marginality of large numbers of lower- and even middle-class wage earners in urban centers, dissatisfied and frustrated by clientelism and the political system in general. This mass of voters believes its aspirations and demands have no way of being heard, much less fulfilled.

A mix of clientelistic and mass political styles in large urban areas may be found in the corporatist manipulation of labor unions and social services by *pelego* politicians and organizers. This differs from the clientelistic style in that the clientelism focuses more on mobilizing voters at the local level, whereas corporatist manipulations (described in the latter part of this chapter) focus more on state and national elections.

The mass/populist appeal finds fertile ground among the voters either not reached through the corporatist structure or alienated by it. This appeal contains a diffuse political message, promising economic development, social justice, job opportunities, economic and social reforms, and a better life for the disadvantaged classes. The content of such messages may be of two types: a studied pragmatism devoid of much ideological content, or a pseudo-Marxist rhetoric of exploitation, foreign domination, and class conflict.[4]

Getúlio Vargas and PTB politicians were, during his second presidency, the first to use this political style. Juscelino Kubitschek also used a populist "developmentalism" style during his term, but he relied heavily on coronelistic and clientelistic mobilization of votes in rural and transition areas. However, the two politicians most associated with the pragmatic style of populism during the 1950s and early 1960s were based in São Paulo—Ademar de Barros and Jânio Quadros—who became bitter political rivals. Barros relied on clientelistic mobilization in the state's interior, but Quadros was almost the anti-politician, charismatic candidate, whose meteoric career is described in Chapter 1.

The more ideological style of populism was especially strong in the 1962 elections during the Goulart presidency. It was concentrated in large urban areas of the Northeast and the Rio-São Paulo-Belo Horizonte triangle. Although the military regime of 1964 purged many of the populist politicians (of both types), the ideological style had a marked resurgence in the 1966 and 1974 elections. Oppression, economic problems, and foreign penetration of Brazil's economy were the key issues of these appeals.

During the 1960s, populist candidates made some use of television, but this was restricted to individual cities with no transmission to interior areas. Political communication was mostly by newspapers, radio, wall posters, paintings, handbills, and interpersonal communication. Television revolutionized political communication in the 1974 campaign, because by then it covered the vast interior areas of most states from their capital cities. Brazil's popular culture and mass media consumption patterns had been heavily skewed toward television since 1970 when the national network was established, so voter mobilization was easy for new-style populists, especially MDB candidates.

Before the 1976 municipal elections, however, the government effectively eliminated television as a campaign tool, forcing politicians to fall back on such traditional methods as outdoor rallies. However, television continued to be the "cool medium" of political communication through news and documentary coverage of events, which affect popular opinion despite "filtering" and indirect censorship by the government. Since 1979, political talk shows and debates have been allowed by the Figueiredo government's *abertura* and have achieved high audience ratings. Even Brazil's popular *telenovela* prime time soap operas have woven social consciousness and political themes into some of their plots.

In many areas, lines of partisan and/or factional divisions may follow socioeconomic cleavages. In small towns, there may be separate social clubs and soccer teams organized by rival factions. In many cases, these divisions may be traced back to the nineteenth century and may involve divisions among (or even within) traditional families. These local rivalries were exacerbated during the *Estado Novo* period, became a "them against us" situation in 1946, and were transformed into PSD-UDN divisions according to which group had been favored/disfavored during the Vargas period. These rivalries were "compressed" into subparty groups in the ARENA party in 1966, and they survive within the new government party (Democratic Socialist) even today.

The discussion of politics and local-level factionalism are part of the daily lives of most Brazilians, as is soccer, the national sport. To accomplish anything of substance on the local level, the machinations of groups and political actors must always be taken into consideration, as many technocrats have found to their dismay when trying to implement state and federal programs.

POLITICAL PARTICIPATION

The franchise was gradually expanded in Brazil from a select elite of *homens bons* (good men) meeting property and income requirements during the Empire, to literate males over 18 during the First Republic, and to all literates over 18 by 1932. Given the low rate of literacy in 1932, a large segment of citizens was excluded. The 1980 census, however, showed that of the population over age 10, only 25.5 percent remained illiterate, compared with 57 percent in 1940. Military enlisted men were barred from voting, and noncommissioned officers were not allowed to be candidates for political office. This sparked the "sergeants' revolt" in Brasília in 1963, and mobilization of these groups by leftist politicians in 1963/64 contributed to the March 31 military coup.

Prior to 1964 and the subsequent tightening of the military regime, there had been much non-electoral political participation. Secondary and university students were very active in student and regular politics, as were urban and some rural workers, and church youth organizations were also involved. By 1970, political participation had been restricted to voting, and protest blanks and invalid ballots reached 30 percent nationwide. This declined to 20 percent in 1974, and 5 percent in 1982.

In Brazil, voting has been obligatory; this produces very high turnout figures: 77 percent in 1970 and 81 percent in 1974, of those registered. In 1970, Brazil's population was 93.1 million, of which 29.0 million (31.1 percent) were registered as voters and 22.4 million cast ballots (24.1 percent). The November 1982 elections produced a higher level of participation, about 90 percent, due to the nation's more literate, older, and more urbanized population—not to speak of the interest generated by direct elections for governor and the climate of political *abertura*.

Levels of political "volunteerism," that is, active engagement in political campaigns and other activities, are lower than in the United States, but they have been on the rise since 1975, when the MDB party began stimulating such grassroots politics. After 1977, student activism began to increase, community organizations and church "basic communities" expanded their memberships, and more independent trade and public employee unions began to appear. By 1979, *distensão* had turned into *abertura*, and the government was hard pressed to keep up with widening involvement in politics. Although the government swung away from liberalization in 1981 and 1982, in an effort to manipulate a government victory in the November 1982 elections (as it had in 1977/78), the political consciousness and involvement of the population remained very high.

POLITICAL SOCIALIZATION

How do Brazilians learn about the political process and how their system operates? Studies of elites[5] and students[6] suggest family and school as important agencies in this process. Pre-adolescents frequently observe family members talking about or participating in politics, and they have had firsthand experience with politics in their home town. Most childhood learning within the family and local environment is diffuse, involving attitude formation about authority patterns and local political factionalism, with a tendency toward negative recollections.

School socialization takes two forms (usually at the secondary level, for those who reach it): classroom learning about political history and civics, and learning from interaction with colleagues and participation in student politics. Prior to the 1967 educational reforms, the content of secondary level instruction in Brazil's recent political history and processes reviewed in detail the nation's social and economic system. After the reforms, the curriculum was "sanitized" into sequences of "Moral and Civic Education" and "Brazilian Political and Social Organizations," and courses on history, social studies, philosophy, and economics were dropped. This produced a post-1968 generation (under age 34 in 1983) virtually without a formal education about their political system.

This gap was partially compensated for through extracurricular learning and through interaction with older colleagues, activism in student politics, and participation in "street politics." After 1968, even this socialization became difficult as student activities were repressed.

For those who do not go beyond primary school, political socialization is mainly through the family, work place, and association with neighbors and co-workers. In recent years, the church had entered the area of political "education" for local parishioners, especially in working-class neighborhoods. This has taken the form of raising the level of class consciousness and of defining the political orientation of the post-1979 political parties in terms of "authentic" representation of the "working class." The latter centers on the Party of the Workers (PT) and, grudgingly, has come to include the Party of the Brazilian Democratic Movement (PMDB), after this MDB successor party protested its exclusion from pamphlets written by the "progressive" clergy.[7]

Work-place socialization has been the province of labor unions, especially those that became more independent of Ministry of Labor control in the late 1970s. For nonunionized workers and those under more controlled unions, this type of socialization has little or no effect.

The post-1964 military regime made no major efforts at mass mobilization or socialization of the population in favor of its ideology and objectives. During the Médici term, some efforts were made to propagandize government programs and the ideology of a *Brasil Grande*. Perhaps the only major socialization program during this period was the national literacy campaign (MOBRAL), which reached into every one of Brazil's 3,991 *municípios*. Using the same methods developed by Paulo Freire during the late 1950s and early 1960s in the MEB literacy campaign, but with a more progovernment content, MOBRAL was able to reach millions of marginalized adults, especially in the more remote rural areas, with the message that the government was doing something for them. The same could be said of the government-controlled unionization of rural workers and the extension of social, health, and retirement benefits to them through the FUNRURAL agency.

This process has produced a political irony. The more underdeveloped, rural regions (especially in the Northeast), which have received the least general economic benefits since 1964, remain the government's most loyal electoral support, while the people of Brazil's developed southern region, who have received more economic benefits, have voted consistently with the opposition over the last 10 years.[8] Although the southern region benefited greatly from post-1964 economic development, the concentration of income distribution was intensified, and too little "trickled down" to the mass of voters, who, with more sophisticated levels of socialization, voted against government party candidates.

Because of truncated socialization imposed in the mid-1960s, the Brazilian regime has produced a generation (of both elite and masses) with skewed political education and an alienated consciousness. Traditionally, even in the nineteenth century, school socialization and student political activity furnished the training ground for Brazil's future political leaders. Political parties had student wings active in socializing and recruiting potential activists within the universities, so that during the 1945–64 period, most national political leaders had held important positions in local, state, or national student political organizations. The differently socialized post-1968 generation will be active in Brazilian politics for the next 30 to 40 years, with unfathomable consequences for the nation.

POLITICAL RECRUITMENT

How does the Brazilian political system select, train, and place persons in political jobs? Traditionally, the route to higher elected office began at the municipal level (councilman and/or mayor) and continued through service in the state legislature and cabinet to the national legislature and to the state governor's mansion. A university education (usually in law) and ties with traditional political families (by blood and marriage) were important to early recruitment and rapid ascent.[9]

After 1945, a base in municipal politics remained an important recruitment factor, but persons with large political clienteles were increasingly recruited directly to the national legislature. During this period, the vast majority of federal cabinet posts were filled by members of the "political class" (members of Congress, ex-governors, or state politicians) in an effort to consolidate interparty and regional coalitions supporting the president. One of the most notable changes after 1964 was a sharp reduction in the number of ministers recruited from the political class by successive military presidents, in favor of military officers and technocrats. Each military president, in turn, depended less and less on political support for his government; and as the political class lost its prerogatives, its participation in the cabinet was reduced—in the name of technical sophistication and efficiency. During the Geisel and Figueiredo governments, this trend began to be reversed, as the necessity for political support and legitimization increased.[10]

During the 1970s, with the indirect election of governors and their selection by the palace group in Brasília, many "technocrats" were placed in charge of state governments in the name of "modern public administration." They (and even their colleagues chosen from the political class), in turn, proceeded to select state cabinet officers predominantly from among techno-bureaucrats, in tune with trends at the federal level, disdaining participation of state politicians, even of the progovernment ARENA party. Many of these state governments were disasters, and some "technocrat governors" even had to be removed from office for mismanagement and corruption beyond levels attributed to their more political predecessors selected by direct popular elections. In 1978, however, most governors selected by the Geisel group were popular politicians in their home states. In the direct popular elections for governor in 1982, the political class reasserted its control of state governments.

One of the objectives of the fiscal reforms implanted by the Castelo Branco government, under Planning Minister Roberto Campos in the mid-1960s, was to put larger resources in the hands of local mayors through the "Municipal Participation Fund," a block-grant program. It was hoped that this would stimulate political ambitions at the local level and help more "authentic" and younger regional-based candidates to defeat traditional, incumbent state and (eventually) national legislators.[11] Because of the changed political climate in 1970 and 1974, this hoped-for recruitment of ex-mayors did not occur.[12] Instead, many federal deputies became candidates for mayor in the 1976 elections. The opposition groundswell in 1974 and 1978 elected a disproportionate number of local councilmen (*vereadores*) to state assemblies and to the federal chamber, thus increasing municipal experience in these bodies.

The Castelo Branco-Roberto Campos strategy finally bore fruit in 1982, when many incumbent mayors stood for state and national legislative office. In addition to regional and popular prestige acquired through administrations bolstered by federal funds, these mayors served six years in office, as opposed to the conventional four-year terms, because the government postponed the November 1980 municipal elections.

While the bulk of career civil servants at the state and federal levels are recruited through competitive examinations, the upper echelons of political appointees are selected on the basis not only of technical competence but also of family networks, business ties, former employment, and state political connections. In addition to these criteria, a special background characteristic has been of prime importance recently—participation in the Superior War College's yearlong training course or in a three-month short course sponsored by participant alumni groups (ADESG) in state capitals and other large cities (see Chap. 5).[13] Such credentials are most important to promotions and ascending transfers from one administration to another.

Since the fundamental changes wrought by the *Estado Novo* in the 1930s, increased political participation has nearly always been controlled and manipulated by the state and its political elites. Serious breakdowns in this control have been treated as threats to the incumbent regime. Thus the emergence of a more politically conscious and autonomous society in the Brazil of the 1980s and the translation of its popular will at the polls into viable political alternatives raise profound questions.

ARTICULATION AND INTEREST GROUPS

The Articulation Process

During the First Republic, most interests were primarily articulated within states, whose representatives would in turn present demands to the federal bureaucracy and/or to the Congress, depending on the action required. Some producing groups had begun to organize, such as the coffee growers and industrialists in São Paulo, sugar producers in Rio de Janeiro and Pernambuco, and meat producers in Rio Grande do Sul. Attempts to organize labor were severely repressed by police. The armed forces, as an institutional group, exerted some influence on national decision makers, but only intermittently. Certain anomic movements in urban areas also influenced policy, such as the riots against mass vaccinations in Rio in 1904.

The 1930 revolution produced large-scale changes in the articulation process by implanting a corporatist model. Under this model, preexisting elite groups were absorbed and accommodated. A series of national institutes tied to a more centralized federal bureaucracy were created for each producing group, such as the Sugar and Alcohol Institute, the Cacao Institute, the Coffee Institute, and soon industrialists were organized into federations at the state level and into national confederations. Emerging groups among the urban proletariat were effectively co-opted and manipulated through labor unions, federations, and confederations, recognized by and subordinate to the new Ministry of Labor. Notably absent were structures to represent rural laborers.

In a certain sense, the 1930 revolution had been anticipationist; in the words of Minas Governor Antônio Carlos, "We must make the revolution before the people do." The new Vargas government believed that under conditions of rapid industrialization, urbanization, and lower-class mobilization, the liberal political institutions of the Old Republic would allow class conflict to build up to an inevitable social revolution.[14] To avoid this danger, the state created the two hierarchies of worker and producer organizations and interposed its new bureaucratic institutions between them to function as organizer, arbitrator, and representative of national interests. The power of recognition under this corporatist model made all the formal groups dependent. However, among the upper classes, informal associations continued to influence decisions through family and private networks.

In 1945/46 democratic political institutions were reestablished, and the vote again became a valuable commodity. However, the corporatist structures of the 1930s were left intact, thus creating a potential for conflict. The Vargas version of state capitalism had been characterized by the socialization of losses and the distribution of benefits, and it was a continuous process of interest accommodation, whereby previous power holders could be induced to make concessions to new power contenders as long as the formers' privileges remained intact. Such a system could be maintained as long as economic growth was such that a concession to one pressure group was not necessarily at the direct expense of another.

The system functioned adequately until the late 1950s, when mobilized elements that could not be accommodated by these networks emerged as populist movements, whose leaders pledged to include them in the distribution of benefits. New laws enacted by the popularly elected Congress allowed participation by radical labor leaders in corporative institutions in addition to their unions, such as in the social security system, which gave them great political leverage. By the early 1960s, inflation had increased, and the economy weakened; thus the system could no longer accommodate all demands, which were on the increase. As a result, many groups broke with their respective corporatist structures and formed their own autonomous organizations to pressure decision makers directly through political action.

The upper and middle classes, and especially the military, came to resent the demands of labor and assumed that its gains would be at their expense. Certain sectors of the military voiced concern over the progressive lowering of their living standard, while inflation and the closing of the gap between wages and salaries led the middle class to believe that it was being reduced to the status of manual laborers. The armed forces tended to link these developments to communism, and a confidential report by the chief of staff to President Goulart in March 1964 stated, "Lenin declared monetary inflation to be a precious ally of communism in capitalist countries."

At this point, the corporatist institutions had lost their capacity to head off incipient class conflict, and the consciousness and independent mobilization of the lower classes had progressed far enough to alarm the privileged. But the masses for the most part remained passive, unorganized, and dependent. Prior to 1930, elections had been fraudulent, but representation had been real. After 1930, elections were honest, but representation became false and manipulated. Thus, in the 1964 "revolution," the military did not actually "seize" power, but rather the civilian political class failed to institutionalize its form of government, and it effectively disintegrated. The military stepped in to fill what it perceived as a dangerous "power vacuum."[15]

Prior to 1964, most extracorporatist interest representation had been channeled through the political class and the Congress. Many groups had succeeded in electing their members to legislative office or in financing the election of spokesmen, called "iron heads" (*testas de ferro*) in Brazilian political slang. This was greatly facilitated by the system of proportional representation and by the hyperfractionated party system (see chap. 4). Upper and middle classes organized the Brazilian Institute for Democratic Action (IBAD) and the Institute for Economic and Social Research (IPES), which were very active in 1962, electing many state and national politicians sympathetic to their demands.[16] When the military stripped the Congress of its constitutional prerogatives of political power and circumscribed the authority of state governors, the interest-representation function of the political class was greatly reduced.

Although the military had acted against the Vargas system, the new military government, far from dismantling the corporatist structures, revitalized and further centralized them within the model of state capitalism. However, these structures were reversed in their representational function. Previously, the corporatist structures had been used to coordinate articulations from the bottom up, with the state as arbiter and manipulator; they now became instruments for political control and top-down communication of decisions made by the military and the technobureaucratic elite.

In many states the regional military commander enjoyed more political power and direct lines of communication with the national government than did the state governor. Many of the commanders wanted to run for state governor in the 1965 and 1966 elections, and President Castelo Branco had to enact stiff ineligibility laws to curtail these ambitions.[17] Thus, for many upper- and middle-class interests (especially those of producer associations) in the states and municipalities, the army chain of command became an effective channel for communicating political demands to the national government. Many of these groups also brought their demands directly to the ministerial and agency bureaucrats in Brasília or Rio who made crucial decisions affecting their sectors. Of course, most proletarian groups did not have the resources to undertake this type of articulation, and in most cases their attempts would not have been welcomed by decision makers.

During the 1964/66 anti-inflation program, the positions of workers' and producers' interests were effectively reversed from what they had been in the early 1960s. Under stiff wage controls with no price controls, real wages declined rapidly, while businessmen and industrialists who could withstand the recession of restricted credit and lessening demand fared better. With even their corporatist structures unable to articulate their demands, urban laborers had no recourse other than protest demonstrations, street riots, and wildcat work stoppages.

With the deepening of the revolution and of the military regime after 1968, even many producer groups' demands went unheeded by national decision makers. With the end of the "economic miracle" in 1973, these groups' situation became worse, and many expressed their displeasure with the government by supporting opposition candidates in the 1974 elections, especially in São Paulo.[18]

Throughout this period, the press (mainly the large daily newspapers in Rio and São Paulo) became the principal articulator of lower-class (and, later, "fenced out" producer-class) demands. However, this channel was stifled from 1969 to 1974 when prior censorship was imposed by the military government.

Another kind of indirect articulation operates through the National Information Service (SNI) established in 1964. Within this largely secret network of informants and information-processing from the local, state, and national levels, a daily intelligence briefing for the president and high-ranking palace staff is prepared. Some demands of certain groups come to the government's attention through this "filtering up" process, which, in some cases, produces "anticipatory" decisions within the traditional model.

With the installation of the Geisel government in March 1974, press censorship was eased, and more authentic trade union leaders were allowed to be elected. Although decision making was even more centralized than in previous governments and Congress remained nearly powerless, the latter began to perform a "tribune" function, and legislators were able to act as intermediaries in the articulation of demands from interests in their states to the appropriate national bureaucracies. These changes were part of the decompression/*abertura* strategy initiated by the Geisel government to enhance its legitimacy and the prospects of the ARENA party in upcoming elections (see Chaps. 1 and 4).

In 1979, the first year of the Figueiredo presidency, nearly all groups had channels through which they could articulate their demands, and more public and private strikes occurred than during the entire 1960–64 period.[19] In 1980, the government decided things had gone too far, and strikes were repressed. Many politicians from producing groups and their representatives formed the new Popular Party (PP) as an alternative articulation channel. On the other hand, sectors within the security forces, unhappy with the liberalization policies, began anonymous bombings of "subversive" organizations as a forceful means of expressing their demands.

Investigations by McDonough,[20] Daland,[21] and Motta[22] suggest that bureaucratic decision makers in the federal government have complex association networks with producing sectors, with the military, and with the political class (through kinship, prior employment, and contacts) and that many have ties to state politics and government. This would indicate a pattern similar to C. Wright Mills's power-elite concept in the United States of America and to W. L. Guttsman's interlocking directorates in Great Britain.

At present, there exists in Brazil a mix of channels of political articulation, whose availability depends on the status and connections of the group or individual involved. At the state level, elected representatives are very active as brokers and intermediaries for local constituents, because the state legislature carries more decision-making force than the national Congress. Such traditional structures as kinship groups, regional affinities, school alumni groups, and "old boy" networks are also active. Producer groups, such as associations of industrialists and farmers and chambers of commerce, are effective. In some states, rural laborers are unionized and able to articulate demands. In all states, the unions representing industrial laborers, white-collar and commercial workers, and public employee sectors are important. Regional military commanders retain much political power and exert influence over decisions at the state level. The church has a larger role in some states than in others, and the ideological inclinations and activism of local bishops vary considerably.

At the national level, the role of the Congress as articulator has increased somewhat since 1979 (see Chapter 3). Many demands from the states are brought directly to Brasília by state governments and their agencies. Representatives of producer groups sit on certain advisory councils and have access to their respective ministries and agencies. However, during the anti-inflation push of 1980–81, most economic policy was determined by a small group within the Ministry of Planning (SEPLAN), headed by Minister Delfim Neto. Rural producer groups have less access and enjoy fewer results than their urban counterparts.

Interest Groups

Organized Labor

As previously discussed, labor began to be organized in the corporatist structure established by Vargas in the 1930s. In the late 1950s and early 1960s, labor unions became more autonomous of government control under the direction of political activists, a fact which contributed to the military overthrow of the Goulart government. It was during this period that rural labor unions were first organized on a large scale. The military government imposed rigid control on unions after 1964, but more independent leaderships emerged in some unions in the late 1970s and began to challenge government policies and corporatist manipulation.

Urban Sector. A docile and productive labor force was a prime factor attracting multinational capital to Brazil's Central-South region during the "miracle" period. Fully cognizant of this critical role, the new and younger labor leadership elected in the late 1970s began to press their demands on employers and the government. These demands mostly involved job security and salary increases. The unions wanted an end to job rotation/salary manipulations under the new Guarantee Fund for Length of Service (FGTS, which accumulates an 8 percent monthly employer contribution in lieu of traditional severance pay) and salary adjustments for the "manipulation" of inflation/indexing data by then Finance Minister Delfim Neto in 1972–73 (to which his successor admitted in the late 1970s). The more dynamic metal-working sector led the way in pressure and negotiations in 1978 and 1979. The president of the local union in São Bernardo, São Paulo, Luis Inácio da Silva ("Lula"), became the articulate representative of this movement with support from church and other activists.

The threat of disruption of this foreign-exchange-producing sector was viewed seriously by the government. Generous settlements quickly followed the strikes in 1979, but in 1980 strikes were declared illegal and were broken by police. The union leaders were removed by the minister of labor and were indicted for violation of the National Security Law. In 1981 and 1982, the threat of repression and massive layoffs (due to the anti-inflationary recession) sharply reduced strikes and union activism.

Some industries, led by Volkswagen, sponsored the internal election of factory workers' councils to negotiate labor-management disputes. Despite labor leaders' calls to boycott these elections in 1981, such councils were established and certainly will undermine the union's role.

In addition to direct labor activism, the labor unions use other channels to press their demands. The Inter-Syndicate Study Group of Socioeconomic and Statistical Indicators (DIESSE) has been very effective in documentation and diffusion of data supporting union economic demands. In 1974 and 1978, several union activists were elected to state legislatures and to the Congress. Volkswagen and some other multinationals were confronted by solidarity pressures from labor unions in their home countries in support of "Brazilian comrades' " demands. Local Volkswagen unions in Germany put heavy pressure on the company; when Prime Minister Helmut Schmidt visited Brazil in 1979, he held highly visible meetings with Lula and other São Paulo labor leaders. Lula and some of his colleagues organized the *Partido dos Trabalhadores* as an autonomous channel for the articulation of union demands (see Chap. 4). They have traveled to Europe and to the United States of America to meet with trade union and political leaders.

Occasionally, Brazil's urban proletariat expresses its demands through anomic demonstrations and riots. Since 1979, the most notable were the "thrashing" of downtown Belo Horizonte by construction workers, the destruction of commuter trains and stations in Rio and São Paulo, the destruction of buses and looting in Salvador, and explosive riots by the unemployed in São Paulo in April 1983.

Rural Sector.   Although the peasant leagues and rural unions were severely repressed by the military government after 1964, rural labor unions were later allowed quietly to organize under Ministry of Labor auspices, and social and labor legislation was gradually extended to rural laborers. In the late 1960s this produced a large-scale expulsion/exodus of peasants from the land to the cities, resulting in the many *boia-fria* (cold-lunch) families that live in precarious conditions on the urban periphery, from where they return as farm day-laborers, recruited and organized by intermediary contractors (*gatos*). Some large, labor-intensive sectors, such as the sugar-cane workers, are well-organized and collectively bargain with landowners and mill operators; in São Paulo even many *boia frias* are organized into unions. The rural unions are served by the FUNRURAL section of the social security system, which provides medical, dental, disability, retirement, and other benefits. This has been a great political asset to government-party elected officials in mobilizing support.

However, many rural laborers are still unorganized and do not receive such benefits. Their basic demands are squatters' rights and conditions to till their own small plots. The conflicts between these peasants and large landowners, land sharks, agribusinesses, and Indians has led to government intervention in many areas. The most notable conflict of this type is in the explosive Araguaia-Tocantins area northwest of Goiás, southeastern Pará, and southwestern Maranhão, where the National Security Council established a special task force in 1980 to resolve the crisis. In the state of Paraiba, after a visit in 1981 by SNI Director Octávio Medeiros, the federal government forced the state to expropriate a large sugar plantation and distribute the land to the workers. In the August 1982 cabinet reshuffle, ex-Chief of Military Household Gen. Danilo Venturini was named to head the newly-created Ministry of Land Tenure Affairs.

At the national level, rural workers are represented by the Confederation of Agricultural Workers (CONTAG), but their most constant and effective support is from the activist sector of the Catholic Church, its local parish priests, and some bishops. The rural labor sector has not been as successful as its urban counterpart in mobilizing electoral support for class representatives because of the deep-rooted *coronelismo* and clientelism still present in many regions.

Producer Groups

Producer groups are not homogeneous, and urban and rural sectors frequently articulate conflicting demands. The diverse groups, however, are aggregated into CONCLAP (Conference of the Producing Classes), with annual conclaves.

Urban Sector.   The *industrialists* are perhaps the most visible and vocal of the urban producer groups and are concentrated in the Central-South region. Their leading organization is the Federation of Industry of the State of São Paulo (FIESP), which is responsible for 60 percent of the nation's GNP. This group's demands generally concentrate on favorable wage policies, credit and production incentives, and expansion of domestic demand for their products. It has ample and direct representation in Congress; its representatives sit on many government advisory councils and have direct access to agency decision makers and economic planners. One might thus assume that industrialist demands would be easily articulated and quickly met by the government, and during the "economic miracle" period, this was so to a great extent. But in times of scarce resources and inflation after 1974, this has often not been the case.

The industrialists' principal complaint in recent years has been with the Inter-Ministerial Price Commission (CIP), which controls the prices of manufactured goods. In 1980, the 13-year reign of 76-year-old Theoboldo De Nigris as president of FIESP ended with the election of 41-year-old Luiz Eulálio Bueno Vidigal Filho. Eschewing any major ideological changes, Vidigal's decisions have been of a more aggressive style, with ample documentation and argumentation. In 1981, he succeeded in getting most price controls removed. However, because of the credit squeeze and decreased demand, profits declined and bankruptcies increased among small- and medium-sized firms producing for the domestic market. Larger firms, like Vidigal's COBRASMA, which produce capital goods mostly for government contracts, fared better.

The *bankers* had been the only group since 1964 with no complaints against the government; at least their articulations and demands were very quiet. Finally in 1980, they complained about the bank workers' strikes and demands and that the government was not dealing forcibly with this problem. Long-standing demands for the removal of government ceilings on interest rates were realized in 1981.

Commercial groups have been hard pressed since 1974 because of declining demand for certain consumer items, the credit squeeze, wage pressures, and the post-1979 recession. A variety of associations represent their interests, from local and state chambers of commerce, store managers' associations, and shopping center organizations to the association of supermarkets.

The commercial and industrial sectors of the national bourgeoisie have long-standing demands against state-enterprise encroachments on the private sector (*estatizacão*). The government began to attend to this demand in

1981 by proposing the sale of some state-owned enterprises to private (and some foreign) investors. Brazilian private enterprise remains, however, much less apprehensive of the demands of the Left than of the state sector and the technocracy.

Foreign business interests share many of the goals of domestic producer groups in the areas of labor and wage policies, price and interest controls, and credit restrictions. The principal differences are in the area of incentives and regulations, which often favor national companies. Many of the multinational firms are more involved in production for international markets and thus are less preoccupied with expansion of the local market. The Volkswagen manager and president of the National Motor Vehicle Manufacturers Association (ANFAVEA) tried to unseat De Nigris from the FIESP a few years ago, and was dubbed the *"pelego* from Volkswagen A.G." by Vidigal. This was a rare example of a representative of a multinational seeking election in a national association of this type. Usually, multinational interests are articulated by foreign chambers of commerce in Rio and São Paulo, by their respective embassies, and through direct bargaining with specific federal agencies.

Because their investments and products for export have been crucial to sustaining both the "economic miracle" and the current balance-of-payments "rollover," the interests of foreign investors have received special attention. Recently, however, some have suffered reverses. IBM fought a losing battle in 1979–81 to gain access to the minicomputer market, which the government reserved for national firms. In 1981, when Volkswagen saw that it was to suffer its first financial loss in 27 years of operation in Brazil, the company sought a variety of relief measures from the government. These were not forthcoming, and the company was told to produce more for export. President Figueiredo was said to have remarked that "VW has made tremendous profits in Brazil over the years—no concessions, let them absorb the loss!"

Although *state enterprises* could be considered part of the government, they constitute an important institutional interest group. Most of their demands center around budget allocations, competition and division of markets, and fiscal controls. In 1980, all were required to take 15 percent budget cuts and to curtail imports, and were subjected to control by a special Planning Ministry section (see Chapter 3). Most of their articulations are made through closed bureaucratic channels and negotiations, but occasionally the press is used to seek broader public support for demands with a more "nationalistic" content. At times, "old boy" and family networks are used, as is the military chain of command.

Rural Sector. The producers of food, industrial crops, and animal products comprise a diverse sector. Certain areas, such as coffee, sugar, soybeans, and cacao, are vital to export earnings and receive special treatment by the government through institutes set up in the 1930s under the corporatist structure. These products are also important to the domestic economy, and a conflict of interest is generated. In the case of coffee and soybeans, this resulted in an export tax with exchange confiscation. The soybean tax was removed in 1978 as an election ploy, but the prolonged protests of coffee producers have gone unheeded.

The basic demand of rural producers concerns a cost-price squeeze like that affecting U.S. farmers. Many agricultural products are considered basic consumer items, and thus their retail prices are controlled. Production credit in Brazil has traditionally been available at very low interest rates (7 percent per annum), but this rate was progressively increased after 1979, especially for larger-scale enterprises.

Nearly every rural *município* has a "rural association" of producers, which are aggregated into agricultural federations at the state level and into the Brazilian Rural Federation. Rural cooperatives have similar associations. Rural interests have always been well-represented in Congress (10 percent of deputies and 13 percent of senators in the 1982 legislature listed their principal occupation as agricultural). ARENA-PDS majorities in most of the less developed regions of the country are dependent on mobilization by landowners; thus the government has been careful in dealing with agricultural policy.

There are cross pressures in this area. The current anti-inflation program counts heavily on the abundance of foodstuffs available at low prices. The national alcohol program, for example, allocates huge resources to spur sugar-cane production and new distillery construction, but in the process, it provokes conflicts of interest: whether to increase sugar-cane production at the cost of foodstuff production, whether to increase alcohol production to ease the burden of imported petroleum or sugar to earn foreign exchange.

Middle-Class Groups

One of the major factors contributing to the political instability of the early 1960s was the inability of the middle class to mediate between other groups in a coherent fashion. Although a majority of Brazil's middle class supported the 1964 military takeover, its frustrated expectations and insecurity have continued to this day. Clearly, the middle class has expanded numerically and proportionately in the past 20 years, as analyses of the 1960, 1970, and 1980 census data have shown. Many writers have commented on the "middle-class" nature of the values and policies of the military regime. Still, many complaints of the middle class are similar to those of the early 1960s: the inflationary spiral erodes salaries and living standards, housing is very costly, quality education is difficult, mobility from lower strata continues, and the quality of urban life deteriorates.

Of middle-class groups, perhaps the *liberal professions* are in the best position and are best organized. Physicians, dentists, lawyers, architects, and engineers, for example, have articulate professional associations and government-sanctioned regional boards to control and police each profession. Many individuals are part of, or are close to, government and thus have direct access to decision makers. Until recently, strikes and protest movements within this group were unheard of, but the progressive proletarianization of the medical profession led to bitter strikes by doctors in public service in Rio and São Paulo in 1980/81, and to well-articulated demands from doctors in residency. Professionals had traditionally been income-tax evaders, but sophisticated techniques of "computer coercion" have forced most to present returns.

Certain sectors of *white-collar* office and commercial employees, such as bank workers and retail clerks, have well-organized unions, bargain collectively within the corporatist model, and receive government-subsidized services through organs like SESC. Recently, however, autonomous movements have appeared outside this structure and have led to wildcat and spontaneous strikes in larger cities. In 1979, white-collar workers were disturbed by many trade unions receiving proportionately larger wage increases, which implied relative status loss and created frustrations.

Public employees at all levels are often stereotyped by their middle-class colleagues as having easy and unproductive lives with near-perfect job stability. This may have been the case prior to changes in labor legislation and in hiring practices effected in the late 1960s, but most public employees hired after the late 1960s have less job stability.

Public-employee demands center on yearly salary adjustments, the plea for the thirteenth-month salary (which other wage earners receive), fringe benefits, and retirement programs. As in most countries, strikes by public employees are prohibited by law in Brazil; but during 1979/80, nearly all states faced strikes by public-school teachers, many of which lasted several months, in addition to work stoppages by other groups.

State-government workers are well-represented in state legislatures, and under proportional representation they carry great weight in many states with inflated bureaucracies. Clientelistic articulations are quite common. In 1981 and 1983, there were mass assemblies of federal employees in state capitals to coordinate a militant, "extrastructural" organization to press their demands, which may forbode problems for the federal government in the future.

In 1979, the government instituted biannual salary increases (in November and May) in an effort to improve the lot of salaried workers. However, a "sliding scale" of percentage increases was built into this new legislation, whereby the increases for lower salary brackets are decreed at higher percentages than for upper brackets.

The Church

Although Brazil has a plethora of denominations, sects, and non-Christian religions, close to 90 percent of the population is baptized as Roman Catholic, making Brazil the world's largest Catholic nation, as Pope John Paul II noted during his two-week visit in 1980.

During the 1930s, the church provided both support and ideology for the corporatist system. In 1964, the church was a main element in mobilizing popular support for the ouster of the Goulart government to prevent the ascension of the "Godless Communists." By the end of the decade, however, church leaders had become alienated from the military government, and many priests, nuns, and lay workers were imprisoned and tortured.

Generational and circumstantial factors contributed to this turn of events. In the early 1960s, many younger priests and lay workers were engaged in youth and workers' movements and in literacy and mobilization campaigns among rural and urban workers. By the late 1960s, many of them, and others influenced by the "Liberation Theology," had achieved leadership positions within the church. At the same time, because of insufficient vocations, many liberal priests and nuns were imported from Western Europe—nearly half the clergy is foreign. In many cases, deprivations of human rights, the economic plight of the "victims of the miracle," and the repression of church workers stirred to action even the more conservative bishops. By 1969, bishops were excommunicating police torturers, and the 200 members of the national Council of Bishops unanimously called for an end to torture and repression and for the normal functioning of the legislature and judiciary. Relations were so strained that in 1972 no church leaders were invited to participate in the sesquecentennial independence celebration. The leftist priests were always a minority, but they carried disproportionate weight because of their activism, and the Brazilian church became perhaps the most progressive branch of Catholicism in the world. During the years of harshest repression, it was almost the only permitted vehicle of dissent.

In many areas, the only effective representatives of peasants, squatters, and the poor are church leaders, many of whom have taken aggressive measures to organize these masses to press their demands and to assert their rights through some 70,000 "church base communities." In urban areas, church leaders have been very supportive of the new, more independent, trade-union leadership, and they have performed an important mediation function and have defused many potentially explosive confrontations. Recognizing the importance of this role, the Geisel government made real efforts to reopen channels of communication with church leaders. These were broadened in 1979 by Justice Minister Petrônio Portela within the Figueiredo *abertura*. The religious have not been won over, however. In its circulars, the church uses the language of the Left, equating the opposition with the people and the government with the rich and the powerful,[23] sometimes declaring flatly, "capitalism is the evil." In 1982, "counterfeit" pamphlets were distributed, mocking the church and its doctrine.

The church articulates demands of an institutional and of a more general nature. Institutional demands concern religious and moral questions, such as the new "Law of Foreign Nationals" decreed in 1980 and the divorce statute adopted by the Congress in 1977. With regard to the former, the church feared not only the general repressive nature of the new decree but also the ease with which foreign priests could be deported or barred, as in the case of the French priests involved in squatters' movements in Pará in 1981/82. In the case of the divorce measure, the severe pressure on deputies and senators threatened excommunication and defeat in the 1978 elections. This public exercise of pressure politics came to naught, but quiet negotiations did produce changes in the "Foreigners' Law" in 1981. Although political activism is formally prohibited by church regulations, many priests participate in party politics, and some are candidates for office.

Besides the armed forces, the church is the only organized group with penetration to nearly every *município* and with a highly organized hierarchy. Thus able to articulate rapidly at any level and to coordinate policy formulation and political action, the church is considered a formidable force by the government, even though the religiosity of the Brazilian population and the ability of the church to mobilize opinion is questionable.[24]

Students

As in many nations, Brazil's student leaders have matured into politicians and top-level government bureaucrats over the years. The "old school tie" has been an important recruitment and articulation channel in Brazil. During the Empire and the First Republic, for example, the São Paulo Law School was an important political training ground for state and national leaders, and its secret fraternal society, *Bucha*, formed an important associational network.

The National Student Union (UNE) was first organized in the mid-1930s, and until its demise in 1964 it was recognized and subsidized by the Ministry of Education within the corporatist system. During the *Estado Novo* period, university students were one of the few groups able to mildly contest the authoritarian regime with impunity, at times encouraged by professors. In 1939, the astute interventor in Minas Gerais, Benedito Valladares, appointed many leaders of the student movement as mayors in newly created *municípios* in the interior, thus harnessing their youthful energies and ambitions.

After 1945, student organizations, both secondary and university and at the state and national levels, became important interest groups, due less to numerical strength than to their politicization and activism. In most university-level elections in large cities, the UDN, PSD, PTB, and other political groups sponsored factions (*alas*). In this way, student politics were an important training ground for future political leaders. Many of Brazil's politicians elected in the 1950s and 1960s had been student militants.

The most frequent demands articulated by the UNE were political rather than educational. The Catholic faction took control of the UNE in the early 1960s, defeating the Marxists. It was at this point that UNE became involved with the mass literacy programs organized by the PDC Education Minister, Paulo de Tarso. In 1963, the UNE joined the labor confederation (CGT), the Nationalist Parliamentary Front (FPN), peasant leagues, and other leftist nationalist groups to form the Popular Mobilization Front (FMP).

Having outlawed the UNE, the Castelo Branco government established the National Directorate of Students, which was disdained by the students and remained a paper organization. The UNE continued to hold clandestine national congresses and in 1968 pressured the suspension of the Ministry of Education/USAID agreement. It helped to organize street demonstrations of more than 100,000 persons, which led to violent government repression and the deepening of authoritarianism with the AI-5. UNE leaders participated in the kidnapping of the U.S. ambassador in September 1969, and they secured the release of many of their imprisoned colleagues.

In the early 1970s, student activism was confined to local university elections in this arena. In 1977, however, various competing leftist factions reactivated student politics in São Paulo and other capital cities and coordinated massive strikes and demonstrations in September. The following year, students clashed violently with São Paulo state military police on the campus of the Catholic University.

In 1979, the UNE was reactivated and held an open national congress in the city of Salvador. Instead of being greeted by repression, the conclave received, within the new *abertura* strategy, complete logistical and "tourism" support from local authorities, like any other big convention of 5,000 delegates. The congress turned into a "Woodstock" and only after a long and bitter dispute was able to establish a loose set of bylaws and to convoke "direct" national elections. In 1980, UNE held another convention and sought recognition by the Ministry of Education and Culture (MEC). Minister Eduardo Portela agreed to meet with UNE leaders informally, but he withheld recognition. Those who succeeded him have refused even informal meetings. In 1982, the government began expulsion proceedings against the Spanish-born UNE president, which were temporarily suspended due to "electoral considerations."

Students have become quite active in the organization of the PT, but they have traditionally been viewed with suspicion by labor leaders. To a lesser degree, students are active in the PMDB. At times, as in the late 1970s, student groups have brought direct political pressure on Congress for specific legislation. In the election year of 1978, competing groups of "biomedical" and medical/pharmacy students descended on Congress in bus caravans from all the states to lobby the passage/defeat of a bill officially regulating the biomedical profession.

For the first time, in 1980, a parallel national association of federal university professors was organized to unite state-level organizations. Its demands center on salary increases, a revised career/promotion structure, and larger education budgets.

The Military

The military is covered in Chapter 5, but it requires brief mention here as an institutional interest group. After the influence and representation function of the political class was curtailed in the mid-1960s, the military command system became an important articulation channel of demands emanating from groups, individuals, and institutions in the *municípios* and states. In addition, the military articulates its own institutional demands (budget, military policy, promotions, and so on) through the hierarchy to the high command and to the president and his staff. Following the ouster of Army Minister Sílvio Frota in 1977 and of General Hugo de Abreu in 1978, military input into political decision making was reduced by the Geisel government. As a result of the Riocentro episode in May 1981, the Figueiredo government was forced to accept a larger role by the military. In 1983, many military leaders became convinced that their budgets might be more generously treated by a civilian regime.

The Technobureaucracy

The public-employee sector at all three levels of government has become more militant since 1979 in pressing its economic demands on the government. Specific bureaucratic agencies make their own institutional demands in the areas of budgetary and economic policy and political decision making. At times, conflicting demands break out into public confrontations.

Following 1980 across-the-board budget reductions, there was a mad scramble among the agencies and public enterprises at least partially to restore their cuts. The Foreign and Finance ministries compete for control of the foreign commerce area. PETROBRAS and the ministries of Mines and

Energy, Industry and Commerce, and Agriculture have conflicting purposes in the National Alcohol Program. Nearly all agencies and enterprises have fought losing battles with Planning Minister Delfim Neto's austerity program, with the notable exception of Education Minister General Rubem Ludwig.

The military was unsuccessful in its efforts to reverse Foreign Ministry decisions to recognize the new government of Angola and to abstain from further efforts to establish a South Atlantic Treaty Organization. Nuclear-energy policy questions, both foreign and domestic, involve the conflicting interests of NUCLEBRAS and ELECTROBRAS (within the Mines and Energy Ministry), plus those of the Foreign Ministry, the Industry and Commerce Ministry, and the armed forces. The state managers, it may be noted, are not recruited from the economically dominant states and have no institutional responsibility to them.[25]

NOTES

1. Victor Nunes Leal, *Coronelismo* (New York: Cambridge University Press, 1977); and Paul Cammack, "O 'Coronelismo' e o 'Compromisso Coronelista'": Uma Crítica," *Cadernos do DCP* (UFMG), No. 5 (March 1979), pp. 1–20.

2. José Murilo de Carvalho, "Barbacena: A família, a política e uma hipótese," *Revista Brasileira de Estudos Políticos*, No. 20 (January 1966), pp. 125–93.

3. Eli Diniz, *Voto e Máquina Política: Patronagem e clientelismo no Rio de Janeiro* (Rio de Janeiro: Paz e Terra, 1982).

4. Francisco C. Weffort, *O populismo na política brasileira* (Rio de Janeiro: Paz e Terra, 1978).

5. David V. Fleischer, "Political Recruitment in Minas Gerais, Brazil (1890–1970)" (unpublished Ph.D. dissertation, University of Florida [Gainesville], 1972).

6. Marcos Antônio Coimbra, *Estudantes e ideologia no Brazil* (Rio de Janeiro: Achiamé, 1981).

7. *Isto É*, September 9, 1981, pp. 22–29.

8. Fabio Reis, ed., *Os partidos e o regime* (São Paulo: Ed. Símbolo, 1978), pp. 289–303; and Bolivar Lamounier, ed., *Voto de desconfiança: eleicões e mudança política no Brasil, 1970–1979* (Petrópolis: Ed. Vozes, 1980), pp. 15–80.

9. David V. Fleischer, "A cúpula política mineira na Velha República: As origens sócio-econômicas e recrutamento de governadores, vice governadores e deputados federais," *Revista de Ciência Política* (FGV), 20:4 (1977), pp. 9–54.

10. Edson de Oliveira Nunes, "Legislativo, política e recrutamento de elites no Brasil, *DADOS*, 17 (1977), pp. 53–78.

11. Antônio Otávio Cintra, "Traditional Brazilian Politics: An Interpretation of Relations between Center and Periphery," in Neusa Aguiar (ed.), *The Structure of Brazilian Development* (New Brunswick, N.J.: Transaction Press, 1979), pp. 127–66.

12. David V. Fleischer, "O trampolim político: mudanças nos padrõs de recrutamento em Minas Gerais," *Revista de Administracão Pública* (FGV), 7:1 (1973), pp. 99–116.

13. Peter McDonough, *Power and Ideology in Brazil* (Princeton, N.J.: Princeton University Press, 1981), p. 67; and Robert T. Daland, *Exploring Brazilian Bureaucracy: Performance and Pathology* (Washington, D.C.: University Press of America, 1981), pp. 275–86.

14. Kenneth P. Erickson, *The Brazilian Corporative State and Working Class Politics* (Berkeley: University of California Press, 1978), pp. 35–40.

15. Michael Wallerstein, "The Collapse of Democracy in Brazil: Its Economic Determinants," *Latin American Research Review*, 15 (1980), pp. 3–40.

16. René Armand Dreifuss, *1964: A conquista do estado; ação política, poder e golpe de classe.* (Petrópolis: Editora Vozes, 1981), pp. 361–96.

17. Ronald M. Schneider, *The Political System of Brazil* (New York: Columbia University Press, 1971), p. 176.

18. Luciano Martins, *Nação e corporação multinacional: A Política das empresas no Brasil e na América Latina* (Rio de Janeiro: Paz e Terra, 1975), pp. 79–91.

19. Erickson, *The Brazilian Corporative State*, pp. 97–130; for the *abertura* period see Maria Herminia Tavares de Almeida, "Nova tendências do moorimento sindicil," in Helgio Trandade, ed., *Brasil em perspectiva. Dilemas de abertura política*, (Porto Alegre: Sulina, 1982), pp. 81–104.

20. McDonough, *Power and Ideology in Brazil*, pp. 69–106.

21. Robert T. Daland, *Exploring Brazilian Bureaucracy*, pp. 273–86.

22. Paulo R. Motta, *Movimentos partidários no Brasil: a estratégia da elite e dos militares* (Rio de Janeiro: Fundaçáo Getúlio Vargas, 1972), pp. 41–44.

23. *Visáo*, August 24, 1981, p. 20. See also Thomas Bruneau, *The Church in Brazil* (Austin: University of Texas Press, 1982).

24. McDonough, *Power and Ideology*, pp. 20–21, 229–30.

25. Ibid, p. 23.

3

Political Institutions

THE PRESIDENCY

The government of Brazil has been headed by a president since the overthrow of the emperor in 1889. During the Old Republic (1889–1930) the president was chosen by direct, nationwide vote (with very narrow suffrage) for a four-year term. The office was almost always alternated between the most powerful states, São Paulo and Minas Gerais, by agreement of the political cliques that dominated the states and the Congress. The power of the presidency was restricted by the states, and politics were rather tranquil except for occasional challenges by outsiders.

Following the revolution led by one of these challengers in 1930, Getúlio Vargas, the powers of the presidency were much expanded. The federal bureaucracy was strengthened and enlarged as the national government took over new functions in management of the economy, labor relations, social security, and state enterprises, while the autonomy of state governments was correspondingly reduced. Vargas met opposition from several state governments, including the Paulista rebellion of 1932, and the Congress was even less docile after 1934. In 1937, however, he used force to remove his opponents from state governorships and to close the Congress. During the *Estado Novo* period (1937–45) the president was a legally unrestricted dictator, who could remove state officers at will. Vargas, with his staff and confidants, directed the affairs of state from the presidential palace.

With the overthrow of Vargas in 1945 and the establishment of a new republican constitution in 1946, the powers of the president, who was directly elected for a five-year term without the possibility of reelection, were much restricted. It is said that President Dutra (1945–51) carried a copy of the constitution in his pocket to determine what he might do. He had good relations with the Congress, which was controlled by his party, the PSD. Vargas, in his second administration (1951–54), found himself increasingly at odds with Congress, which forced him several times to change ministers and which might have impeached him following the scandals of 1954 had he not removed himself. The scope of the presidency was enlarged, however, notably by the creation of Petrobras and Electrobras, charged with near monopolies in their sectors of the economy.

During the interim after Vargas's suicide, the presidency reached a low ebb as successive acting presidents were impeached. But Juscelino Kubitschek (1956–61) was able to reconsolidate the office, expanding its staff and broadening its involvement in economic development. He maintained generally good relations with the Congress, although strains were developing before the end of his term. He generally adhered to the constitution, although he occasionally prohibited critical broadcasts by Carlos Lacerda.

Jânio Quadros was an extreme individualist at odds with the leadership of the parties, and he came into sharp conflict with the Congress during his seven-month administration (1961). He hoped to achieve much stronger authority by his dramatic resignation. After Quadros's failure, João Goulart became president, with much reduced powers, under a parliamentary system. From September 1961 to January 1963, administration was in the hands of a prime minister nominated by the president but serving at the direction of Congress. After Goulart's powers were restored by plebiscite, the legislature continued to be self-assertive. Toward the end of his term, late 1963/early 1964, Goulart was demanding basic reforms, including land reform, and powers to effect them, but the Congress refused.

Although the Second Republic saw a tremendous increase of federal intervention in the economy and, correspondingly, of the bureaucratic apparatus, presidential powers were contained and were often frustrated by the Congress and by the decentralized federal system. The federal budget, in particular, was usually quite remade by Congress, making it very difficult for the executive to implement any consistent program.

Among the first acts of the military regime in 1964 was to concentrate authority exclusively in the presidency and high command. The (purged) Congress could only approve (or theoretically reject) the budget submitted by the executive, and law-making power passed, under several institutional acts, almost entirely to the president, who was de facto chosen by the high command. President Castelo Branco (1964–67) cancelled the mandates of many politicians, intervened in various states, and gave the Ministry of Planning additional powers over the economy. The establishment of the National Information Service and its extension into state and local governments also increased the effective powers of the presidency. The Congress was briefly closed by federal troops in November 1966. Castelo Branco generally spared the judicial system, although he "packed" the Supreme Court from 11 to 16 justices.

The presidency of Costa e Silva (1967–69) instituted the severest authoritarian regime since Vargas's *Estado Novo*. After the Congress endeavored to protect one of its members in December 1968, it was dissolved, and Institutional Act 5 gave the president nearly absolute powers. The Supreme Court and other judicial bodies were purged, and many more persons were removed from office. When Costa e Silva was incapacitated by a stroke, the military ministers assumed the presidency. After a balloting process within the upper ranks of the officers' corps, Gen. Emílio Médici was chosen to serve as president until March 1974.

Médici, facing waves of protest and violence that had been growing since 1968, "deepened" the revolution, with increased censorship, repression, and terroristic counterterrorism. However, Médici continued the trend of Costa e Silva away from Castelo Branco's detailed involvement in government. Médici delegated power within the executive, in a "committee" system reminiscent of Eisenhower's, keeping to himself only major political decisions.[1]

Gen. Ernesto Geisel, chosen by the High Command to succeed Médici, had a broad understanding of both foreign and domestic problems and was assisted by the remarkable General Golbery as his chief advisor. Consequently, Geisel restored close presidential supervision of the government, conferred regularly with his ministers, and expected them to follow high standards of performance.[2] As he excluded the high command from decision making, reduced repression, and gradually liberalized the regime, Geisel had better relations with the Congress than had Médici; but they were strained at times, and Geisel reacted strongly, as with the "April Package" in 1977 after the Congress had balked at following his directions.

Geisel succeeded in choosing his successor, João Baptista Figueiredo, without consulting the high command. Figueiredo, taking office in March 1979 for a term extended to six years, continued the general directions of the Geisel presidency with the assistance of Golbery. He maintained detailed control of political and administrative operations, although he somewhat decentralized authority and gave more scope to interministerial councils than had Geisel. Figueiredo leaned on a tripod consisting of the Chief of the Civil Cabinet, Leitão de Abreu (replacement for Golbery de Couto e Silva); the minister of planning, Antônio Delfim Neto; and the chief of the National Intelligence Service, Octavio Medeiros. Other very influential persons included the chief of the military cabinet, General Rubens Ludwig, and the minister of justice, Ibrahim Abi Ackel.[3]

When President Figueiredo suffered a heart attack in 1981, his military aides first hesitated, then allowed Vice President Aureliano Chavez to occupy the presidency temporarily, the first civilian to do so since 1964.

In 1985 a president is to be chosen by others than the high military authorities for the first time since 1961. The electoral college to meet on January 15 is to consist of the 69 senators, 479 deputies, and 138 delegates, six from each state legislature. The latter were included to improve prospects for the government party, which is stronger in the less populous states.

THE FEDERAL BUREAUCRACY

A large number of ministers and advisors (including planning staff, the SNI, and the president's military and civilian households) form with the president a sort of managing committee. There are numerous councils (such as the National Security Council, the Council of Industrial Development, the National Research Council, and so on) as well as many advisory and normative commissions, all represented in the presidential palace.

The bulk of federal bureaucracy is organized into the following ministries: Air Force, Agriculture, Education and Culture, Army, Finance, Industry and Commerce, Interior, Justice, Navy, Mines and Energy, Social Security, Health, Foreign Relations, and Labor and Transportation. There is also a ministry without portfolio of debureaucratization and one for land tenure, both of which will presumably end with the Figueiredo administration, and the Department of the Administration of Public Service (DASP), an autonomous agency. In 1982, Ester de Figuereido Ferraz, named to head Education and Culture, became the first woman minister in Brazilian history.

Each ministry is organized into three distinct sectors, directly under the ministers: the general secretary (usually a career civil servant) handles administrative detail; the chief of staff manages the minister's appointments, document flow, and political coordination; and the Department of Internal Security (DSI) supervises security and intelligence matters within the ministry in cooperation with the SNI. Usually the head of the DSI is a retired army colonel, while the chief of staff is a close personal confidant of the minister.

Loosely associated with each ministry are a plethora of public corporations, research enterprises, foundations, and autonomous agencies, whose heads are appointed by the president and whose tenure depends on the latter's confidence, not the minister's. A ministry may set up one of these "autonomous agencies" to circumvent bureaucratic restrictions. Ministry of Foreign Relations pay scales could not attract many of the technical (not foreign service) staff needed, so the Viscount of Cabo Frio Foundation was established as an adjunct agency to hire the technicians. The Ministry of Agriculture's old National Department of Agricultural Research (DNPEA) was notoriously lethargic and ineffective, so in 1973 it was transformed into the Brazilian Enterprise for Agricultural Research (EMBRAPA), operated on a cost-effective production basis. When the Ministry of the Army decided to go into arms production, a public corporation (EMBEL) was organized. Because of their autonomous budgets and activities in the private sector, these agencies have nearly escaped central fiscal control. When austerity measures were adopted in 1980 by the planning minister to control federal expenditures, a special watchdog coordination (SEAP) had to be set up to supervise these agencies.

Traditionally, admission to the federal bureaucracy was by public examination and political appointment. Once permanently appointed, the public servant served for life, barring drastic misconduct. The middle echelons have become a favorite haven for many intellectuals (such as Machado de Assis) as a means to support themselves. Many temporary political appointees often found ways to secure permanent appointment. In 1938 DASP was organized and charged with rationalizing the federal bureaucracy and with developing training mechanisms, evaluation and promotion procedures, and so forth. This was not overly successful, as a 1964 survey indicated that only about one-third of 700,000 public employees performed useful functions.[4]

Since the early 1970s, most appointments to the federal bureaucracy have not been permanent. Under the Consolidation of Labor Legislation (CLT) norms, they have been given fixed-period-of-service contracts, sometimes through subcontractors. Those admitted by way of the CLT are usually selected through competitive examinations, but they may be terminated with 30 days notice through the indemnization rules of the Guarantee Fund for Length of Service (FGTS). Thus job stability is not what it used to be in the federal service. Employees can be either temporarily "requisitioned" or permanently hired by another ministry or agency.

Upper-echelon political appointees are temporary and are mostly recruited from outside the federal public service; some may come from state or local government. These appointments are usually "reviewed" by respective DSIs, which may cause some problems. In 1979, some 30 such appointments made by the new Education Minister were vetoed by the DSI in view of SNI information.

The public service before 1964 was plagued by low pay. Although job security was high, employees could usually find higher-paying jobs in the private sector; and many did, as a second or clandestine job. Many federal workers were on 20-hour workweek schedules and so could easily hold a second job. In an effort to upgrade the federal bureaucracy, post-1964 governments provided a full-time, higher-pay option to most employees, while making pay schedules competitive with the private sector in middle-management positions for those with high technical qualifications. A university degree became an important factor in promotion.

This restructuring produced a so-called "technobureaucratic elite," charged with reorganizing the federal service and the nation's development.

Most "technocrats" have advanced or graduate degrees (many from foreign universities) in economics, planning, administration, engineering, and other technical areas. During the months previous to a government transition, there is a considerable circulation (called "musical chairs") of these technocrats from one agency to another.

As is discussed in Chapter 5, the Brazilian military has one of the fastest promotion tracks in the world. After 1964, the federal bureaucracy began receiving a new type of employee, the active duty or retired officer. Officers could also get a two-year leave of absence to take a civilian bureaucratic position, after which they had to return to active duty or opt for retirement. Many officers took such leaves, especially to organize and "sanitize" certain areas of the federal bureaucracy in the early phases of the 1964 revolution. However, a job in the civilian bureaucracy also became attractive to officers, especially to colonels, faced with retirement after being passed over for promotion three times. This second salary was often more than the military pension. Although this was done before 1964, it became much more common after 1964, as the "system" cared for its own through "old boy" networks throughout the federal service.

By 1972, most of the central federal bureaucracies had moved to Brasília, although some subsections remained in Rio. However, a large part of the federal bureaucracy is located in the interior in subsections and agencies charged with regional coordination, such as SUDAM in the Amazon and SUDENE in the Northeast, which work closely with state and local governments.

Federal employees are represented by the Brazilian Association of Civil Servants (ASCB), which periodically negotiates with DASP. Although DASP provides some in-service training for federal bureaucrats, the traditional academic training ground for public administrators has been the Getúlio Vargas Foundation's Brazilian School of Public Administration (EBAP) in Rio, and its branch in São Paulo, which recently reduced operations. Many federal employees are able to attend night classes in their home cities and thus receive university degrees, usually in law, administration, or economics.

In 1981, the federal bureaucracy counted some 468,000 employees, and there are nearly 2 million in state and local governments. The federal bureaucracy now has slightly more CLT employees (51.6 percent) than traditional, civil-service appointments; two-thirds are men, and 37.3 percent have had some university education.[5]

In June 1980, President Figueiredo signed an executive order putting a hiring freeze on the federal executive, an austerity measure that many states adopted. Already faced with a recession and with increasing unemployment in the private sector, the middle class now found this traditional haven effectively blocked.

The Ministry of Debureaucratization, headed by Hélio Beltrão (who had been associated with Carlos Lacerda and was Costa e Silva's planning minister), has succeeded in streamlining some of Brazil's traditional bureaucratic procedures, but its most significant action has been to select some 40 or 50 state enterprises for sale to domestic or foreign private capital. This should serve a variety of purposes: to reduce federal budget deficits, to secure badly needed resources (especially foreign exchange) for the federal treasury, and to respond partially to the demands of the national bourgeoisie for reducing the role of state capitalism in the economy. However, the sale of state enterprises to foreign capital would not be as well received by these groups and by nationalist military officers.

Based on his interviews with managers of public corporations and with upper-echelon bureaucrats, McDonough concluded that in 1972/73 this group was quite conservative in ideology and that it placed more emphasis on economic development than on social or political development.[6] However, Daland, on the basis of his lengthy research on the federal bureaucracy (since the late 1950s), concluded pessimistically that it has not performed well as an agent of modernization and of promoting economic development, because of lack of training, incompetent leadership, and organizational constraints—which are firmly rooted in the nation's traditional political culture.[7]

THE CONGRESS

Composition

During the Empire, Brazil was a constitutional monarchy with a bicameral parliament. The Chamber of Deputies was elected periodically when the emperor dissolved it. Elections were by two stages, and the electorate was severely limited. Proportional, district, and mixed electoral systems were tried at various times for the lower house. Senators represented the states and were appointed for life terms from three-name lists submitted to the emperor.

After the overthrow of the Empire in 1889, the new republican constitution established a bicameral legislature after the U.S. model. Three senators were directly elected from each state to staggered nine-year terms, while deputies were elected to three-year terms. Legislators were selected and nominated by each state political machine. Rarely would an independent candidate be elected, and usually these renegades would be unseated by the "certification committee."

Following the 1930 revolution, the national legislature was closed until December 1933 when a constituent assembly was convened to elaborate the

1934 constitution. During these four years, Brazil experimented with a system of proportional representation with professional (or functional) representation. Approximately one-third of the lower house was indirectly elected by functional groups in the society: producing classes, workers, public servants, and professionals. During the *Estado Novo* period, the Congress remained closed.

With the fall of Vargas in 1945, the constitution of 1946 established the Congress essentially as it is today. Although it was buffeted by regime crises of the 1950s and 1960s and by the years of military government, legislators have been elected every four years with no interruption. The legislature elected in 1982 is the tenth session.

As in the First Republic, the 20 states and Federal District each elected three senators to staggered eight-year terms. The Chamber of Deputies continued the system of proportional representation but dropped the fascist-inspired system of functional representation. As in Philadelphia in 1789, one of the crucial questions in Rio de Janeiro in 1946 was that of determining how the size of each state delegation in the lower house was to be calculated, the more populous states opposing the smaller ones, the latter generally being less developed as well. A bracket system of unequal representation was adopted, based on the population of each state. This guaranteed a minimum number for the smallest states, while progressively larger population brackets reduced the delegations of the larger states (São Paulo and Minas) from what they had been in the First Republic.

The military government established representation according to population rather than number of voters in order to increase the weight of the poorer states. It also erected new states in the interior to improve its position in the Senate. As a result, in 1982 the North and Northeast, with less than one third of the voters, had 56 percent of Senate seats and over 40 percent of the Chamber. São Paulo state is grossly underrepresented, not only in the Senate but also in the Chamber, where it has one-eighth of the seats for one-quarter of the national population. In 1982 the number of deputies was increased from 420 to 479, benefiting mostly the North and Northeast. Each state was to elect at least eight.

Congress and the President

With Vargas effectively retired to São Borja, the politicians meeting in 1946 expanded the Legislature's powers somewhat. Constitutional amendments needed two-thirds of both houses, and executive decree-laws were subject to review. The Congress had independent taxation, expenditure, and civil-service powers, "extrabudget" and extremely powerful subpoena and investigative authority, and strong immunities.

From 1951 through 1964, all presidents and vice presidents had been members of Congress, and usually half of their cabinet ministers were drawn from the Legislature. Because of the party list system of proportional representation, a legislator did not resign his seat to occupy such a position but rather took a leave of absence, while the next alternate on the list (in order of votes accrued) would take his place. These substitutions were very common as legislators would "feather their nests" in executive positions (both state and federal) between elections, while giving the alternates in their party some experience. During this period, presidential appointments were not subject to legislative approval (save judges and ambassadors who required Senate approval), but officials were at times forced to resign by pressures from the Congress.

Following Vargas's suicide in 1954, the legislature was called upon to impeach two presidents in 1955. The first was Acting President Carlos Luz, who took over when Vargas's vice president, Café Filho, had a slight heart attack and who was maneuvering to prevent the recently elected Kubitschek from taking office in January 1956. Café Filho tried to return to office and to continue the conspiracy against Kubitschek, but he was in turn impeached by Congress.

Six years later, in August 1961, Congress was faced with another regime crisis. President Jânio Quadros resigned because of frustrations in his relationship with Congress, hoping to be recalled with enhanced powers because Vice President João Goulart was unacceptable to the military. However, Congress enacted a constitutional amendment establishing a parliamentary system, which reduced Goulart's presidential powers sufficiently to satisfy the military. This system of divided powers did not work well, however, and Goulart was able to regain full power. His "basic reforms" were frustrated by a recalcitrant Congress, and Goulart was attempting to circumvent Congress by issuing decrees on land reform and other matters when the military removed him from office.

In April 1964, Chamber President Ranieri Mazzili temporarily occupied the presidency, but it was the military that effectively filled the power vacuum with Institutional Act 1, which made the High Command the supreme power.

Military governments after 1964 successively reduced the powers of Congress by depriving the members of immunity, purging obstreperous members, establishing a simple "approve or disapprove" budget vote, and prohibiting Chamber and Senate officers from serving consecutive two-year terms. Later legislation established that members voting against party leadership could lose their mandates. This eliminated roll-call voting and produced the so-called "standup-sitdown" bloc voting. Finally, the Congress was reduced in its legislative functions by the *decurso de prazo* rule, whereby an executive bill is submitted with a time limit (30 or 45 days) for deliberation by the Congress. If it has not been acted upon during this period, the bill is automatically passed. Thus, if the government party cannot count on votes to pass a bill of this type, its leadership resorts to an exodus to prevent a quorum for deliberations. This device was frequently used after 1975, when government majorities were more precarious within the Congress, and especially in 1980/81 following the reorganization of the party system.

During the Médici period (1969–74), the Congress was very subservient to the executive; less than 10 percent of Legislature-initiated bills were passed, in contrast to 100 percent of executive-initiated bills. In the early 1960s, prior to the military takeover, the Congress passed some 85 percent of its own bills and 95 percent of executive bills.[8]

Traditionally, the Congress had two effective means of monitoring and controlling the executive. One was requests for information and the subpoena power of Chamber and Senate investigative committees, *Commissão Parlamentar de Inquérito* (CPI). Prior to 1964, the use of these powers had sometimes caused the fall of ministers and bureaucrats and had contributed to the demise of President Vargas in 1954. The military government curtailed these powers after 1964 by placing a limit on the number and duration of CPIs and by making their creation more difficult. Once the opposition party regained a minority larger than one-third, which it did in 1975 during the Geisel administration, it could constitute CPIs, which examined such delicate questions as the nuclear energy program, the role of multinational corporations, drug abuse, torture, repression, and state capitalism.

Congressional monitoring of executive performance is also aided by the *Tribunal de Contas da União* (TCU), and by the Federal Tribunal of Accounts, similar to the U.S. General Accounting Office. The TCU passes judgment on the accounting and spending procedures of federal agencies, reports mismanagement and other illegalities to Congress, and assesses penalties.

In 1980, government and opposition deputies sponsored legislation that would have partially restored Congressional prerogatives as well as those of individual legislators. This effort was defeated by the government through the "exodus" technique previously described. However, a reduced version of this bill was passed by a government majority in June 1982. By 1982, in order to secure passage of its bills, the government had to threaten that deputies of the government party would lose their seats if they failed to vote correctly.

Given this environment and restrictions on the Congress, what, if any, is the role of the Brazilian legislature in the current political system?

First, through the post-1964 period, the Congress has served to legitimize the regime. The popular will has received some expression through regular legislative elections every four years. Second, the Congress has performed as a forum of political communication for the government and the opposition. The ARENA and MDB established foundation-type think tanks within the Congress, which have organized a number of national symposiums on critical issues. The executive seemed to welcome them, and many agency bureaucrats participated. During the most repressive years, when other channels of communication were censored and silenced, the Congress stood alone in this regard. After 1974, the Congress and the political class became the focal point of negotiations between opposition and government and provided the climate for the *abertura.*

Third, while the press was impeded from performing the watchdog function of monitoring government implementation of its own programs, the Congress was able to provide some feedback in this regard. After 1975 the press vigorously reassumed this role. In elaborating legislation, the Congress has at times contributed to the improvement of executive bills that would have been disastrous in practice. On these occasions, instead of allowing the Congress to perform its legislative function, the executive would withdraw the bill from consideration and completely rewrite it, incorporating the suggestions and criticisms made in Congress, and then resubmit "its" bill. The Senate also has the right to formally approve executive appointments of federal judges, of the governor of the Federal District, and of ambassadors, as well as to pass on foreign loans incurred by state and local governments.

The new Congress installed in 1983 (with nearly 60 percent turnover in the Lower House) regained some of its autonomy as part of the negotiations of the May 1982 "Package," including stronger immunities and more liberty to select its own presiding officers. Because the government party (PDS) lost its majority position in the Chamber of Deputies (5 seats shy of the 240 majority figure), in order to pass its bills, the government will be forced to negotiate transient coalitions almost on a case-by-case basis, none of the smaller parties having agreed to a permanent coalition. Thus the Brazilian legislature will play a somewhat more significant role in the political system, but without a return to its full powers and prerogatives of the pre-1964 period.

THE JUDICIAL SYSTEM

The present legal system evolved from Roman law, with important influences from the French, Portuguese, and German systems. Traditionally, individual rights were protected by such guarantees as habeas corpus, trial by jury, and the writ of security (*mandado de segurança*), on which a judge has to rule within 72 hours when a person has submitted a petition for relief. After the 1964 revolution, these guarantees were often suspended, and the jurisdiction of the civilian judiciary was reduced as the military courts enlarged their role in the area of subversion and internal security.

There is no Brazilian network of federal courts as there is in the United States. Each state has its Court of Justice (*Tribunal de Justica*) and district courts presided over by appointed, civil-service judges. On appeal, cases go to the Federal Court of Appeals (*Tribunal Federal de Recursos*) in Brasília and finally to the Supreme Court (*Supremo Tribunal Federal*, STF).

There are four parallel court hierarchies which deal with matters pertaining to civil, labor, electoral, and military law. The STF is the final instance of appeal of all four systems.

The Supreme Court is composed of 11 judges, native Brazilians over age 35 who are appointed by the president with Senate confirmation. Many cases are decided by three committees of judges. Decisions are by majority, and deliberations and discussions are public. The STF has jurisdiction over cases involving the federal government and its employees, between states and local governments, and concerning foreign governments or international agencies. It also hears cases against members of Congress within the National Security Law. During the Médici and Geisel terms, several legislators were tried and some were convicted under this law. In 1981, two deputies were tried for having slandered the armed forces, but they were released.

Historically, the STF was nearly immune to the crosscurrents of Brazilian politics. In 1863, the Visconde de Sinimbu retired four justices whose rulings had offended the emperor. In 1931, the Vargas revolutionary government retired six STF members. President Castelo Branco, although unhappy with many STF decisions—especially the granting of habeas corpus to politicians imprisoned by the government, such as Miguel Arraes—did not intervene directly by purging judges. However, Castelo Branco's AI-2 added five justices to the high court.

Relations between the STF and the executive worsened during the Costa e Silva government. The military was outraged at the court for declaring portions of the National Security Law unconstitutional and for freeing students and other political prisoners in 1968. On January 16, 1969, three STF judges were among those removed in the second wave of AI-5 purges. Two other judges resigned in protest.

Recently, the STF has recouped most of its autonomy and former prestige as an independent branch of government. Castelo Branco appointed mostly UDN politicians to the court, but subsequent governments have appointed jurists and lawyers from within their administrations.

The Superior Electoral Court (TSE) is the final instance in the hierarchy of local and regional electoral courts. This system established in the 1930s, came into its own after 1945. It is charged with the registration of voters, parties, and candidates, and with printing ballots, supervising elections, and tabulating the vote. In 1971, the electoral courts were given the added responsibility of feeding, housing, and transporting voters who reside great distances from their polling places during elections.

The TSE has played a role in several important political decisions. In January 1948, the TSE declared the Brazilian Communist Party illegal because of its foreign connections. In 1950 and 1955, it decided upon the legality of presidents elected with less than absolute majority. In 1965, Marshal Lott was declared ineligible to run for the governorship in Guanabara because his voting residence was in the neighboring state of Rio de Janeiro. More recently, the TSE ruled in May 1980 that the Ivete Vargas faction, and not that of Leonel Brizola, would be provisionally registered as the Brazilian Labor Party. As a result, both factions lost strength. In January 1982 the TSE demonstrated its independence by refusing to prohibit the fusion of the PP and the PMDB, and in the height of the campaign an electoral judge forbad the broadcast of a speech by the president.[9] It is a remarkable testimony to the electoral system that the military government, even when political action was largely repressed, never tried to falsify electoral results.

The Superior Labor Court (TST) has 17 judges, 11 appointed for life and six "temporary" members appointed to three-year terms. Individual employee-employer disputes are first heard by local boards of conciliation, consisting of one judge and one representative each for labor and management. They are heard on appeal by the Regional Labor Courts (TRTs), which also have original jurisdiction over collective labor disputes. Some TRTs have five judges, others three, with representation of both labor and management.

With the reemergence of a more independent trade-union movement in Brazil since 1975, the labor court system has played a more important role. Most notably, in 1979, the TRT in São Paulo, instead of decreeing a salary-increase settlement, admonished labor and management to return to the bargaining table. Because of the new, complicated salary legislation involving inflation indexes and productivity calculations, the labor courts' role in labor disputes has become more complex and more based on econometric data.

The Superior Military Court (STM) dates from the nineteenth century and traditionally had jurisdiction over trials of military personnel. Following the 1964 revolution, however, the STM's role was enlarged to include all cases involving subversion, corruption, and internal security that initially stemmed from military investigating commissions and that were later prosecuted under the National Security Law.

The STM is also at the apex of a hierarchical system of lower military courts. It is composed of 15 judges, 10 military (from the three branches of the armed forces) and five civilian judges. Some of the latter have tended to be more conservative and hard-line than some of the former. During Geisel's presidency, many of his former military colleagues on the STM were outspoken proponents of a political liberalization and amnesty. During 1979, the STM eliminated many cases against exiled political figures, including Leonel Brizola, thus permitting their return and subsequent participation in politics.

In 1981, the STM made two very important decisions. First, the trial and condemnation of "Lula" and his fellow labor leaders by the Military Court in São Paulo for their role in the 1980 strikes under the LSN was declared a mistrial because their lawyers had not been present at the proceedings. Second, on a close decision, the STM decided not to continue the investigation of the April 30 Riocentro bombing, instead filing the report of the First Army investigating commission.

The independence of Brazil's judicial system is also being reasserted through a series of cases stemming from physical torture by federal and state authorities. In the state of Paraná, a person who lost an eye and was crippled at the hands of state security forces received a favorable indemnization judgment from the civil courts. The widow of Wladimir Hertzog, who was tortured and died at the Second Army headquarters in São Paulo in 1975, received a favorable judgment in her suit against the federal government, a decision which is still on appeal. In these and similar cases, no accusations or judgments were made against individual defendants, but rather against a state or the national government.

THE FEDERAL SYSTEM

The relationship between national government and the states and *municípios* has been a difficult problem throughout Brazil's political history. Even during the colonial period, the Portuguese crown had great difficulty asserting its authority over the provinces and local municipal governments. One of the most important questions during the early independence period was that of centralization vs. decentralization. Dom Pedro I's troubles with the powerful provinces of São Paulo and Minas Gerais contributed to his resignation. Historians have marveled at the fact that Brazil was able to maintain the integrity of its huge territory during the regional secessionist rebellions in Bahia, Pernambuco, Pará, and the south through the ensuing regency period. A unitary system prevailed during the reign of Dom Pedro II, whereby the emperor appointed the provincial governors, who appointed the local administrators; both had elected legislative bodies, however. Although the emperor was adroit at balancing political forces through these appointments, by the 1880s São Paulo and Minas began to chafe under centralized control because of their new wealth from coffee. The desire for provincial autonomy was one of the most important factors contributing to the downfall of the Empire and to the advent of the First Republic in 1889.

The republican constitution of 1890 established a very decentralized federalism. The states elected their own chief executives, called "presidents," by direct popular vote and established their own constitutions, tax laws, and state military forces. The townships also had autonomous governments with elected officers. States could levy taxes on interstate commerce, contract foreign loans directly, and maintain representatives in foreign countries. Most taxation prerogatives were reserved for the state and local governments.

Although the larger states were free to run their governments without federal interference, many of the smaller states suffered federal intervention during this period as the national government tried to maintain its allies in power. However, the lines of communication and control of the central authorities were precarious; and often as not, the "outs" regrouped for a counterattack and became the "ins" again.

This fostered the system of mutual support between the state government and local political chiefs in the interior (*coronéis*). Because of economic dependence, rural voters were effectively controlled by the local bosses, who offered electoral support to the state government in return for political autonomy and for "spoils" such as public works, but especially for jobs as police chiefs, judges, school principals, tax collectors, and so on. The *tenentes* saw these corrupt electoral and political practices as impeding the nation's progress and development in the 1920s and sought to eliminate them with the 1930 revolution. Except for the short-lived democratic period of 1934–37, Brazil reverted to a unitary system after 1930. Vargas appointed an interventor in each state, who in turn named local mayors; and he greatly centralized and strengthened the national government, especially the armed forces, which had been considerably weaker than the state militia during the First Republic.

Although *tenentes* were appointed interventors in some states, civilian governors were indirectly elected by the state assemblies by 1935. Before closing the Congress and decreeing the authoritarian *Estado Novo* in 1937, Vargas carefully isolated and forced the resignation of "independent" governors in the important states of Bahia, São Paulo, and Rio Grande do Sul. The 1930 revolution had been made in the name of curing the political vices of the old regime, but Vargas essentially removed the "ins" in most states, who were replaced by "outs" who were loyal to him and who were representative of the same political and economic elite that had dominated the states.

The 1946 constitution returned Brazil to a federal system of government but retained most of the centralized features of the federal administration. States were granted full political autonomy to elect executives and assemblies by direct popular vote, as were the *municípios*, many of which were dependent on state government for direct grants.

In 1964, the autonomy of state government facilitated the military revolution, crucial military and political support against the Goulart government coming from the governors in Minas, São Paulo, and Guanabara. But once Castelo Branco was in power, these three governors turned against the revolution, and their autonomy was destroyed. In the last direct elections for governor, in October 1965, several "contesters" were elected, to the consternation of some of the military. Although the elected governors were allowed to take office, Castelo Branco decreed a reform of the party system and the indirect election of future governors by state assemblies. Further, in the name of national security, the mayors of all state capitals and 77 other *municípios* designated as national security areas were to be appointed by the state governor. In practice, state governors were selected by the president and his close advisors.

The federal government also had a hand in the security apparatus of the states. After 1964, state secretaries of security were active-duty army colonels on a two-year rotation, except for São Paulo, where Governor Maluf in 1979 named a civilian from the state's criminal justice system. However, even Maluf maintained an army officer as commandant of the state military policy forces (PM). Following the opposition victory in key states in the southern region in 1982, President Figueiredo signed a decree in January 1983 allowing the newly-elected governors to name a career officer from within the ranks of the state PM as commandant, subject to approval by the Army Minister. Collaboration between the State Department of Political and Social Order (DOPS) and the Federal Police was reduced, and the operations of the latter were beefed-up in the states.

Under the 1964/65 tax/revenue sharing reforms, revenues from the sales tax collected at the municipal level (where the goods were manufactured) were remitted directly to Brasília, whence they were disbursed to the states and *municípios* according to complicated formulas based on population and on the amount of tax collected. Under severe pressure from the states, the government undertook a tax/revenue sharing reform in 1983 to return to collection of sales taxes where the goods are consumed, to the benefit of the less developed states, especially in the Northeast. To compensate losses by the more developed producer states (São Paulo, Minas Gerais, and Rio de Janeiro), a certain percentage of the Tax on Industrial Products (IPI) will be returned to the states. At the same time, state finance and planning secretaries are closely monitored by their counterpart ministries in Brasília.

Despite such restrictions, politics is a very serious game in most states and *municípios*. State legislators play a much more active role in elaborating and passing legislation and in representing constituents' demands than do their federal counterparts. This state-federal difference is due to factional divisions at the state level, which at times have made possible coalitions to defeat the governor. State deputies are consequently taken more seriously by governors than are federal legislators by the president.

In November 1980, the lengths of the terms for mayors and councilmen were extended for two years, as early elections were judged "inopportune" by the Figueiredo government, with the new party system less than a year old and public sentiment running against the government. Thus, concurrent local, state, and federal elections were held in November 1982, and many mayors, having mobilized support during six years in office, mounted serious challenges to incumbent state and federal deputies. However, those elected to local office in 1982 will again have six-year terms, thus setting the elections out of phase again, with the next state and federal elections scheduled for 1986 and local elections for 1988.[10]

One reason Castelo Branco and his planning minister, Roberto Campos, instituted the ad valorem tax reforms in the mid-1960s and eliminated the state governments as redistributors was to provide local mayors with more adequate resources. It was hoped that these mayors, especially those from larger interior cities, could thus create a sufficient political base to work a "grassroots" revolution by unseating traditional and perennial state and federal deputies in subsequent elections. Because of the adverse political climate, this did not occur in 1970, but it was beginning to take place in 1974 and 1978 and was an important factor in 1982.

Throughout two lengthy authoritarian periods in the twentieth century, Brazil's local political institutions have seen their roles and prerogatives reduced by centralizing federal executives. However, these institutions survived and adapted to each new environment. The increased, centralized role of the federal executive in finance and economy will doubtless be essentially retained, but by the mid-1980s the states and *municípios* may have recovered much of their importance, just as they did in 1945–46 after the Vargas dictatorship.

NOTES

1. Peter Flynn, *Brazil: A Political Analysis* (Boulder, Colo.: Westview Press, 1978), pp. 473–75.

2. Ibid.

3. Carlos Chagas, "The Unstable Tripod of Power in the Planalto", *Estado de São Paulo*, July 18, 1982, p. 4; *JPRS* September 3, 1982, p. 28.

4. Alexandre de Souza Costa Barros, *The Brazilian Military: Professional Socialization, Political Performance, and State Building* (Ph.D. dissertation, University of Chicago, 1978), p. 197.

5. *Isto É*, August 5, 1981, pp. 66–69.

6. Peter McDonough, *Power and Ideology in Brazil* (Princeton, N.J.: Princeton University Press, 1981), pp. 138–42.

7. Robert J. Daland, *Exploring Brazilian Bureaucracy: Performance and Pathology* (Washington, D.C.: University Press of America, 1981), pp. 5–6.

8. Sérgio Abranches and Glaucio D. Soares, "As funçôés do legislativo," *Revista de Administração Pública* (1973): 90–92.

9. FBIS Latin America, September 8, 1982, p. D1.

10. *Latin American Regional Reports, Brazil*, July 2, 1982, p. 1.

4

Political Parties and Electoral Process

Based on her research on the Brazilian parties and electoral system in 1958, Peterson described what she had observed as "institutionalized confusion."[1] This chapter describes and analyzes this "confusion" during three distinct historical periods: the multiparty system established with the 1946 constitution, the two-party system organized in 1965 after the Second Institutional Act, and the new multiparty system formed in 1979–80.

HISTORICAL BACKGROUND

During the Empire (1822–89), the franchise was limited to propertied males, and electors were selected in a two-step process to the lower house of parliament, controlled alternately by aristocratic Liberal and Conservative parties under the aegis of the emperor. The Old Republic (1889–30) extended the franchise to all literate males, and elections were direct on all levels, from municipal councilmen to president. In the federal system, state and local oligarchies had considerable autonomy. State-level Republican parties were organized, and the largest states of Minas Gerais and São Paulo virtually ran the country, but no parties were organized at the national level. However, dissident parties did organize in some states.

In 1930, the São Paulo political machine tried to retain control of the presidency, which by custom should have been rotated to Minas Gerais. The outcome was a revolution led by the Liberal Alliance and the victory of Getúlio Vargas of Rio Grande do Sul. He ruled Brazil until 1945, mostly without benefit of political parties and elections, although elections were held in 1933 and 1935 under a mixed system that included occupational (functional) representation.

Six years after Vargas closed Congress in 1937 and decreed the *Estado Novo*, a group of politicians and intellectuals from Minas Gerais issued the *Manifesto dos Mineiros*, calling for elections and a return to constitutional democracy. With the return of the Brazilian Expeditionary Force from Italy, stronger demands were voiced within the military. On February 28, 1945, Vargas issued an "Additional Act" that stated that the electoral process would be put in motion within 90 days. This was done on May 28, and elections for constituent assembly and president were set for December 2.

THE MULTIPARTY SYSTEM: 1945–65

The New Parties and Elections, 1945–46

On April 7, 1945, a heterogeneous group of opposition factions met at the Brazilian Press Association (ABI) in Rio to form an anti-Vargas front, including pre-1930 politicians, dissidents from Vargas's *Estado Novo*, and socialists. From this anti-Vargas front emerged the *União Democrática Nacional* (UDN), which chose its presidential candidate, Brig. Eduardo Gomes, at its August convention. Many original "front" participants also organized their own parties: A. Bernardes, the Republican Party (PR); A. Barros, the Popular Representation Party (PRP); Raul Pilla, the Liberator Party (PL); and A. Pereira, the *Partido Comunista Brasileiro* (PCB).

The pro-Vargas forces, under the guidance of the Vargas-appointed interventor, held a large meeting in Belo Horizonte on April 8 to organize the *Partido Social Democrático* (PSD). Similar conclaves were held in all states, as each interventor summoned his followers to form a new party. War Minister Eurico Gaspar Dutra was named the PSD presidential candidate at its July 1 convention.

The urban equivalent of the more rural-based PSD, the *Partido Trabalhista Brasileiro* (PTB), was organized by Vargas's Ministry of Labor and by its "official" labor organizations, established during the *Estado Novo*, in effort to counteract successful Communist Party efforts in these unions and to attract lower-class voters in the urban-industrial areas of the Central-South.

Dutra was elected by 53 percent of the 6.2 million votes cast, Gomes being second with 33 percent. Proportional representation (PR) was retained for the election of 286 federal deputies, and two senators were elected from each of the 20 states and from the federal district. Due partly to the addition of female voters, the electorate rose from 1.5 million in 1934 to 7.4 million in 1945, out of an estimated 9.2 million eligible voters. The franchise was, and still is, restricted to literates.

As shown in Table 4.1, the PSD had a comfortable majority in 1945, as well as in the first legislative period (1947–51), with the UDN, PTB, and PCB running second, third, and fourth.

Because the smaller, less developed rural states held a majority within the PSD, the 1946 constitution adopted a minimum representation formula for the lower house, which favored the smaller states to the detriment of the largest states that had held control in the First Republic: São Paulo and Minas Gerais.

The PR system used initially gave the "remainders" to the lead party in each state, but in 1950 the de Hondt system was adopted, dividing the remainders among all parties proportionately to their total vote. As shown in Table 4.1, chamber size was open-ended and increased to 326 in 1954 and to 409 in 1962, following the respective decennial censuses. The two senators per state elected in 1945 served eight-year terms, while the third senator elected in 1947 served an initial four-year term. Three new senators were added when the Acre territory achieved statehood in 1962. Deputies served four-year terms.

Voting was by individual ballots for each office. Ballot papers, printed by the candidates, were placed in plain envelopes before being dropped in the ballot box. This practice lent itself to corruption and voter manipulation, and it was later replaced by "general" or long ballots printed by the electoral court system.

Brazil began this multiparty period with 10 parties represented in the Chamber, but with the PSD in a hegemonic position. By 1963, there were 13 parties, and the PSD had lost its dominant position and was rivaled by the PTB in a system of moderate pluralism.

The Populist Parties were characterized by a direct, mass appeal to the electorate, in the populist mode, with no fixed ideology or well-defined political program. They ranged from the personalist populism of Ademar de Barros's PSP and the "antiparty" populism of Jânio Quadros to the orthodox *trabalhismo* (laborism) of the PTB—tied to official manipulations through the Labor Ministry and social security institutes—and the "alternative *trabalhismos*" of the Socialist Labor Party (PST), the National Labor Party (PTN), the Rural Labor Party (PRT), and the Renovating Labor Movement (MTR). Their common thread was a diffuse message of progress and development aimed at the working and lower-middle classes in urban areas.

TABLE 4.1. Party Strength in the Chamber
of Deputies, 1946–63[1]
(by percent)

Political Party	Constituent Assembly 1946[2]	Legislative Session				
		1st 1947[3]	2nd 1951	3rd 1955	4th 1959	5th 1963
PTB	7.7	8.2	16.8	18.4	20.2	28.4
PSD	52.8	52.3	36.8	36.2	35.3	28.9
UDN	27.6	26.3	24.8	22.4	21.5	22.2
PSP	1.7	2.6	7.4	9.5	7.7	5.1
PDC	0.7	0.7	0.7	0.9	2.1	4.9
PTN	—	0.3	1.6	1.8	2.1	2.7
PST	—	—	3.0	—	0.6	1.7
PR	3.5	3.9	3.6	5.2	5.2	1.0
PL	0.4	0.3	1.6	3.1	0.9	1.2
PRP	—	—	0.3	1.2	0.9	1.2
PSB	—	—	0.3	0.9	2.8	1.2
PRT	—	—	0.3	0.3	0.6	0.7
MTR	—	—	—	—	—	0.7
PCB	4.9	4.6	—	—	—	—
ED	0.7	0.7	—	—	—	—
TOTAL	100.0	100.0	100.0	100.0	100.0	100.0
(N)	(286)	(304)	(304)	(326)	(326)	(409)
Fragmentation Index[4]	0.635	0.646	0.767	0.772	0.778	0.780

[1]The data are not exactly congruent to those of the TSE due to deputies elected by coalitions and those who changed party labels after taking office. The party affiliations are, therefore, those reported in the *Annals of the Chamber of Deputies* at the start of each legislative session.

[2]Constituent Assembly elected on December 2, 1945.

[3]After the supplementary elections of January 19, 1947.

[4]This index is from Douglas Rae, *The Political Consequences of Electoral Law* (New Haven: Yale University Press, 1967), pp. 46–64. The formula used:

$$F.I. = 1 - \sum_{i=1}^{N} p_i^2$$

N is the number of parties, and P_i is the proportion of seats occupied by the "ith" party.
Source: Compiled by Fleischer.

The Brazilian Labor Party was made up of union bosses (*pelegos*) associated with Ministry of Labor administrators of union affairs, pensions, and social security, with professional politicians of the Getúlista movement, and more or less doctrinaire ideologues. The group grew steadily from 22 deputies elected to the Constituent Assembly to 116 deputies and 18 senators in 1963, thus rivalling the PSD as the largest party in Congress. Vargas managed to stay on top of the three factions until his death in 1954. After being elected vice president in 1955, João Goulart took hold of labor relations and strengthened the syndicalist sector. After becoming president in 1961, Goulart achieved a tenuous leadership of the PTB, in competition with more extreme radicals led by his brother-in-law, Leonel Brizola.

Although the PTB was called the "party of laborers," most of its elected representatives came from middle- and upper-class backgrounds: public servants, journalists, lawyers, and teachers. They had lower levels of education and of localism and a very efficacious recruitment style, being elected to Congress at very young ages and after short political careers.

The MTR was an offshoot of the PTB. Rebelling against the impossibility of making the PTB the representative of legitimate labor interests, it drew away a fraction of labor votes, electing one senator and three federal deputies in 1962.

The second most important "progressive" party, the *Partido Social Progressista* (PSP), was organized by Ademar de Barros, a medical doctor and son of a coffee grower who had been Vargas's interventor in São Paulo (1937–41). Barros engineered the fusion of three small parties in 1946 to form the PSP, which became the fifth-ranking party nationwide, with six deputies. With the backing of the PCB, Barros won the governorship of São Paulo in 1947. In 1950, Barros agreed to support Vargas's reelection bid in return for the latter's support in 1955. Suicide broke this pact, so in 1955 Barros was forced into a three-way race with the PSD-PTB and the UDN, which he lost.

Barros lost gubernatorial races to Jânio Quadros and his coalition in 1954 and 1958, and presidential bids in 1955 and 1960. But in 1957 he was elected Mayor of São Paulo, and he finally returned to the governorship in 1962, defeating Quadros by a mere 100,000 votes. The PSP was the fourth party in Congress by 1964, when Barros broke with Goulart and joined the conspiracy, hoping to enhance his presidential chances in 1965. These elections were canceled by President Castelo Branco, who eventually purged the São Paulo governor in 1966.

PSP deputies came from a variety of occupational backgrounds: agriculture, health, business, journalism, and even military—perhaps the most diverse mixture of all parties. Administrative and elective careers were equally frequent. The PSP recruited "outsiders" without local/regional ties from diverse economic sectors, who used politics as a means of "striking it rich" or improving their business interests.

There were several smaller labor-populist parties. The PST had support mostly in the northeast, where it contributed to the radicalism of the early 1960s. It elected 13 deputies in 1962. The PTN, which became the most consistent supporter of Jânio Quadros, also found most of its support in the northeast. It elected 16 deputies in 1962. The Rural Labor Party (PRT), based in São Paulo, managed to elect three deputies in 1962.

Ideological Parties

Five parties were noted for well-elaborated and fixed doctrines, which were translated into programs of political action. The most important of Brazil's ideological parties, the *Partido Comunista Brasileiro*, was organized in 1922. Its most illustrious adept was Luis Carlos Prestes. A captain in the army engineering corps, Prestes participated in the 1924 *tenentes* revolt and led the "long march" of the "Prestes Column" across thousands of miles of Brazil's interior, eluding government troops for 18 months before seeking exile in Bolivia and, later, in Buenos Aires. He refused to participate in the 1930 revolution, thinking it too moderate. He joined the Communist Party in 1931 and traveled to Russia, where he worked as an engineer until 1935. Back in Brazil, he helped to organize the leftist National Liberation Alliance (ANL). Under the leadership of Prestes, the party led the disastrous military insurrection of November 1935 (the *Intentona*), as a result of which the party was repressed until 1945.

The PCB opposed the Vargas government in early 1945, but after its leaders were released from prison, the party abandoned the anti-Vargas front. However, instead of backing the "official" Dutra candidacy, the PCB took to the streets in the *queremismo* campaign, whose slogan was "We want Getúlio," seeking his continuation in office in an attempt to get Vargas to repeat his ploy of 1937. After Vargas was deposed, the PCB ran its own candidate, engineer Yeddo Fiúza, who polled 8.7 percent of the vote.

The PCB elected 14 deputies and one senator (Prestes) in 1945 and stood in fourth place behind the PTB. Various estimates put PCB membership at 200,000 nationwide. In 1947, however, the party actually polled 32,000 fewer votes than in 1945. Its strength increased only in the federal district. Elsewhere, the PCB elected 46 state deputies in 15 states and contributed decisively to the election of Ademar de Barros in São Paulo.

The Dutra government declared the PCB illegal in May 1947, which was confirmed by the STF in January 1948, and its members lost their mandates, except for a few who had been elected by other parties. The accusation was that the PCB was an antidemocratic party following foreign orientation, but it was made within a context of the Cold War, which brought pressures on Latin American nations to outlaw local Communist parties.[2]

After 1948, the PCB operated clandestinely, always managing to elect elements on other party slates, especially that of the PTB. During the presidency of Goulart (1961–64), the Communist Party, although legally banned, was able to work openly and effectively, so that Goulart relied on Communist support to a considerable extent. In 1964 Prestes made a famous statement to the effect that "we now control the government and we soon will be the government"—a statement that contributed to the military coup and that Prestes recognized as euphoric optimism upon returning from exile in 1979.[3]

The majority of PCB deputies were laborers from the industry-transport sector, plus workers in health and journalism; thus they had low levels of university education. They had few local roots, as most were elected in Rio and São Paulo, having migrated there from the North and Northeast. Following the denunciation of Stalin's excesses in 1956 and Prestes's reassertion of party leadership in 1958, many dissidents left the party and in 1962 organized the *Partido Comunista do Brasil* (PC do B), which adopted a militant pro-Chinese line.

Brazil's socialist movement originated in the 1890s, had a brief resurgence in the 1930s, and reappeared in 1945 with two separate factions. A group of socialist intellectuals took part in the anti-Vargas, UDN front in April 1945, and 63 members of this group published the manifesto of the Democratic Left (*Esquerda Democrática*, ED) in August. That same month, a Trotskyite faction began publishing the *Vanguardia Socialista*. At a national convention in April 1947, the two factions joined to form the *Partido Socialista Brasileiro* (PSB).

The 1950 election was a near disaster for the new party. Its presidential candidate, João Mangabeira, polled fewer than 10,000 votes, and it elected only one federal deputy and one senator. One of the PSB's problems was its inability to assume an ideological position independent of its chief rivals on the left, the PCB and the PTB. However, the PSB gained by its association with Quadros in São Paulo and reached its high-water mark by electing 10 federal deputies in 1958. But the party broke with Quadros in 1960 and backed Lott for president. The PSB elected only four federal deputies and one senator in 1962.

Despite socialist ideology, most PSB deputies came from the national bourgeoisie—commerce, banking, and finance—in addition to lawyers and professors, who were perhaps more responsible for party doctrine.

The Christian Democratic Party (PDC) had antecedents in the 1890s when conservative and monarchist elements attempted to form a Catholic party, and there was a Catholic Electoral League in the 1930s. The Christian Democratic Party was formally organized in 1945, and it elected three deputies. The party associated itself irregularly with the rise of Jânio Quadros in São Paulo. Its fortunes were on the rise through 1962, as it was becoming more like a classical Christian Democratic party in the style of the moderate-reformist, modernizing Italian and Chilean parties. It might have evolved into a major centrist party, with support from the urban middle-classes and from a Catholic labor movement had the military government not truncated its development.

The Popular Representation Party (PRP) was founded by Plínio Salgado in 1932 as the *Ação Integralista Brasileira* (AIB), which tried to impose a tropical version of the fascist-corporatist model in Brazil. The AIB provided "shock troops" in street skirmishes with the leftist ANL before 1937, as Salgado hoped to be named education minister by Vargas. But in December 1937, Vargas outlawed all parties and political movements, and the AIB tried a palace "putsch" in May 1938. Vargas severely repressed the AIB, and Salgado found asylum in Salazar's Portugal until 1945.

Upon the "Führer's" return in 1945, the AIB membership was much reduced from some 60,000 in the 1930s. Outside of Rio Grande and Paraná, the PRP rarely put up separate party slates, entering coalitions with the conservative parties. The PRP increased its federal deputies from one in 1950 to five in 1962.

The PRP tried to finesse its fascist AIB origins, presenting itself as a nationalist anticommunist party that favored a corporatist form of government and functional representation. This "Christian socialism" also condemned "savage capitalism." A personalist type of ideological party, the PRP recruited a small but dedicated elite cadre instead of a mass following. Salgado was always proud of his adepts, who were well-placed in state and federal government as well as the armed forces.[4]

Conservatives

The UDN stalwart, Carlos Lacerda, once said that the *Social Democratic Party* was neither a party, social, nor democratic. It was hastily organized in 1945 by the *Estado Novo* political machines in each state, aggregating many *coronéis*. The 1946 PSD delegation reflected this background, with eight former interventors, many senior officials, and several Vargas and Dutra relatives.

From its dominant position in 1946/47, the PSD receded from majorities to pluralities, so that by 1963 it held 29 percent of the Chamber and 35 percent of the Senate. Similar but smaller declines were noted at the state level, especially in the southern region.

Oliveira observed the PSD to have an "ideology of the general interest,"[5] which involved the pragmatic distribution of jobs, financing, and other public favors to allies. This ideology was best elaborated by Kubitschek's "developmentalism," which attempted to integrate agrarian and industrial interests. However, the conflict between these interests in the early 1960s caused the disintegration of the PSD, with structural transformations, demands for agrarian reform, and increasing economic dependence.

Cardoso described the São Paulo PSD as a "weak-conservative cliente-listic party tied to the federal bureaucracy, financial capitalists and rural leaders." Carvalho found the Minas PSD to contain many doctors, dentists, and pharmacists,[6] occupations well-suited to organizing clientele in small- and medium-sized interior cities. The majority of PSD deputies were law-yers, health professionals, public servants, and businessmen. Perhaps these deputies represented rural interests, but they were not of that sector; rather, they were recruited from the bureaucracy, from clientelistic professions, and from the national producing classes.

Always close to the nerves of government, the PSD maintained a plural-ity in Congress during the full period and lost control of the executive only twice: 15 months in 1954/55 and seven months in 1961. In 1964, the mili-tary's choice for Castelo Branco's vice president was José Maria Alkmim of the PSD *mineiro*.

The *National Democratic Union* (UDN), a party of "eternal opposi-tion," had its roots in the antigovernment movements of the 1920s, in the oligarchies deposed in 1930, in the *Partido Democrático* and the UDB, and in those persecuted by Vargas interventors during the *Estado Novo*.

After defeat in 1945, the UDN was split into two factions: the "eternal vigilance" and the "eternal compromise." The latter participated in Dutra's "union" cabinet and even in Vargas's second government. Although E. Gomes lost a second presidential bid in 1950, the UDN dominated the Café Filho successor government. In 1955, the party chose another *tenente*, Juárez Távora, who achieved broader coalition support, but who lost nar-rowly to the Kubitschek/Goulart slate.

Falling back on a strategy of pragmatic coalition-building in the 1958 state elections, the UDN made gains in preparation for the 1960 presidential election. At the November 1959 national convention, Carlos Lacerda led the drive in favor of Jânio Quadros, who was already endorsed by some smaller parties. The intransigent group urged caution with regard to Quadros, who had "betrayed" the UDN in the 1955 anti-Kubitschek conspiracy. They fa-vored yet another *tenente*, Juraci Magalhães, governor of Bahia. The *janis-tas* won out, and the Quadros/Campos slate was approved. In the ensuing UDN vs. PDC-MTR dispute over Ferrari's vice presidential candidacy, Qua-dros resigned both parties' nominations and returned only after all parties declared that he would be under no political obligation to them if elected.

Quadros's loose ties with the UDN were further strained as he tolerated the "Jan-Jan" ticket splitting campaign and by his March 1960 visit to Cuba. The "antiparty" populist won by a landslide, but Goulart was elected vice president over Campos. Despite this "victory," the UDN continued to suffer its "opposition complex," because although the party had supplied Quadros with three ministers, it had little control over his program. The party was split into three factions: the ultraconservative, "orthodox" wing; the *Bossa Nova* group, which tried to cooperate with Quadros and which participated in the Nationalist Parliamentary Front (FPN); and the anti-Communist but nonconservative group led by Lacerda. After Quadros's resignation, the UDN felt obliged to participate in the parliamentary cabinets, but it became Goulart's most virulent opposition in 1963, and in 1964 turned to conspiracy.[7]

Cardoso found the UDN *paulista* to be of "the traditional middle class, with links to the traditional landed aristocracy, no longer economically dominant."[8] Soares[9] and Benevides[10] identify this "split personality" between the urban middle class, who set UDN policy in high-rise offices, and the rural chiefs, who decided elections.

As in the case of the PSD, the data on deputies diverge somewhat from the UDN's traditional image. Instead of elements from the national bourgeoisie, the UDN elected deputies from the legal, health professional, and agrarian sectors. The UDN was fairly successful in states like Minas, Bahia, and Paraiba, but where another party effectively raised the opposition banner (PTB in Rio Grande and the PSP and PTN in São Paulo), the UDN was weak.

The oldest party of this period, the *Partido Republicano* (PR) was founded in 1870. Having dominated national politics during the First Republic, the PR survived the 1930 revolution and *Estado Novo* in the person of its leader, Artur Bernardes. Bernardes, who had been governor of Minas (1918–22) and president (1922–26), was a staunch foe of foreign investments and in 1953 played a pivotal role in congressional approval of the Petrobras petroleum monopoly.

With Bernardes's death in 1955, the PR began a decline that by 1963 left the party with its four *mineiro* deputies. Even if there had been no AI-2, the PR would have probably disappeared from national politics in the 1966 elections.

The *Partido Libertador* was organized in Rio Grande do Sul in 1928 as successor to the *Partido Federalista*. The PL supported the *Alianca Liberal*, but after the *Estado Novo*, it became a conservative anti-Vargas party led by Raul Pilla. The PL's program contained three basic elements: the secret ballot, the vote for women, and the parliamentary system. By 1946 the first two had been adopted. Pilla proposed the adoption of the parliamentary system as a solution to the 1955 crises to no avail, but in the more severe regime crisis of 1961 the idea was adopted.

In 1946 Pilla was the lone PL deputy, but the party rose to a zenith of 10 in 1954, suffered reverses in 1958, and made a slight comeback in 1962, reflecting the ups and downs of the presidential system.

The Crisis of the Party System

Long before the AI-2 in 1965 applied the "coup de grâce," the multi-party system was undergoing severe crisis in the early 1960s. Six reasons are frequently cited:[11]

First, the electoral decline of the conservative parties forced the PSD to share power with the PTB and later to seek a tacit alliance with the UDN against Goulart.

Second, electoral fragmentation as a threat to the PSD-PTB coalition was a contributory cause, although, as shown in Table 4.1, the fragmentation index registered its biggest increase in 1951. This alliance was in fact weakened for political reasons by "orthodox" PSD and PTB "conciliators" who joined the UDN against Goulart.

Third, the lack of party discipline and cohesion produced crises only when associated with ideological radicalization. Weakness of party loyalty and "label switching" was sometimes a problem. Another aspect of party indiscipline was the proliferation of intraparty factions, which weakened the three larger parties. The party system was further debilitated by the formation of two ideologically polarized supraparty blocs, which drew legislators from all parties.

The Nationalist Parliamentary Front was formed in 1956, after the nationalist battles over Electrobras and Petrobras. The PTB (40 percent) and PSD (23.5 percent), followed by a UDN faction (11.8 percent), were the main FPN elements in 1959–63, but five other parties also contributed. Leadership was shared by Leonel Brizola and Sérgio Magalhães during the battles for Goulart's "Basic Reforms." After 1964 some 40 FPN members were purged.

In 1959 the Democratic Parliamentary Action (ADP) was organized to combat the FPN within the Congress, and parallel movements were promoted in the states by the Brazilian Institute for Democratic Action (IBAD) and the Institute for Social and Economic Research (IPES), coordinated by Col. Golbery do Couto e Silva.[12] Most ADP members came from the UDN (31.1 percent) and from the PSD (29.7 percent), confirming the conservative alliance that weakened the PSD-PTB alliance, but the PSP (12.2 percent) and the PTB (8.1 percent) also contributed, as did the six smaller parties.

Fourth, electoral alliances and coalitions at all levels grew steadily from 25 percent of federal deputies elected in 1950 to 38 percent in 1962. This mechanism usually favored the smaller parties, and the UDN generally fared better than the PSD or PTB. These larger parties usually participated in order to "cut losses" and to better combat regional rivals. In some states, a bipolar tendency evolved, while in others, further fragmentation of the party system occurred. Those elected by coalition tended to be very distant from their party program, if it still existed by 1962.

Fifth, as voting is legally obligatory, voter apathy and alienation, which reached 18 percent in 1962, are manifested in Brazil by casting blank or void ballots. Schwartzman explains that as rural-urban migration increased, direct control of voters decreased and marginalization increased;[13] denied normal channels of participation, this mass became alienated, especially in proportional representation elections. However, this phenomenon may be more a consequence than a cause of the party system crisis.

Sixth, the politics of personalism can weaken any party and stifle the emergence of "new blood." On the other hand, the lack of national leaders, as shown by UDN dependence on military candidates and the disarray of the PTB after Vargas's death, can also weaken parties.

When the UDN finally "elected" a president, he was not a *udenista*. Goulart could never consolidate his leadership of the PTB, even as president. Ademar was the only PSP leader, and the party would have had less success without him, but the party spent itself for his election as president and reelection as governor. After 1960 the principal objective of the PSD was Kubitschek's reelection in 1965, which resulted in a series of tactical errors. Many of the small parties became personal vehicles for a succession of politicians. The electoral system also permitted the candidates' "dropping in" from one region or state to another, which decapitated local party leadership and left its organization in disarray.

Final Considerations

The multiparty phase, which began with the limited pluralism of three relevant parties in 1946, had advanced to moderate pluralism with five relevant parties by 1963. Because of the more stringent minimum thresholds adopted by new party legislation in July 1965, coalitions would have been precluded and only the PTB, PSD, UDN, PSP, and perhaps the PDC would have survived the 1966 elections, had it not been for AI-2.

Several factors contributed to the evolution of this party system: the maintenance of the PR system with tolerant minimum thresholds and unequal representation in 1946; the increasing polarization of producer and proletarian classes plus the alienation of the latter, which in the Central-South (especially São Paulo) gave rise to many of the smaller, personalist parties; the dichotomy of the "ins" and "outs," in some areas dating from the Empire, which determined party affiliations in 1945; the legacy of decentralization superimposed on regional political cleavages, which divided the major parties; and a structure of political opportunity that favored coalition building to achieve state and national executive office.

By 1965, the multiparty system had lost its viability and political effectiveness through its own inertia, and it probably would have been reduced to more compact proportions in 1967. All 13 parties were organized by elites from the top down, and, with the possible exception of the PCB, none had organized "grassroots" movements.

THE TWO-PARTY EXPERIMENT: 1966–79

During 1964, Castelo Branco governed with a loose coalition in Congress, based on ADP leadership, which was transformed into a slim majority of 205 deputies as the *Bloco Parlamentar Revolucionário* (BPR) in March 1965, thus reinforcing the bipolar tendency. The BPR, however, proved unstable and failed to approve a number of government measures in 1965. Despite restrictions placed on candidate selection and the coercive environment, Kubitschek's PSD won five of the 11 governorships in the October 1965 elections.

Although under severe pressure from the hard-line military to "close the system" because of such "negative" results, Castelo Branco was able to keep his promise that those elected would take office. But he could do so only at the price of deepening the authoritarian system by decreeing AI-2, which abolished the parties, provided for indirect elections of governors in 1966, and began a new wave of purges that were most severe among PTB legislators, as shown in Table 4.2.

The Two-Party System

The new legislation called for the formation of "temporary" parties from the top down by at least 120 deputies and 20 senators. Thus, a maximum of three new parties could have been formed, but in practice some 250 deputies and 40 senators rushed to join the new progovernment party, the National Renovating Alliance (*Alianca Renovadora Nacional*, ARENA), and government leaders had to persuade several senators to join provisionally the new opposition party, the Brazilian Democratic Movement (*Movimento Democrático Brasileiro*, MDB), so it could meet these quotas.

In many states, traditional political enemies from the former party factions were forced to "cohabit" within ARENA, necessitating complex "coexistence" criteria and producing chronic instability within the party in most states.

Of the three larger former parties, the ex-UDN was most coherent; 90 percent of its deputies and 100 percent of its senators joined ARENA. Nu-

TABLE 4.2. Pre-1966 Party Affiliations of Federal Deputies and Senators, 1966–71

Pre-1966 Party Affiliation	1963	AI-1 and AI-2[1]	1966–67[2]			1967–71[3]		
			ARENA	MDB	Total	ARENA	MDB	Total
Deputies								
PTB[4]	119	37	34	75	109	34	50	84
PSD	118	11	80	44	124	83	39	122
UDN	91	02	84	10	94	105	14	119
PSP	21	04	20	04	24	13	08	21
PDC	20	03	15	05	20	18	05	23
PTN	11	01	08	05	13	06	07	13
PST	07	05	03	01	04	01	02	03
PR	04	01	04	00	04	04	00	04
PL	05	00	03	00	03	04	02	06
PRP	05	00	06	00	06	04	00	04
PSB	05	03	01	02	03	02	01	03
PRT	03	00	02	02	04	01	00	01
Subtotal	409	67	260	148	408	275	128	403
Unknown	—	00	00	00	01	01	05	06
Total	409	67	260	148	409	276	133	409
Cassados	—	67	—	—	—	28	66	94[5]
Senators								
PTB[4]	19	1	06	13	19	03	10	13
PSD	23	1	17	06	23	18	05	23
UDN	16	0	16	00	16	19	01	20
PSP	02	0	02	00	02	03	00	03
PDC	01	0	01	00	01	03	00	03
PTN	01	0	00	01	01	00	01	01
PL	02	0	01	01	02	01	01	02
PRP	01	0	01	00	01	00	00	00
PSB	01	0	00	01	01	00	01	01
Subtotal	66	2	44	22	66	47	19	66
Cassados	—	2	—	—	—	00	04	04[5]

[1]Cassados removed by AI-1 (1964) and by AI-2 (1965–66).
[2]Realignment among surviving members of the 5th Legislature, elected in 1962.
[3]Legislators elected to the 6th Legislature in November 1966.
[4]Includes legislators of the MTR splinter party.
[5]Cassados removed by the AI-5 after December 16, 1968.
Source: Compiled by Fleischer.

merically, the largest bloc within ARENA, the ex-UDN played a dispropor-
tionate role in national and state politics after 1964, leading Dep. Tancredo
Neves to call the government of the revolution the *"Estado Novo* of the
UDN."

The ex-PSD was more divided; 65 percent of its deputies and 74 percent
of its senators joined ARENA, while the rest joined the MDB out of loyalty
to the purged Kubitschek and due to regional incompatibilities. This ambivalence reflects the split that occurred during the Goulart period, when more
conservative PSD members joined the UDN in opposition.

Nearly 70 percent of ex-PTB legislators joined the MDB. The remaining
34 deputies and six senators who jointed ARENA, popularly nicknamed *bi-
gorrilhos* (bogeymen), were concentrated in Pernambuco, São Paulo, and
Ceará.

Most of the ex-PSP deputies (83 percent) and both of its senators joined
ARENA in early 1966. After Ademar was purged, some stood for election
with the MDB in November, but they returned to the government fold in
1970.

Most of the ex-PDC and ex-PST went to ARENA; the ex-PTN and ex-
PRT were divided; two-thirds of the ex-PSB joined the MDB; while all of the
ex-PR and ex-PRP joined ARENA.

The 1966 elections were held in three stages, In the September indirect
elections for governor, the PSD won six of the 12 governorships, the same
proportion as in 1965. In October, the Congress indirectly elected Costa e
Silva (Castelo's army minister) and Pedro Aleixo (former UDN, MG) as
president and vice president, respectively. Finally, in November, the voters
balloted for federal and state legislatures plus municipal offices. The MDB
emerged in a weaker position than in 1966, and the ARENA elected two-
third majorities in each house. In 1967, the biggest changes affected the ex-
UDN and the ex-PTB, the revolutionary "ins" and "outs," with the former
gaining 25 Chamber seats, and the latter losing the same number.

National Renovating Alliance

In a sense, ARENA was the party of the state governors, like the presidents in the First Republic, except that ARENA governors were selected in
Brasília and ratified by state legislatures instead of the more autonomous,
decentralized process prior to 1930. This situation created severe factional
strains in the party at the state level. They were partially contained by use of
the *sublegenda* (the system whereby a party might present up to three candidates for mayor or senator, the votes for all of whom would count toward the
election of the most voted-for individual) and by continuation of the PR system, but they made the party instable and weak.

The ARENA's occupational profile included farmers (Minas and Central West), professionals (Rio Grande, North, and Rio), teachers (Rio and Rio Grande), and business managers (North). The progovernment party was more locally oriented but less educated (due to its Rio and Northern sections). ARENA deputies from Rio Grande, Minas, and Rio had the longest careers and were elected to the chamber at the oldest ages, in contrast with colleagues from the Central-South and North. In all areas except Rio, ARENA deputies preferred elective careers. Local political experience was strongest in Rio and São Paulo.[14]

Brazilian Democratic Movement

In most states, MDB leadership was drawn from the ex-PSD and ex-PTB, but the former dominated the national leadership. The MDB was able to elect only one state governor, in Guanabara (which was fused with the old state of Rio de Janeiro in 1975). The party suffered severe losses in 1970 and discussed the possibility of self-dissolution, but it made a spectacular recovery in 1974 (see Table 4.3).

The MDB concentrated its recruitment among lawyers, business managers, and public servants and had fewer farmers but more teachers and journalists than ARENA—occupations conducive to political mobilization and communication. MDB deputies had shorter careers and younger chamber-entry ages than ARENA deputies. Opposition deputies favored elective careers slightly over administrative, a tendency more pronounced in the South than in the North.

The Electoral System and Decompression

The military government arbitrarily changed the rules of the electoral and political games several times in an attempt to favor the progovernment party, ARENA. Each change, in its turn, won immediate benefits for ARENA, but the MDB would rebound and make further gains, thus necessitating more changes.

After the 1970 elections, the government set municipal elections out of phase with the general elections, eliminated the *sublegenda*, and established "tied voting" for state and federal deputy, all in the name of "strengthening" the parties and making them more authentic. With a more open political climate under President Geisel, whose government was plagued by an economic downturn, the MDB was able in the 1974 elections to increase its Chamber delegation from 28 percent to 44 percent, to elect 16 of 22 senators, and to win majorities in six state assemblies.

TABLE 4.3. Pre-1966 Party Affiliations of Federal Deputies and Senators, 1971–79

Pre-1966 Party Affiliation	1971–75			1975–79			1979		
	ARENA	MDB	Total	ARENA	MDB	Total	ARENA	MDB	Total
Deputies									
PTB[#]	17	32	49	13	42	55	16	36	52
PSD	52	22	74	64	28	92	60	37	97
UDN	79	08	87	69	14	83	70	13	83
PSP	12	04	16	08	06	14	09	07	16
PDC	16	03	19	13	05	18	14	08	22
PTN	03	05	08	00	05	05	01	03	04
PST	02	00	02	03	00	03	02	00	02
PR	08	02	10	10	03	13	10	03	13
PL	03	00	03	03	00	03	00	00	00
PRP	05	00	05	03	00	03	04	00	04
PSB	02	02	04	01	02	03	01	04	05
PRT	00	00	00	02	02	04	02	02	04
Subtotal	199	78	277	186	110	236	189	113	302
Unknown	25	08	33	18	50	68	42	76	118
Total	224	86	310	204	160	364	231	189	420
*Cassados**	—	—	—	00	06	06	—	—	—
Senators									
PTB[#]	03	01	04	02	02	04	02	05	07
PSD	23	04	27	20	06	26	19	07	26
UDN	26	00	26	20	01	21	15	03	18
PSP	03	01	04	03	01	04	00	00	00
PDC	03	01	04	01	01	02	02	02	04
PST	00	00	00	00	01	01	00	01	01
PL	00	00	00	00	01	01	00	01	01
PSB	00	00	00	00	01	01	00	01	01
Subtotal	58	07	65	46	15	61	39	20	59
Unknown	01	00	01	02	03	05	03	05	08
Total	59	07	66	48	18	66	42	25	67
*Cassados**	—	—	—	01	00	01	—	—	—

[#]Includes legislators of the MTR splinter party.
Cassados removed by the AI-5 under President E. Geisel.
Source: Compiled by Fleischer.

Faced with the prospect of the MDB repeating this feat in 1978 and thus winning majorities in Congress and electing governors in the key states of São Paulo and Rio Grande do Sul, Geisel recessed the Congress in April 1977 and decreed electoral law changes, dubbed the "April Package" (Pacote de Abril). For the 1978 elections, one of the two Senate seats would be indirect as would the gubernatorial election by gerrymandered state "electoral colleges." The basis for calculating the size of the states' delegations in the Chamber was also to favor ARENA strongholds in the Northeast. This exercise in "political engineering" enabled the government to maintain control of the key governorships and of a majority in the Senate, but it had no impact on the ARENA position in the Chamber, which remained at 55 percent.[15]

Abertura

Pres. João B. Figueiredo took office in March 1979 without the exceptional powers his three predecessors had enjoyed, but he decided to enhance his government's legitimacy and space of maneuver by enacting a rapid sequence of reforms that kept the opposition off balance: release of political prisoners, general amnesty allowing the return of all exiles, and new legislation permitting the formulation of new parties in 1980. Despite an earlier initiative, adopted in late 1978, permitting "voluntary" formation of new parties, none were formed during 1979, although negotiations were intense.[16] To end this impasse, the government introduced legislation abolishing the two existing parties, which was duly approved by ARENA majorities in late 1979.

Conclusions

During the first phase of the two-party experiment (1966–74), the party system was of the "hegemonic" type, but in the second phase, when ARENA majorities were reduced, the system could be classified as "dominant party competitive." The most important historical factor was the inertia from the multiparty system, especially in the case of ARENA, which by 1979 was much more fragmented by former party cleavages than was the MDB. On the other hand, the MDB suffered from ideological factionalism with its "authentic," "neo-authentic," and "moderate" wings.

By 1979, Brazilian society had become increasingly polarized, with higher levels of consciousness, thus strengthening the MDB as the electoral channel for opposition to the regime. For this reason, the 1974 and 1978 elections were like "plebiscites" in which the electorate voted "yes" or "no" vis-à-vis the government. Therefore, although ARENA had comfortable majorities in 1979, government political strategists thought that a return to a multiparty system would offer a release from the two-party "straightjacket" in preparation for the 1982 elections.

TABLE 4.4. Party Realignment in the National Legislature, 1980–1982, by ex-Party Origins of Deputies and Senators

Current Party Affiliation	Chamber of Deputies[1]			Federal Senate[1]		
	ARENA	MDB	Total	ARENA	MDB	Total
March 1980						
PDS	201	24	225	36	1	37
PMDB	3	91	94	1	16	17
PP	25	43	68	4	3	7
PTB[2]	1	22	23	0	1	1
PT	0	5	5	0	1	1
Undecided	1	4	5	1	3	4
March 1981						
PDS	191	21	212	34	2	36
PMDB	5	108	113	1	19	20
PP	26	40	66	7	3	10
PDT	0	10	10	0	0	0
PTB	3	2	5	0	0	0
PT	0	6	6	0	0	0
Undecided	6	2	8	0	1	1
December 1981						
PDS	192	22	214	35	2	37
PMDB	10	111	121	1	19	20
PP	26	41	67	6	4	10
PDT	0	9	9	0	0	0
PTB	3	1	4	0	0	0
PT	0	5	5	0	0	0
August 1982						
PDS	196	28	224	35	1	36
PMDB[3]	32	136	168	7	20	27
PDT	0	9	9	0	1	1
PTB	3	11	14	0	2	2
PT	0	5	5	0	1	1
Total Seats	231	189	420	42	25	67

[1]ARENA and MDB figures are for February 1979, before any changes took place. Includes results of 1978 elections.

[2]Prior to the PTB/PDT schism in May 1980 of the Ivette Vargas/Brizola factions.

[3]The fusion of the PP with the PMDB took place in February 1982.

Source: Compiled by Fleischer.

THE RESTORED MULTIPARTY
SYSTEM

Survey research in March 1979 revealed that 92 percent of MDB and 85 percent of ARENA legislators favored a multiparty system with more than three parties.[17] Both parties were fraught with internal cleavages, especially the MDB, which palace strategists thought ripe for "implosion." During the legislative recess (1979/80), the mad scramble was on to organize new parties. As in the party reform of 1965/66, party reorganization was from "the top down" by current legislators but with less stringent quotas; only 42 deputies and seven senators needed to sign up to create a new party. This rule was later softened to allow the formation of "temporary party blocs" within the Congress with no minimum quotas.

The New Parties

The realignment process is analyzed in two stages in Table 4.4, from March 1980 through August 1982.

The Brazilian Labor Party

Since early 1979, "historic" and more recent *trabalhistas* had been organizing a new *Partido Trabalhista Brasileira*, although they were divided into rival factions led by Leonel Brizola and Ivette Vargas, grandniece of Getúlio. Whereas there were 52 ex-PTB deputies in 1979 (16 ARENA and 36 MDB), only 22 ex-MDB deputies and one senator plus one ex-ARENA deputy joined the new PTB bloc in 1980. Two-thirds of this bloc was concentrated in three states: Rio Grande (8), Bahia (5), and Rio (3).

These rival factions were not compatible and filed separate registry petitions with the Superior Electoral Court (TSE), and in a surprise political decision on May 12, 1979, the court awarded the acronym "PTB" to the Ivette faction, even though the Brizola faction had 22 of the bloc's 23 duputies.

The Democratic Labor Party

Undaunted by the TSE decision, the Brizola faction immediately resubmitted its registry petition under the name *Partido Democrático Trabalhista* (PDT), but by 1981 the bloc had been reduced to 10 deputies. Those deserting the PDT returned to the successor opposition party, the Brazilian Democratic Movement (PMDB). Besides Brizola, the PDT has attracted other notable former *cassados*, such as Doutel de Andrade, Darcy Ribeiro, and Neiva Moreira.

In the 1982 campaign, Brizola showed some of the qualities that had made him top winner in the 1962 election. His victory in Rio de Janeiro raised the PDT, with 6 percent of the national total, to third place among the parties. In the wake of the elections, the PDT moved to merge with what was left of the PBT—a merger rejected by the PT.

From the point of view of the military and conservatives, the charismatic Brizola represented the most dangerous force on the political horizon, and the strongest threat of the return of the political forces against which the military acted in 1964. The PDT propounded a democratic socialist ideology in the West European vein and maintained contacts with the socialist Second International.

The Workers' Party

The *Partido dos Trabalhadores* is the only one of the new parties to be organized from the "bottom up," outside the legislature and political class in 1978/79, by labor union leaders Luis Ignácio da Silva (*"Lula"*), Jacó Bittar, and Olívio Dutra.[18] These union leaders were of a younger generation, independent of Labor Ministry manipulations and tired of decades of labor policies dictated by *trabalhista*, "populist," and "progressive" politicians said to be "representatives" of the working class. After a frustrated attempt by São Paulo intellectuals to form a Popular Democratic and Socialist Party (*Partido Popular Democrático e Socialista*, PPDS) in 1977 and fruitless meetings with members of the ex-MDB "authentic" faction, the union leaders decided to organize their own party of the workers, in which politicians and/or students would not be accepted as leaders but as suspiciously received supporters.

However, this "grassroots" approach would have been a "via crucis" for the PT, given the complicated new party organization legislation. So when the chance to constitute a PT bloc with five deputies and one senator from the ex-MDB "authentic" faction appeared, the union leaders opted for this alternative, which permitted provisional registry with the TSE and representation in Congress.

By 1981, the PT stood at six deputies and was fighting off bitter takeover attempts at the precinct level by leftist students and radical groups. Early in 1981, Lula and other PT leaders visited Europe and the US to meet with Mário Soares, Felipe Gonzalez, François Mitterrand, Willy Brandt, and Polish Solidarity leader Lech Walesa.

During 1981, the future of the PT seemed uncertain because Lula and 11 other labor leaders were appealing three-year prison sentences under the National Security Law for having led the bitter São Paulo strikes in 1980. However, in April 1982, the Superior Military Court declared the military court system incompetent to judge the case, enabling these leaders to stand for and to actively participate in the November 1982 elections.

Lula has claimed that his is the only real party of change, and it certainly represents a relatively dynamic force on the stage. PT candidates ran very poorly, however, even in the industrial districts; the workers seemed to regard it as a hopeless cause. Its ideology is vaguely socialistic.[19] It would like to consider itself revolutionary, and it calls the PCB and the PC do B revisionist, but it seems to have only a general idea of the workers' power. Its principal hope was that a worsening economic situation would bring a stronger rejection of the established order.

The Popular Party (*Partido Popular, PP*) brought together ex-ARENA dissidents, led by Dep. Magalhães Pinto, and ex-MDB moderates, led by Sen. Tancredo Neves. This new party of the center was conceived by Justice Minister Petrônio Portela as a "third force" that would operate as an "auxiliary" government party at the national level but that would be a strong opposition contender at the state level by providing the dissident ex-ARENA factions with an electoral vehicle for the 1982 elections.

Table 4.4 shows that one-third of the PP deputies had no affiliations with the old multiparty system, and, as shown by Table 4.5, 45 percent were from the ex-UDN and ex-PSD. Regionally, the PP is concentrated in Minas and Rio de Janeiro (58 percent). In the latter, the party is based on the efficient machine of Gov. Chagas Freitas and Dep. Miro Teixeira, national PP secretary general.[20]

The PP was able to recruit eight former ARENA governors who were at odds with incumbent state administrations. Popularly nicknamed the "party of the bankers," the largest PP contingent was from the commerce-banking sector, but liberal professions and public servants were also well represented. Their administrative experience exceeded that of all new parties, and their careers were quite long. The PP was a well-organized party of seasoned politicians skilled in the arts of maneuvering, bargaining, and coalition building. At the end of 1981, however, in reaction to the changes in electoral rules pushed through by the government, the PP (or a large majority of the party) merged with the PMDB to form a semiunited opposition.

The Party of the Brazilian Democratic Movement

During the initial realignment in 1980, the ex-MDB lost more than half of its original 189 deputies—70 to the three new opposition parties, 24 to the new progovernment party, and four undecided—as well as eight of its 25 senators—a small compensation for the three deputies and one senator it received from the ex-ARENA. In March 1980, the *Partido do Movimento Democrático Brasileiro* (PMBD) was left with 94 deputies and 17 senators.

TABLE 4.5. Pre-1966 Multiparty Affiliations of Legislators by New Parties in 1981

Pre-1966 Affiliation	PDS	PMDB	PP	PDT	PTB	PT	Undecided	Total
Chamber								
PTB	15	15	2	8	2	0	0	42
PSD	41	23	14	1	0	1	1	81
UDN	47	6	16	0	0	0	0	69
PSP	6	1	7	0	1	0	0	15
PDC	15	4	1	0	0	0	0	20
PTN	2	1	1	0	0	0	0	4
PST	2	0	0	0	0	0	1	3
PR	10	1	2	0	0	0	0	13
PRP	4	0	0	0	0	0	0	4
PSB	1	1	1	1	0	1	0	5
PRT	1	1	0	0	1	0	1	4
N.a.	68	60	22	0	1	4	5	160
Total	212	113	66	10	5	6	8	420
Senate								
PTB	3	4	0	—	—	—	0	7
PSD	15	4	5	—	—	—	1	25
UDN	15	2	2	—	—	—	0	19
PDC	1	2	1	—	—	—	0	4
PST	0	1	0	—	—	—	0	1
PL	1	1	0	—	—	—	0	2
PSB	0	1	0	—	—	—	0	1
N.a.	1	5	2	—	—	—	0	8
Total	36	20	10	—	—	—	1	67

Source: Compiled by Fleischer.

By March 1981, the PMDB picked up an additional 19 deputies and three senators, standing at 113 and 20 respectively. Most returned from the Brizola bloc and a few from the PP. The party attracted such notable ex-*cassados* as Miguel Arraes, Mário Covas, and Almino Affonso.

Comparing the ex-MDB in 1979 with the PMDB in 1981 regarding ties with the old multiparty system, one finds that 21 of the 36 ex-PTB and only 14 of the 37 ex-PSD deputies left the ex-MDB, plus half of the ex-UDN and ex-PDC and nearly all of the ex-PSP group. Except for the ex-PSD, this was nearly an across-the-board exodus, leaving the latter and post-1965 elements in command of the PMDB. The PMDB has more lawyers, teachers, journalists, and other professionals than the MDB had; and the latter's "losses" were from the sectors of health, public service, and the military—a clear division between "mobilizers" and the more "traditional" politicians. The new opposition party had more political experience and localism and was slightly younger than the ex-MDB in 1979.

Despite its critical losses, the PMDB emerged in 1982 as the chief focus for opposition to the military-dominated government. As such, it sheltered some rather radical elements, including some allegedly affiliated with the illegal PCB. The PMDB was perhaps the chief beneficiary of antigovernment feeling generated by the effort of the ruling group to perpetuate itself by changing electoral laws. The decision in December 1981 of the PP, which had been regarded as a potential coalition partner for the PDS, to merge into the PMDB meant that in many states there was but single viable opposition party. In 21 of the 23 states, the campaign for governor in 1982 was practically reduced to the former two-party competition between the PDS and the PMDB.

The Democratic Socialist Party

The new progovernment party, the *Partido Democrático Social* (PDS), with a name ironically close to that of the old PSD, is essentially the ex-ARENA with a few "new clothes" in that 89 percent of its deputies were from the ex-ARENA in 1980. In the initial realignment, the government party lost much less than the ex-MDB; the loss of 29 ex-ARENA deputies (25 to the PP) was compensated for by attracting 24 "opposition" deputies from the ex-MDB. The government's majorities were reduced from 55 percent to 53.6 percent in the chamber and from 63 percent to 52 percent in the senate. The maintenance of the government's majority position of 225 deputies and 37 senators was due to co-opting some of the ex-PSD group from the PP, as well as to the loyalty of most "bionic" senators. In 1981, the PDS was eroded to levels barely above minimal majorities. In the Chamber, most of these "erosions" became "undecided," and in the Senate they joined the PP.

In comparison with the PDS, the ex-ARENA lost teachers, lawyers, and professionals, while the latter gained elements from the "producing classes" (agriculture, business, and industry transport). The PDS has slightly less political experience, education, and localism, and its members are slightly older than the ex-ARENA. The ex-UDN and ex-PSD continued to divide leadership in the PDS, with 47 and 41 deputies, respectively, and 15 senators each.

The Brazilian Communist Party

An analysis of Brazil's current spectrum would not be complete without mentioning the *Partido Comunista Brasileiro*. Although it was not legally registered, exiled members of the party were allowed to return, the central committee has held numerous meetings, the party newspaper is freely published and distributed, and many PCB leaders have been interviewed on television. Veteran PCB Secretary General Luis Carlos Prestes, now in his 80s, returned to suffer his own *abertura*. His Stalinist line was out of step with the "Eurocommunism" style of the majority of the central committee, which removed him from leadership in May 1980. In the 1982 elections, the PCB was able to elect a few candidates on PMDB slates. However, when the party attempted to hold a congress in São Paulo in December, federal police arrested and briefly imprisoned General Secretary Giocondo Dias and more than 80 others, including members of the Central Committee, and delegates, thereby indicating limits of *abertura*.

THE 1982 ELECTION

Campaign, 1982

During 1981, the government's strategy of "divide and conquer" appeared to be working well, as numerous candidates for governor and senator had surfaced in most states. During President Figueiredo's health-related leave of absence in October, the Congress defeated the *sublegenda* section of the electoral reform. In November, the government retaliated by submitting a massive, more hard-line, electoral reform package, prohibiting coalitions, obligating parties to field complete slates, and obligating voters to vote straight-party tickets in an effort to stem the opposition tide in most states and to retain PDS absolute majorities in Congress after the November 15, 1982 elections. In doing so, the government rejected the strategy of possible PDS-PP cooperation, forcing PP leaders to opt for reincorporation with the PMDB at their December 20 convention. Although the PDS had a viable majority, the "November Package" was passed the "hardball way," *decurso de prazo*, on January 9, 1982.

A second "package" was sent to Congress in May 1982 to safeguard the government against a possible opposition majority. This raised the required majority for constitutional amendments to two-thirds, postponed the (indirect) election of the next president from October 1984 to January 1985, and added to the electoral college six delegates chosen by the majority party in each state. This greatly overrepresented the smaller and poorer states in which the official political machine was more effective. The survival threshold for small parties (at least 5 percent overall and at least 3 percent in nine states) was postponed in order to keep them from joining a united opposition. Additionally, the chamber was enlarged from 420 to 479 seats, and parliamentary immunities were slightly improved. For the 1986 elections, there was established a mixed district-proportional representative system somewhat like that of the Federal Republic of Germany. Under this system, half of the federal deputies would be elected by single-member districts by simple plurality, while the other half would be chosen by proportional representation on a state-wide basis. The PDS was able to pass this legislation by a narrow majority without recourse to *decurso de prazo*.

The government also tried to improve its prospects by imposing a ballot requiring the voter to write the name or number of the chosen candidates in blank spaces without party labels. All candidates who voted had to be of the same party.

The campaign aroused intense interest as the most important in twenty years and the first opportunity for the opposition to gain a real share of power. For a large majority of the election, it was the first opportunity ever to vote for state governor. Posters covered all available spaces, the press commented heatedly and lengthily, and there were endless meetings with samba bands. Television played a key role, especially through political debates, until broadcast electioneering was severely restricted, after September 15, under the *Lei Falcão*, banning broadcast speeches for sixty days before the election. Frequent public opinion polls heightened interest in the contest. The appeal was largely personalist, however; there was little ideological heat, nationalist or populist. Government and opposition both promised a better life for the masses.

The fight for the governorship of Rio de Janeiro caused most excitement. Leonel Brizola, onetime firebrand who contributed to the fall of Goulart in 1964, candidate of the PDT, came from behind to overtake the PTB and the PMDB candidates; in turn he was nearly passed in October by the PDS candidate.

Pres. Figueiredo threw himself into the fray, as some of his military predecessors had done, stumping and speaking on behalf of the PDS, the motto of which was, "lend a hand (*mão*) to João." The government tried in many small ways to influence the voters, from appropriate public works to holding off tax collections, granting loans, promising cheap milk, rice, and beans, and providing food for the poor. The nationalized pawn service returned wedding rings without payment. Radio and television stations received gratuities, and public servants were expected to support the PDS. Some irregular practices were reported, such as the illegal transfer of voters, multiple registration, and registration of minors. The SNI was reported to have manipulated election boards in some locales. But irregularities were probably not more than in previous elections but better reported in the atmosphere of *abertura*, and they were not enough to substantially change the results.

Election Results

The military-engineered experiment in democratization was generally successful. Nine-tenths of the electorate of 50 million went to the polls to select among 55,000 candidates. Broadly speaking, the moderates won. The prestige of the government and Pres. Figueiredo was raised. The PDS kept control of the Senate and of a majority in the future electoral college and won 235 seats, just 5 seats under a majority, in the chamber. There was no antigovernment coalition, but the opposition could be pleased with raising its governorships from one, Rio de Janeiro, to 10, including 60 percent of Brazil's population and paying 72 percent of its sales taxes. It could also boast a majority of the popular vote and large majorities in all the more advanced states except Rio Grande do Sul and Santa Catarina.

The PDS did best, as expected, in rural and poorer areas, and the tied ballot apparently helped it to sweep the Northeast. However, in most other states, there seemed to be a reverse effect, popular opposition candidates for governor giving the PMDB control of local offices. PMDB victories owed much to PDS factionalism in several states. Leonel Brizola won in Rio de Janeiro by an ample margin, although for a time it seemed that he might be cheated by fraud involving the SNI. Thanks to Brizola, the PDT showed itself more than a splinter party. Brazil, however, seemed almost to have a two-party system, as in the days of ARENA or MDB. The government, swallowing Brizola's victory, was gratified that Lula's radical PT made a feeble showing. The workers preferred the PMDB; only in São Paulo did the PT have any real strength.

The major result of the election was that, barring a new coup, the military leadership would have to pay considerably more attention to the elected politicians. The strength of the opposition in both the Congress and the state governments meant that the federal authorities had not merely to consult but also to bargain in order to implement their plans. The PDS controlled the electoral college (see Table 4.6), but this could be jeopardized by a mere twenty defections. As the PDS would choose its candidate by secret ballot early in 1984, a civilian president became a real possibility. On the other hand, the direct election of the president, desired by a large majority of the population, seemed excluded by military distrust of perhaps the most appealing candidate, Brizola.[21]

Economic troubles, a breakdown of order, or a return of extremism could bring the military back in to politics. But for the time being, it seemed that Brazil was ending an era of centralization and authoritarianism, like the Vargas dictatorship, and returning to more decentralization, pluralism, relaxation, and open political life, with all the inherent advantages and drawbacks.

FIGURE 4.1. Results of the 1982 Elections

Roraima

Amapá

Amazonas

Pará

Maranhão

Ceará

Rio Grande do Norte

Paraíba

Piauí

Pernambuco

Alagoas

Acre

Sergipe

Rondônia

Mato Grosso

Bahia

Goiás

Minas Gerais

Mato Grosso do Sul

Espírito Santo

São Paulo

Rio de Janeiro

Paraná

PDS

Santa Catarina

PMDB

Rio Grande do Sul

PDT

FINAL CONSIDERATIONS

Political parties in Brazil have never functioned to relate popular desires to political outcomes. They have usually been tools for the manipulation of the state. During the Empire and the First Republic the parties represented only a narrow political elite. Under Vargas's *Estado Novo*, the parties were outlawed. Since 1946, the parties have become somewhat more responsive to popular desires because of the expansion of the electorate. Nonetheless, with few exceptions, Brazil's political parties since 1946 have been elitist and organized from the top down. Successive governments have been able to manipulate the formation of major parties during realignment periods, such as the PSD and PTB in 1945, the ARENA in 1966, and the PDS in 1980. During the first multiparty period, most of the smaller parties were personalist vehicles, and this seems to be the case in the current multiparty phase. With the exception of the PMDB and PT, no parties have done much "grassroots" organizing.

TABLE 4.6. Results of the November 1982 Elections by Party

	PDS	PMDB[a]	PDT	PTB	PT	Total
Governors[b]	13	9	1	0	0	23
Senators[c]	46	21	1	1	0	69 (35)[d]
Federal Deputies	235	200	23	13	8	479 (240)[d]
Electoral College Delegates[e]	78	48	6	0	0	132
Electoral College Composition[f]	359	269	30	14	8	680 (341)[d]
Proportion of Party Vote (%)[g]	41.5	44.0	6.1	4.7	3.7	100.0

[a]The PP entered a fusion with the PMDB in February.

[b]The PDS governor of Rondônia was appointed, thus only 12 PDS governors were popularly elected.

[c]Includes the 44 senators elected in 1978. In the new state of Rondônia, the PDS elected all 3 senators.

[d]Figures in parentheses indicate the absolute majority.

[e]Six representing the majority party in each of the 22 state legislatures. As the PDS and PMDB each elected 12 state deputies in the state of Mato Grosso do Sul, this state has no electoral college delegates.

[f]The electoral college will elect the next president in January 1985. Includes all senators and federal deputies, plus the 132 state delegates.

[g]Excludes blank and void ballots. Percentage calculated for total vote cast for the five parties.

Source: Report of TSE.

Although national integration has progressed since 1945, the factions remain strong at the state level. Both the electoral system and the loss of power by the national legislature and by the political class in general after 1964 contributed to the inability of the party system to aggregate political interests and demands and to present viable political programs. With a few notable exceptions (PCB, PRP, PDC, and PL), most parties have been devoid of political ideologies and doctrines. These factors, coupled with internal ideological divisions, weakened party cohesion during all three periods.

Successive civilian and military governments have been skilled in the practice of "preemptive anticipationism." When new activism of civil society challenged the incumbent regime, its strategists heeded the basic idea of the 1930 conspirators: "We must make the revolution before the people do!" Each in the series of transformations of the Brazilian party system was, in its turn, part of this strategy.

NOTES

1. Phyllis Peterson, "Brazil: Institutionalized Confusion," in Needler (ed.), *Political Systems of Latin America* (New York: Van Nostrand, 1964), pp. 463–510.

2. Ronald H. Chilcote, *The Brazilian Communist Party: Conflict and Integration, 1922-1972* (New York: Oxford University Press, 1974), p. 58.

3. Prestes in 1982 claimed that this phrase was taken out of context of a speech he made in Recife in early 1964, and was used by his PCB colleagues against him after the military coup of March 31, 1964. Prestes claims he really said, "We are exerting influence on the government through our control of the labor unions." Dênis de Moraes and Francisco Vianna, *Prestes: Lutas e Autocríticas* (Petrópolis: Ed. Vozes, 1982), p. 172.

4. Alzira Vargas, *Getúlio Vargas, meu pai* (Porto Alegre: Editora Globo, 1960), pp. 91–116.

5. Lúcia L. Oliveira, "O Partido Social Democrático: Notas de Pesquisa," *DADOS*, No. 10 (1973), pp. 146–53.

6. Fernando H. Cardoso, "Partidos e Deputados em São Paulo," in Cardoso & Lamounier (eds.), *Os partidos e as eleições no Brasil* (Rio de Janeiro: Paz e Terra, 1975), p. 53; José Murilo de Carvalho, "Barbacena: A família, a política e uma hipótese," *Revista Brasileira de Estudos Políticos*, No. 20 (January 1966), p. 183.

7. René Armand Dreifuss, *1964: A conquista do estado; ação política, poder e golpe de classe* (Petrópolis: Ed. Vozes, 1981), pp. 261–80. See also, Maria Victória M. Benevides, *A UDN e o Udenismo: Ambiguidades do Liberalismo Brasileiro* (Rio de Janeiro: Paz e Terra, 1981).

8. Cardoso (1975), "Partidos e Deputados em São Paulo," p. 54.

9. Glaucio D.D. Soares, *Sociedade e política no Brasil* (São Paulo: DIFEL, 1973), p. 99.

10. Maria V. M. Benevides, *O Governo Kubitschek—desenvolvimento economico e estabilidade política, 1956-1961* (Rio de Janeiro: Paz e Terra, 1976), p. 46.

11. Maria do Carmo Campello de Souza, *Estado e partidos políticos no Brasil (1930-1964)* (São Paulo: Alfa-Omega, 1976), pp. 141–42.

12. Dreifuss (1981), *1964*, pp. 101–04, 162–72.

13. Simon Schwartzman, "Twenty Years of Representative Democracy in Brazil," in Alker, Deutsch & Strotzel (eds.), *Mathematical Approaches to Politics* (San Francisco: Jossey-Bass, 1973), pp. 148–53.

14. David V. Fleischer, "A Evolução do bipartidarismo brasileiro, 1966-1979," *Revista Brasileira de Estudos Políticos* 51 (July 1980), pp. 166–74.

15. David V. Fleischer, "Renavação política, Brasil 1978: eleições parlamentares sob a égide do 'Pacote de Abril'," *Revista de Ciência Política* (FGV), 23:2 (1980), pp. 78–81.

16. Maria D. G. Kinzo, "Novos partidos: o início do debate," in *Voto de desconfiança: eleições e mudança política no Brasil, 1970-1979* ed. Bolivar Lamounier (Petrópolis: Ed. Vozes, 1980), pp. 231–38.

17. Luiz Bahia, Olavo B. Lima, Jr., and Cesar Guimarães, "Perfil social e político de nossa legislatura," *Jornal do Brasil*, April 22-24, 1979.

18. Luis Ignácio da Silva, "Interview," *Latin American Perspectives*, 6:4 (Fall 1979), pp. 90-100; José Álvaro Moisés, "Current Issues in the Labor Movement in Brazil," *Latin American Perspectives*, 6:4 (Fall 1979), pp. 51-70; José Álvaro Moisés, "PT: una novedad histórica?," *Cuadernos de Marcha* (México), (Sept./Oct. 1980), pp. 11-19; and Mário Pedrosa, *Sobre o PT (Partido dos Trabalhadores)* (Rio de Janeiro: Editora Ched, 1980).

19. Eli Diniz, "Máquina Política e Oposição: O MDB no Rio de Janeiro," *DADOS*, 23 (1980), pp. 335-61.

20. *Visáo*, October 12, 1981, p. 15.

21. *Isto É*, December 15, 1982, p. 37.

5

The Military

ORGANIZATION

The Brazilian armed forces are not large, comprising about 280,000 men, or 0.2 percent of the population. There is theoretically a draft, and youths must register at age 17 to be summoned at age 18, but only a small fraction of eligibles are taken. Expenditures on the forces are also a modest percentage of the GNP. In 1958, in the times of Kubitschek, they received 2.8 percent; populist regimes reduced this to 1.7 percent in 1964. The military in power cut itself a larger slice, 2.9 percent in 1967. Since then, however, military expenditures have grown more slowly than the economy as a whole, and their percentage of GNP has shrunken to less than one percent.[1] Brazil devoted in 1981 about 7 percent of national government spending to the armed forces, compared with 64 percent in Argentina. Brazil is about number 100 of 140 countries in the proportion of population in the armed forces.[2] The cost of the armed forces is larger, however, than indicated by budget figures, because the state-dominated economy provides good positions for many former officers.

The army is by far the dominant force, with 182,000 officers and men, vs. 49,000 in the navy and 50,000 in the air force.[3] The army is divided into four major commands, based in Rio de Janeiro, São Paulo, Porto Alegre, and Recife, plus several military regions, each with its own staff. The regional commander is still a political power in his domain, and he can build a base for further advancement.

Regionalism

Each state has its own militia, and these were formerly important. Up to the revolution of 1930, the state militias were quite independent of the federal government, had their own heavy arms, and together outnumbered the federal army. The São Paulo *Força Pública* had a French mission in 1906, well before the federal forces.[4] The militias played an important role in the conflicts of 1930 and 1932 and a secondary role in the revolution of 1964. The military government placed them under strict federal command, with an active-duty army colonel as state cabinet secretary for public security.

The army is still somewhat regional, however. The youths drafted for a one-year stint are usually kept near home. This practice saves money on travel and board, makes it easier to plan an emergency call-up, and lessens the rural-urban migration that overcrowds the cities. Most of the lower officers also serve in their home state.[5] A negative result is that the army is not so important an agent of national unification as is sometimes claimed. Moreover, the unity of the army has been questionable. The top command could not carry out measures unacceptable to regional commanders, who had to take into account the feelings of their troops. This potential for dissidence was most obvious when the forces in Rio Grande do Sul helped override the efforts of the military ministers to veto the presidency of Goulart in 1961, and when they insisted on an early plebiscite to restore the powers of the presidency in 1962. When the commander in Minas Gerais opened the attack in 1964, the decisive question was which way other generals in the various regions would turn. Since 1964, however, regionalism has been reduced.

Class Considerations

The army is sharply divided between officers and enlisted men in terms of economic and social status and education. The two groups are entirely distinct; there is no gateway from below into the officer corps. The army prefers to draft literate urban youths, but the ordinary recruits come from the less-advantaged classes. The officers, to the contrary, receive a great deal of education. The noncommissioned officers stand between. They, particularly the sergeants, have career standing and are professionalized through the Sergeants' School.[6]

Because of what may be considered a class difference between enlisted men and officers, there has been a potential for conflict. In the 1920s, the *tenentes* looked to the lower ranks for support for their insurgency against the hierarchy. In 1935, the enlisted ranks of many units rebelled under Communist leadership. In 1963–64, the Goulart government played on an old grievance, the enlisted men's lack of the rights to vote and to be elected, rights enjoyed by officers, and sought to organize and mobilize the ranks against the generals. In a showdown, however, the army obeyed orders, although the navy was paralyzed.

Much has been written of the class origins of the officers as a presumed basis for their politics. The professionalization of the military, especially since 1945, has greatly reduced upper-class representation in the officer corps, because it is much easier for youths of rich families to go into well-paid civilian positions than to start at the bottom of the career ladder, entering the academy along with their social inferiors and moving upward through a series of often-disagreeable posts at modest pay—there being no lateral entry. As late as 1942–43, 20 percent of entering cadets were of upper-class background; by 1962–66, the figure was only 6 percent,[7] and the percentage has tended to decrease under the military regime.

Poverty and malnutrition, on the other hand, make it difficult for poor boys to obtain secondary education and to prepare themselves for the entrance examination. Consequently, an overwhelming majority, perhaps about nine-tenths, are of middle- or lower-middle-class origins, many of them from large families. The military career represents for them the best opportunity for advancement, and the officers like to regard themselves as neither populists nor aristocrats but as representatives of the real nation.[8]

Nearly half the entrants 1962–66 were from families of military or civil-service background, Stepan found. For that reason, the governmental city of Rio de Janeiro, with 4 percent of the population of Brazil, furnished 40 percent of the cadets. Rio Grande do Sul was next most overrepresented, because of its strong military tradition. Few came from São Paulo because of the relative abundance of opportunities in the civilian economy, while the impoverished Northeast was underrepresented for the opposite reason: poverty preventing boys from obtaining an adequate preparatory education.[9] The officers' corps is emphatically not associated with the industrial elite.

There was a strong tendency toward the formation of an hereditary military caste because more than nine-tenths of cadets were from military secondary schools, which are free for sons of military men. In 1966, however, a law was passed to broaden recruitment. In particular, the three top graduates of civilian secondary schools were made automatically eligible for entry to the military academy. In the following years, the percentage of cadets of civilian background rose to nearly half. It may be supposed that the intellectual level of the young officers was also raised.

Training and Promotion

The graduate of the four-year academy, in order to qualify for the rank of captain, must pass a one-year course at the Junior Officers' School. To

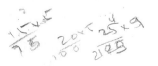

qualify for major requires another year's study. To rise to colonel or general, one must go through the highly selective Command and General Staff School, a three-year course. Generals ordinarily, but not obligatorily, also attend the Superior War College (ESG) for one year. Along the way, academic performance is quite important for promotion.[10] This prolonged education with indoctrination separates the military from civilian elites and makes the values of officers those of their organization to a greater extent than in any other profession, except perhaps religion.

There are strict up-or-out rules, strengthened by Castelo Branco following the U.S. model, and officers can remain in grade only for a limited time. Obligatory retirement ages range from 59 for colonel to 66 for four-star generals. The rule long prevailed that a general passed over three times had to retire, but in August 1980 this was changed to require retirement if passed over once.[11] At least a quarter of the positions of each general rank are changed each year. This flux and renovation of military command contrasts with the persistence of civilian politicians and contributes to military distrust of civilian leaders.

The president makes promotions to the top ranks, but he is restricted to a three-name list prepared by the High Command, and he must consider seniority in the upper echelons. However, President Figueiredo had a unique opportunity to replace the entire High Command in 1981 because of retirements under the rule that no one can remain a general more than 12 years. His choices included two of his brothers.

Ministers and Advisors

A large majority of presidential advisors since 1964 have been military men, and no president has been in a position to disregard his fellow officers. The president is assisted by his three military ministers, who command the respective forces; by the chief of the Military Household (*Casa Militar*), who acts as his personal military advisor; by the High Command; by the General Staff; and by the National Security Council.

The High Command consists of four-star generals, the minister of the army (formerly minister of war), the chief of staff, the commanders of the four armies, and five chiefs of sections of the ministry. The High Command has tried since the days of the *Estado Novo* to monopolize army decision making, resisting the idea that any subordinates might be entitled to a voice.[12] The High Command speaks mostly through the National Security Council, composed of the three military ministers, the chief of staff of the armed forces, the chiefs of staff of the three forces, the vice president, and principal civilian ministers; the chief of the Military Household is its secretary.

The National Security Council is important for studies and policy rec-ommendations, as well as for discussion of current proposals; the president is reluctant to go against it or its military members. It is reported that the nuclear program was initiated by the secretariat of the National Security Council. In 1974, the military members of the council were a minority in opposition to the recognition of the People's Republic of China; President Geisel refrained from simply overriding them but asked for reconsideration, and he acted only after five of the seven changed their votes.[13] In 1980, the military members of the council favored rapprochement with the Chilean Pinochet government, despite the unsuccessful opposition of the Foreign Ministry.[14]

Security Organs

A very influential branch of the military is the Brazilian counterpart of the U.S. Central Intelligence Agency, the National Information Service (SNI). It began as the continuation of General Golbery's anti-Communist organization, the Institute of Research and Social Studies (IPES), which played a considerable role in the overthrow of Goulart; and it was founded by Castelo Branco shortly after taking office, with Golbery as its director. Two of its heads, Médici and Figueiredo, have become presidents—and Me-deiros is regarded as a potential president. Its chief is normally a close advi-sor of the president, as General Octávio Medeiros of Figueiredo.

The budget and staff of the SNI are secret, but it supervises and coordi-nates the intelligence services of the three branches of the armed forces: the Army Information Center (CIE), which supplies all commanders with confi-dential assessments of policies; the Detachment of Operation and Informa-tion (DOI); and the Center for Internal Defense Operations (CODI). The latter two, established by Médici as part of his war on terrorism, have repre-sentatives in the command of each army.[15] The SNI has its own National Intelligence School to rival the Higher War College.

The SNI is very influential through its control of security clearance. Moreover, it has branches in each ministry to assure proper attention to na-tional security goals.[16] These consist of about 30 SNI officials, headed by an ESG graduate, who form a Division of Security and Information. They are subordinate to the minister but supervised by higher authorities of the SNI. There are also affiliates of the SNI in most official agencies and in the ad-ministration of the various states to coordinate (or subordinate) state re-gimes and to oversee policies for conformance to the goals of the military regime. There may be as many as 50,000 persons in the SNI system, including informants.[17]

At least potentially, the security apparatus is a sort of government within the government. It influences both policies and appointments at all levels through its control of information. It is something of an administrative agency, overseeing policies from land reform to nuclear energy and the disciplining of state enterprises.[18] The president cannot easily defy it. Its units seem to have undertaken a countercampaign of violence after Figueiredo took office, as evidenced by occasional bombings of leftist bookstores and the like; and they are immune to prosecution, just as they cannot be brought to account for actions, such as torture, of repressive years.

The Military Club

An organization formerly important for the formation or expression of military policy is the Military Club in Rio. In the 1880s, the club rang with republican rhetoric and played a major part in the overthrow of the monarchy. In 1954, the ouster of Vargas was decided in a tumultuous session at the Military Club. In the 1950s and 1960s, it was the most important locale of debates over national policy between the leftist-nationalists and the moderates, and elections to its governing positions were the best barometer of military sentiment. In 1963, the Military Club became a center of criticism of the Goulart government, and its president, Augusto Pereira, was briefly imprisoned.[19] Since 1964, the military government, desirous of no competition outside its circle, has discouraged political activism in the Military Club. It has, for the most part, succeeded. The elegant club in Rio and its counterparts wherever there is a military unit have thus lost their direct political importance. They remain, however, a social focus for officers, a place where new lieutenants meet the colonel's daughter whom they are likely to marry and where officers exchange views—part of the apparatus encapsulating the military from civilian life.

POLITICAL ROLE

The political role of the armed forces in Brazil has been quite as strong as in other Latin American republics in recent decades, but the Brazilians come from far behind. The early history of Spanish American republics was dominated by military forces because they were by far the strongest organized force emerging from the protracted struggle for independence. Brazil became independent with no need for military action, and the army was looked down on in the years after 1822 as a reminder of colonial oppression. Civilian politicians sought consistently to reduce military expenditures, considering them wasteful and the personnel under arms as a threat to freedom.

Military manpower and budget were pruned in half after 1830, and they were not permitted to recover the old levels until the Paraguayan War (1865–70). Following the buildup in that conflict, the military again was cut down to its lowest level, taking only 8 percent of government expenditures in 1878–79.[20] This neglect was a major reason for discontent and the coup of 1889.

Having joined with the republicans to overthrow Dom Pedro II, the army acquired a certain sense of moral superiority and compensated for its previous low status by ruling directly until 1894 and by maintaining a sort of oversight through the years of the Old Republic. The constitution of 1891, like subsequent constitutions, required the military to obey civilian authority, that is, the president, "within the limits of the law," a provision that was approved by civilians as restricting potential dictators but that invited the generals to decide what the law was. There also developed the thesis of the "moderator" role of the armed forces, as a fourth—and in effect supreme—power in the state, standing over and guaranteeing the legality and constitutionality of the presidency, legislature, and the judiciary, somewhat as the emperor had stood over his government.

Although three presidents of the Old Republic were marshals or generals and many officers went into the Congress and state governments, the armed forces were not a coherent, autonomous organization but, to a large extent, were the instrument of political groups.[21] Despite a training mission from Prussia prior to World War I and from France after it, discipline and hierarchy were breached by many mutinies. Insubordination culminated in the *tenente* movement of the 1920s, especially active in 1922 and 1924. Junior officers rebelled in 1922, specifically because they believed the military honor was besmirched by a (forged) letter attributed to a leading presidential candidate, Artur Bernardes, generally because they felt suffocated under a narrow oligarchy. The *tenentes* were the more embittered by their relatively harsh punishment after the mutiny was put down because previous insurrections had been treated very gently.

The armed forces came to political maturity under Getúlio Vargas. The revolution of 1930 was more of a military movement than a personal campaign of the defeated presidential candidate, and the authoritarian regime required a firmly united military force as a major arm of the state. The army was seared by the Communist uprising of 1935, in which dissatisfied noncoms had a major part; thereafter, the forces were usually united in anticommunism, and the officers were apprehensive of politics in the ranks. The armed forces became dominant with the dissolution of Congress and of political parties by the *Estado Novo* of 1937. However, the actual job of closing the Congress in November 1937 was entrusted to police forces of the Federal District.

The *Estado Novo* made the army an agency of national reconstruction, and it undertook many developmental activities, such as opening interior frontier regions, building roads and railways, and promoting education and literacy, at least among recruits. Vargas placed many officers in high administrative posts and associated the military with industrialization; the germ of Petrobras, for example, came from the need to provide fuel for the armed forces. The forces were glad of the mission, because they increasingly saw industrial development as the basis of national strength and approved of the technocratic, rather than commercial or political, approach to problems. At the same time, they saw themselves better prepared than civilians to manage great enterprises.

Teaching and fulfilling patriotic duty, the armed forces developed a sort of ideology rationalizing their role. Their ideals had long been influenced by the Positivism of Auguste Comte, which was popular among intellectuals from the last decades of the nineteenth century and which furnished the slogan on the Brazilian flag since the beginning of the republic: "Order and Progress." Positivism stood for the value of reason in the best nineteenth-century tradition of optimism. It looked to a higher society, based on science and material progress, to be achieved by social planning imposed by beneficent authority, in practice most likely the military. The Positivists were antislavery and prorepublic, and many of them had hopes for social and political improvement through the armed forces. Vargas was influenced by Positivism, which was a partial rationale for his dictatorship. Gen. Goes Monteiro elaborated for Vargas's regime ideas of National Security; the responsibility of the armed forces for all aspects of national life; morality and education for patriotism as well as strictly military strength—a doctrine anticipating the more articulated idea of Security and Development of the ESG.[22]

In 1945, the soldiers, converted to democracy by their wartime experience, removed the dictator who had given them a large national role, but they continued to be the arbiter of politics. Their mentality was somewhat alien to that of the republic, as they formed a relatively autonomous group within society, unfriendly to civilian values, relatively duty-bound, anticommercial, and somewhat ascetic. Although they shrank from intervention in politics because of the negative public image acquired thereby, with consequent effects on the quality of recruits, they agreed on the incapacity of civilian politicians and the need for better social discipline, and they felt repeatedly called upon in 1945, 1954, 1955, 1961, and 1964 to pass judgment on constitutional questions.

The controversies of 1945–64 entangled the military in political questions in new ways and to a new degree, as the army undertook to make decisions that properly should have been made within the framework of the constitution. They were encouraged to do so by civilians, and each party looked to the military not to stay out of politics but to support its partisan interests. Military opinion was consequently much divided, the more so as a high officer was a candidate in each presidential election (unsuccessful except for Dutra in 1945). That hardly anyone was killed through five military interventions reflects the Brazilian tradition of limited conflict. At crucial times, the generals in effect voted and respected the majority decision; those who saw themselves in a minority on an issue would back down, and no reprisals followed.

Since 1964, the military view has been fairly well equivalent to the official, but differences have not ceased. There was an example of military infighting in the Castelo Branco administration over who, navy or air force, was to control the planes on a newly purchased aircraft carrier. The carrier was immobilized for many months by the disagreement, and Castelo Branco had to decree a compromise: the navy got the planes but the air force was compensated with antisubmarine helicopters.

There have naturally been many clashes of personality and frustrated ambitions. For example, late in the Geisel administration, Gen. Frota tried to secure the succession. He was a hardliner, but that the quarrel was personal became clear as the "hard-line" faction supported a reformist opposition candidate, General Bentes Monteiro, against Geisel's preference, Figueiredo.

The recurrent division during the military government, however, has been more or less ideological. Some, the "hard-line," were more concerned with making their revolution, imposing discipline, and changing society; others looked primarily to economic development and were more prepared to make concessions to economic interests and to civilian institutions. This also corresponded roughly to the division between those preferring reliance on national resources and state enterprise against those prepared to welcome foreign investment (mostly U.S. at one time) and to favor private enterprise under guidance. The hardliners were frequently junior officers, impatient with their seniors' lack of revolutionary enthusiasm. The navy also tended to support the hard line.

The hard-line faction was able to threaten the tenure of Castelo Branco and Costa e Silva. Geisel could discipline those who did not wish to give up the torture of prisoners, and he effectively isolated the High Command from political decision making, but there continued to be an undercurrent of opposition to his more liberal policies, and he had to discipline generals who insisted on pushing nationalistic themes. In April 1980, it was reported that leaders of the auto workers' strike were arrested by the Second Army without the authorization of the central authorities.

A major reason for the renunciation of power by military regimes is factionalism; the difficulty of securing general compliance in the absence of constitutional legitimacy. Arbitrary authority invites arbitrary rejection, and the necessity of making many political choices is inevitably divisive. Factionalism does not seem to have grown in the Brazilian Armed Forces since 1964, however; rather it has diminished or retreated behind the public stage with the fading of revolutionary feeling. Most officers were probably politically indifferent so long as their careers were secure. All could agree on the necessity to combat subversion, broadly defined, on the need for rapid development, and on the value of making Brazil fully independent and projecting its presence and influence in the world.

THE SUPERIOR WAR COLLEGE

A major reason for the fair degree of harmony of Brazilian officers is their extensive and well-coordinated educational curriculum. In particular, since 1950, the attitudes and motivation of the armed forces have been much influenced, or at times largely shaped, by an institution that originally seemed of little importance, the Superior War College (*Escola Superior de Guerra*, ESG).

After World War II, Brazil, like the United States, set about improving high-level, national-security institutions. A Joint Services General Staff was set up, and a National Security Council was formed to advise the president. To improve the training of high officers, the ESG was established in 1949, in imitation mostly of the United States War College, then only three years old, and with the help of a U.S. military mission. Veterans of the Brazilian Expeditionary Force, including Gen. Oswaldo Cordeiro de Farias, took the lead in its formation. Classes began in 1950, and the school has subsequently expanded in importance and in size, taxing the small old building it occupies in Rio—a move to Brasília has been long proposed but has been much resisted by those who prefer life in the old capital.

The commandant of the ESG is a four-star officer and thus a member of the High Command. The command was rotated among the three services up to 1964, but since then has mostly gone to army men. The High Command has jurisdiction over the ESG, but its guidance is only general. The military ministers participate in the governing board, and there is a partly civilian consultative commission.[23]

The staff, formerly taken from among the high officers, has recently been composed mostly of graduates, plus a few civilian scholars. Ministers sometimes lecture to classes.

About 120 students (called "temporary members," *estagiários*, to avoid the separation of students and teachers), aged 35–55, come for a one-year course. Civilian students were brought into the ESG because of the desire to pursue economic and social studies and to train a civil elite whom the military could trust. At first civilians were very few, but their number gradually increased to well over half. Since 1973, women have been admitted; in 1980 there were nine. The civilians are picked from lists of eligibles submitted by institutions. The ESG wants persons of diverse backgrounds and professions. Bankers, industrialists, civil servants, and professionals figure prominently; some classes, such as labor leaders, are de facto excluded because of the prerequisite of a university education. Some officers come from other Latin American countries. Four officers from the ESG go each year for a two-year course at the U.S. Staff College.

The work of the ESG has been essentially different from that of the U.S. War College, because the Brazilians felt the need not only to apply resources militarily but also to create them, not only to guide the armed forces but also to make a nation capable of sustaining strong armed forces. There have always been staff and command courses for officers, but from the beginning and increasingly in the 1960s, the ESG turned to the broader or internal aspects of national security (subversion, terrorism, propaganda) and to the development necessary for basic security,[24] for the benefit of civilian as well as military members.

Courses have embraced the whole range of national problems, economics, education, natural resources, the fuel question, banking, and so forth. Attention has been given from time to time to current events, such as the Iranian revolution, and to Brazilian political affairs, particularly the *abertura*. The school promotes not merely academic instruction but a greater sharing of experience and ideas—a reason for not calling the one-year members "students." It claims an undogmatic approach, encouraging free expression and discussion. At the end of the course, temporary members present papers, the best of which are published. Trips are organized to study conditions throughout Brazil and in other Latin American countries, and refresher courses are offered a few years after graduation.

There is a great effort to create a school spirit in and around the ESG, with many trophies, emblems, and cultivated traditions, down to the button worn by graduates. More important is the extension of the influence of the ESG through other institutions. Its chief impact on officers probably comes through the Command and Staff School, which follows ESG teachings. In 1971, a school was established for the SNI to train military and civilian personnel and to formulate doctrine for the intelligence branch; it is closely allied with the ESG.[25] There are other extensions of the ESG, such as the Brazilian studies program required at all Brazilian universities. In 1973, the ESG began extension or correspondence courses for graduates and nongraduates.

Every effort is made to keep the alumni of the ESG together and, through them, to spread the doctrines of the school and to educate the nation, to "multiply the ESG," as it is put. Some 4,000 graduates of the ESG, mostly civilians from the ESG Graduate Association (*Asociacão de Diplomados da ESG*, ADESG), form the nucleus of a political elite.

The ADESG has been conducting courses since 1962; in 1980 they were held in three- or four-month cycles in 23 branches in 17 cities, each bringing in from 100 to 150 students for four hours of instruction nightly. Students are preferably local leaders in various occupations, probably with higher education, nominated by ADESG members. They discuss issues in the light of the general philosophy of the ESG, "Security and Development," using as a text the *Basic Doctrine*, published by the ESG. Lecturers make the circuit of the locals. Under the motto "One heart and one spirit for Brazil," courses treat, for example, the Brazilian family, education and national security, the needy child and birth control, energy policy, and agricultural development. There are also lectures for outsiders. There were more than 30,000 participants from 1962 to March 1979; and they were held together by weekly luncheons, in the style of U.S. civic groups, discussion groups, refresher courses, and other activities, forming a sort of social-political order comparable to lodges in the United States. They also have a magazine, *Security and Development*.[26]

The teachings of the ESG, thus spread among a large number of influential people, have undoubtedly done much to make military government more effective and more acceptable. ESG influence, however, is not apparently so much on policy as on general philosophy and the formation of a self-aware, politically minded elite. To some extent, it serves to bring civilian ideas into the armed forces and to keep the forces aware of the thinking of the country. Mostly, however, it disseminates armed forces' thinking to the community. Civilians attending the ESG or its subsidiaries—politicians, businessmen, and so forth—are pleased to come into the company of the powerful officers and to share their thinking.

Within the armed forces, the ESG has had some success in generating a common philosophy and a set of principles. Its training prepared some generals in 1964 to intervene and, more significantly, to feel themselves capable of managing the country. In 1964, 60 percent of the generals who had attended the ESG were actively anti-Goulart, whereas only 15 percent of those who had not been through the ESG were in that category[27]—partly because Kubitschek and Goulart removed unfriendly officers from command positions by assigning them to the school. The generals affiliated with the ESG dominated the government of Castelo Branco, and the ESG provided an orientation for the new military regime. Since then the immediate influence of the school may have declined, but most generals attend it, and graduation from it probably leads to better appointments. Presidents Castelo Branco, Geisel, and Figueiredo are alumni; Costa e Silva and Médici are not.

The key role of the ESG is to be the ideological guide of the armed forces and, since 1964, of the government, a role which is the stronger because of what the military regards as the deficient study of national problems in Brazilian universities.[28] Study groups of the ESG make policy proposals to the armed forces; more important, the ESG is charged by law with the formulation of the official ideology, an authority to fix national directions suggestive of that of the central committee of the Communist party-states.[29]

The motto on the wall of the school is less ambitious and less authoritarian: *Nesta casa se estuda o destino do Brasil* ("In this house we study the destiny of Brazil"). Under the ideological guidance of Golbery do Couto e Silva, an outstanding intellectual, it developed and refined the doctrine of National Security, or Security and Development (S and D) as it has been called since the military assumed the responsibilities of government. Since 1975, the school has published biennially a lengthy handbook, written by instructors in consultation with higher authorities, called *Basic Doctrine.*

SECURITY AND DEVELOPMENT

The Brazilian military-dominated government has evolved a rather sophisticated ideology and rationalization of its purposes and role, the details of which have been formulated and published by the ESG. It is rationalistic but elitist and temperately authoritarian, different in spirit and purpose from democratic political theory and also from Brazilian clientelistic politics. It is not basically new; much of it is practically a restatement of traditional military values, fleshed out with technocratic concepts.[30] In large part, it goes back to nineteenth-century Positivism; National Security and Development are practically synonymous with Order and Progress and the ideas developed to rationalize the *Estado Novo.* Prior to the revolution of 1964, the administration of Kubitschek was guided by the ideas basic to the more recent doctrine: the need for development to assure national security and to defeat subversion and the superiority of the community to the individual.[31]

The broad purpose of S and D is to guide toward the securing of the "Permanent National Objectives," which, according to the constitution of 1969, are to be fixed by the National Security Council.[32] The goal is the preservation of the national community; as stated by Golbery, the world is a very dangerous place, with new dimensions and kinds of conflict constantly arising, and "Brazil at present has only one choice: to become great or perish."[33] Basic principles were set forth at the time of founding of the ESG: National security rests on the whole nation; Brazil has the potential of great power but has been held back by conditions that can be changed, the acceleration of Brazil's progress requires cooperative work and better means of securing harmony; one step toward this goal is the education of the elite.[34]

S and D is intended to be not dogma but doctrine, not so much a set of fixed answers to questions as an approach to problem solving.[35] It should avoid arbitrariness and remain flexible and subject to improvement; its practitioners are invited to question old ideas and to bring up new ones in free debate, as long as the permanent national objectives are served.[36] There are none of the claims of perfection or intolerance of deviation frequently seen in Marxist movements, nor is there a thesis of necessary struggle within society; on the contrary, the belief that society should be essentially harmonious within the nation permits acceptance of differences.

In the view of S and D, the ability to achieve the permanent national objective is to be analyzed, measured, and improved in all aspects—economic, social, psychological, demographic, scientific, educational, and so forth—and the authorities are concerned with the moral as well as physical health of the population. Most attention, however, goes to economic development, which refers primarily to industrialization; this is at once the object and the source of political power.[37] The immediate and strongest purpose of economic growth is to serve the national security, although this has the ultimate purpose of serving the common welfare. Concerning the means to economic growth, the thinking of the ESG has always been pragmatic, wishing to make use of state enterprise if necessary but to avoid it if inefficient. On practical grounds, it has sought the cooperation of foreign capital, frequently to the displeasure of the nationalists. On the other hand, it has favored central economic planning.

One purpose of development is to reduce dissatisfaction and social disharmony,[38] but the philosophers of the armed forces have not felt able to rely on this slow and uncertain remedy. The military used force to liquidate what it regarded as subversive politics, and this purpose, especially during the first decade of power, ranked close to development. National Security seemed to require saving the nation from itself, or from its subverted elements, or from the psychological and guerrilla war carried on by communism, which is seen as both an internal and an external danger.[39] This meant, of course, neglect of individual rights in favor of the interests of the community as perceived by the elite.

More broadly, the priority of the community is a central tenet of S and D. National security is a function of the whole national capacity, to be mobilized by the state, while economic development is the task of all classes and sectors, requiring discipline and sacrifice. The individual has importance only in the realization of the community, which stands morally superior over all. The state is the expression of the collective and is its moving force by virtue of centralized authority. Dissent must be restricted to prevent irrational exploitation of individualism, demagoguery, and radicalism.[40] It is the duty of the state to weld the nation together for the common purposes, whether or not people are so disposed.

In this way, liberalism and social democracy are harmful, leading to disintegration of the state; and popular democracy is incompatible with rapid development.[41] There is consequently no question of asking or allowing people to decide the basic questions of national objectives and locus of power. Democracy, indeed, is understood more as constitutionalism than as an expression of the will of the masses.[42] It is recognized, however, that power, to be effective, must be legitimate or generally accepted.[43]

In theory, at least, S and D includes representative democracy as a fundamental goal. Among the permanent national objectives established by the National Security Council are . . .

> to establish a national community, politically, socially, economically, and culturally integrated; to guarantee the exercise of complete national independence; to maintain territorial integrity; to foster democratic representative government; to preserve social peace and national prosperity; and to project the national personality in the concert of nations.[44]

More specifically, political parties and legislatures are regarded as a proper means of people-government communication, and it is legitimate for parties to express divergent opinions with the purpose of gaining political power.[45] Aside from these concessions, however, democracy is treated in S and D more as a purpose than as a form of government: national security should serve the general welfare, and the elite should express the interests and aspirations of the people, while helping them to realize true understanding of their needs.[46] Democracy means the state serving the people instead of the reverse.[47] Democracy seems to be equated with the health of the society:

> First, the unceasing search for a moral, rational society providing a lifestyle characterized by respect for the dignity of the human being and for equality of opportunity for all; second, the adoption of a political system based on the values of and characterized by the continual perfection of political representation and public opinion, as the bases legitimating democratic institutions, and by the adaption of these institutions to the national society.[48]

For an undefined period, however, the people need to be guided and educated by the elite. The word "elite" in this connection is no more pejorative than the word "party" or "vanguard" in the context of a Communist state, and political and technical elites should work together to set goals and find means of securing the common good.[49] Great historical movements have always been the work of elites, which should listen to the people and consider their true interests but which should form proposals and policies in their, the elites', judgment.

Why the elite is elite and who should be elite the doctrine does not make clear, but the leaders of the armed forces are obvious candidates. They see their institution as "the people in uniform," a nonclass body qualified to arbitrate between rich and poor,[50] while development requires the military to guarantee order and security. The armed forces also have the advantage of unity; the failure of elites to work together for the good of Brazil was always the greatest handicap, from the military view, holding back the nation.[51] S and D further institutionalizes the cohesion of the armed forces, giving them a basis for action without placing themselves at the service of civilian groups. Under the doctrine, the armed forces are thus an essentially political organ, making politics instead of being the object of politics, and the nation should be organized on military lines, with strong central government responsive to the armed forces and with the discipline necessary for maximum productivity and results. Security then serves development,[52] just as development serves security.

NOTES

1. *SIPRI Yearbook 1980* (Stockholm: Stockholm International Peace Research Institute, 1980), p. 24; *Foreign Broadcast Information Service, Latin America*, September 17, 1981; *Latin American Weekly Report*, October 8, 1981, p. 11.

2. Wayne A. Selcher, "Brazil in the World: Ranking Analysis," in *Brazil in the International System: The Rise of a Middle Power* (Boulder, Colo.: Westview Press, 1981), p. 3.

3. International Institute for Strategic Studies, *The Military Balance 1979–1980* (London: 1979), p. 77.

4. D. A. Dallari, "The Força Pública of São Paulo," in *Perspectives on Armed Politics in Brazil*, ed. Henry H. Keith and Robert A. Hayes (Tempe, Ariz.: Arizona State University Press, 1976), p. 80.

5. Alfred Stepan, *The Military in Politics: Changing Patterns in Brazil* (Princeton, N.J.: Princeton University Press, 1974), pp. 13–14.

6. Ibid., p. 159.

7. Ibid., p. 31.

8. Alexandre de Souza Costa Barros, "The Brazilian Military: Professional Socialization, Political Performance, and State Building," (Ph.D. dissertation, University of Chicago, 1978), p. 364.

9. Stepan, *The Military in Politics*, pp. 36–39.

10. Ibid., pp. 50–51.

11. *Latin American Weekly Reports* 80 (December 12, 1980).

12. Edmundo Campos Coelho, *Em busca de identidade: O exército e a política na sociedade brasileira* (Rio de Janeiro: Forense-Universitária, 1976), pp. 117–18.

13. Walder de Goés, *O Brasil de General Geisel: estudo do processo de tomada de decisão no regime militar-burocrático* (Rio de Janeiro: Nova Fronteira, 1978), pp. 32–36.

14. *Latin American Regional Report, Brazil*, October 17, 1980.

15. *Veja*, June 3, 1981, p. 22; *Jornal do Brasil*, May 9, 1981, p. 3.

16. Barros, *The Brazilian Military*, pp. 215–16.

17. Goés, *O Brasil de General Geisel*, p. 52; Carlos Chagas, "The System Ever More Rigid," *O Estado de São Paulo*, February 7, 1982, p. 4; Joint Publications Research Service, *Latin American Weekly Report*, March 8, 1982, p. 22.

18. *Latin American Regional Report, Brazil*, August 6, 1982, p. 1; Carlos Chagas, "The Unstable Tripod of Power in the Planalto," *Estado de São Paulo*, July 18, 1982, p. 4, *JPRS*, September 3, 1982, p. 28.

19. Robert A. Hayes, "The Military Club and National Politics," in *Perspective on Armed Politics*, ed. Henry H. Keith and Robert A. Hayes (Tempe, Ariz.: Arizona State University Press, 1976), pp. 140–55.

20. Coelho, *Em busca de identidade*, pp. 34–35, 39, 47.

21. Ibid., p. 168.

22. Ibid., pp. 103–04, 114.

23. Carlos Henrique Rezende de Noronha, *A Escola Superior de Guerra* (Rio de Janeiro: Superior War College, 1979), pp. 12, 19.

24. Ibid., p. 17; Antônio de Arruda, "História da Doutrina de ESG," lecture delivered at the Superior War College, Rio de Janeiro, March 10, 1980, p. 31.

25. Goés, *O Brasil de General Geisel*, p. 54.

26. Dept. de Ciclos e Estudios, *Instruções gerais ás delegações* (Rio de Janeiro: Superior War College Graduate Association, 1980).

27. Stepan, *The Military in Politics*, p. 184.

28. Arturo Valle, *Estruturas políticas brasileiras* (Rio de Janeiro: Editora Laudes, 1970), pp. 55–56.

29. Fernando Pedreira, *Brasil político, 1964–1975* (São Paulo: Difel, 1975), pp. 33–34.

30. Coelho, *Em busca de identidade*, p. 165.

31. Mirim Limoeiro Cardoso, *Ideologia do desenvolvimento—Brasil, JQ/JK* (Rio de Janeiro: Paz e Terra, 1978), passim.

32. *Doutrina Básica* (Rio de Janeiro: Superior War College, 1979), p. 112.

33. Golbery do Couto e Silva, *Geopolítica do Brasil* (Rio de Janeiro: José Olímpio, 1967), pp. 22, 24, 66.

34. Noronha, *A Escola Superior de Guerra*, pp. 7–8.

35. *Doutrina Básica*, p. 13.

36. Ibid., pp. 20–21.

37. Ibid., p. 65.

38. Coelho, *Em busca de identidade*, p. 173.

39. *Doutrina Básica*, p. 217.

40. Coelho, *Em busca de identidade*, p. 173.

41. Pedreira, *Brasil político*, pp. 168–69.

42. *Doutrina Básica*, pp. 46–47.

43. Ibid., p. 59.

44. Goés, *O Brasil de General Geisel*, p. 34.

45. *Doutrina Básica*, pp. 106, 111.

46. Ibid., pp. 34, 185.

47. Ibid., pp. 64–65.

48. Ibid., pp. 50–51.

49. Ibid., p. 109.

50. Stepan, *The Military in Politics*, p. 42.

51. Arruda, "História da Doutrina de ESG," p. 8.

52. Coelho, *Em busca de identidade*, pp. 165–67.

6

Brazil and the United States

Brazil is geographically the counterpart of the United States in South America, the natural leader of the continent by virtue of size and population. For this reason, and because Portuguese Brazil has felt itself a little at odds with Spanish America—especially the sometimes bitter rival of Argentina—the United States and Brazil have generally respected one another and have maintained good relations. The United States has seen Brazil as its best friend in Latin America and has been Brazil's best friend in the world. The two powers have never had a serious quarrel or a major conflict of interest. When, in the latter 1930s and in the early 1960s, they seemed heading toward conflict, it was primarily for ideological reasons, and in both cases, the drift was turned around to exceptionally close relations. Since 1967, relations have tended to cool, even to chilliness at one time; Brazil, however, is probably still the country of South America that harbors the least resentment for the United States.

The infant United States was the inspiration for the proindependence conspiracy of Tiradentes in 1789. The United States, unlike European powers not constrained by consideration for the feelings of Portugal, was the first nation to recognize independent Brazil. Brazil at the same time welcomed the Monroe Doctrine and several times in the nineteenth century endorsed its application, although Spanish America has ranged from skeptical to hostile.

During the nineteenth century, U.S.-Brazilian relations were troubled by a few minor misunderstandings, arising from shipping questions, a U.S. excursion in the Amazon region, which the Brazilians regarded as potential imperialist spying, and so forth. During the U.S. civil war, Brazil, as a slave-holding nation, was favorable to the Confederacy, and a U.S. warship captured a Confederate vessel in a Brazilian harbor. But these were only minor disturbances in the generally tranquil relations between the two powers. The most important U.S. influence was ideological, nourishing the feeling that the imperial form of government was inappropriate in this hemisphere. This was a basic factor in the overthrow of the empire in 1889. The United States gave relations with the new republic an excellent start by granting recognition in the phenomenally short time of four days.

During the nineteenth century, there was little economic penetration of Brazil by the United States. From the middle of the nineteenth century, the United States became the largest buyer of Brazilian coffee, but Britain was the chief supplier and holder of most foreign investments. There was correspondingly much more friction with and animosity toward the British, who were several times rather high-handed toward Brazil. The U.S. economic stake in Brazil remained minor until the First World War and became dominant only during the Second.

U.S.-Brazilian relations warmed to special cordiality during the foreign ministership of the Baron of Rio Branco (1902–12). He undertook generally to side with the United States in world and Latin American affairs in return for U.S. support against Brazil's neighbors, with which he was trying to settle border controversies. Argentina about this time was emerging as the chief Latin American critic and rival of the United States, so it was the more satisfying for the Brazilians to support U.S.-sponsored Pan Americanism and to promote hemispheric solidarity, acting as a bridge between the United States and Latin America.

Rio Branco also wished to use the United States to displace British influence; the axis of Brazilian diplomacy was shifted from London to Washington, where it remained, so far as Brazilian diplomacy has had any clear orientation. In 1906, Elihu Root, regarding Brazil as the cornerstone of policy toward Latin America, sealed the "special relationship" by picking Brazil for his first foreign visit as secretary of state.

In 1917, Brazil was the only major Latin American country to follow the United States into war with Germany. The war greatly reduced the positions of both Britain and Germany in Brazil and improved that of the United States. The first was never able to recover its shares of Brazilian trade. The decade following the war was rather uneventful, but the U.S.-Brazilian entente lost some of its significance because of the increased attention of both countries to European affairs. Brazil was active in the League of Nations in its first years. However, the Brazilians felt entitled by size to a permanent seat in the League Council, along with the great powers. When this was refused, Brazil became, in 1926, one of the first countries to abandon the League.

ALLIANCE

In 1930, the supporters of Getúlio Vargas overthrew the staid and corrupt Old Republic. In the first years of Vargas's rule, relations with the United States were excellent, as Franklin Roosevelt inaugurated his Good Neighbor Policy, to the warm approval of Brazil. U.S.-Brazilian trade flourished, and Brazil was the first nation to sign a reciprocal trade agreement in accordance with Roosevelt's plan to chip away tariff barriers.

Brazil, however, shared in the tensions generated by the worldwide depression of the 1930s—tensions leading to growing ideological and political conflict and, ultimately, to world war. The fall of the oligarchic republic set Brazil adrift constitutionally and ideologically, and antidemocratic, also anti-U.S., forces burgeoned; both Communists and fascists (*Integralistas*) seemed a real threat to the established order. The Communists reached for power in November 1935 but were crushed. *Integralistas* thereby gained considerable strength. Together with a pro-German sector of the officers' corps and with the Nazi-oriented German colony in the southern states, they made a potential for the first truly fascist state of the Americas, until they were severely repressed after an attempted coup in May 1938.

From the mid-1930s until the war and blockade, Germany waged a strong contest with the United States for economic and political influence in Brazil.[1] German bilateralism challenged U.S. multilateralism, and the former scored points despite the greater capacities of the U.S. economy. The German government could take indefinite quantities of agricultural and mineral products the Brazilians were unable to place on the world market and pay for them in blocked marks, usable only to buy German manufactures. The Germans gave bargains for political purposes, to gain entry and influence and to create dependency on the German market. As a result, German sales to Brazil rose sharply and, in 1938, even slightly exceeded those of the United States. The Nazis also offered cut-rate weapons to Brazilian forces eager to modernize, while the United States was reluctant to furnish armaments that were becoming necessary for the rearmament of the United States and its European friends.

The establishment of the *Estado Novo* in 1937 was generally viewed in the United States and Europe as a fascist coup. Vargas abolished parties, dismissed the Congress, censored the press, and exalted his own image; he seemed at least a fair facsimile of another fascist dictator. Vargas made much of nationalism, which was directed more against the United States than any other country—the theme of the enslavement of Brazil to international finance was much heard in the 1930s. Vargas was obviously inspired by the example of such successful leaders as Hitler and Mussolini; he exalted stern fascist virtues, looked down on decadent democracy, and talked of "improvident liberalism and sterile demagoguery."[2] Most of Vargas's higher officers were pro-Nazi, impressed by German efficiency, by the ability to supply arms—Brazil placed a large order in 1938—and perhaps by the Nazi medals that most of the generals accepted.[3]

The canny Vargas, however, was not prepared to foreclose options sooner than necessary or to commit Brazil to a losing cause. Soon after setting up the *Estado Novo*, he named as foreign minister his good friend, the very able and also pro-U.S. Oswaldo Aranha, who remained at the helm until August 1944, when Brazil had fully joined the Allies in the war. Vargas earlier had proposed military cooperation with the United States; he had turned to Germany only when the United States failed to offer assistance. Vargas also frustrated and infuriated the Nazis by outlawing the promising Nazi movement among Brazilians of German descent, Brazilianizing German schools, closing Fatherland clubs, and insisting that ethnic Germans behave as Brazilians. At the same time, he welcomed U.S. investment.

In 1940, as the United States was edging toward war and the Germans failed to conquer England, Vargas stepped down on the side of the United States. The U.S. Congress had finally decided to provide arms for Brazil for fear that the Axis might acquire a trans-Atlantic bridgehead in the northeastern bulge, and the United States provided financing for Vargas's pet project, the Volta Redonda steel plant.

The Brazilian public reacted emotionally to Pearl Harbor. In January 1942, Brazil broke relations with the Axis powers. This was against the wishes of many senior officers, but thereafter collaboration with the United States progressed rapidly in step with arms deliveries. In August 1942, Brazil entered the war after the Germans sank numerous Brazilian ships at a cost of more than 600 lives.

Brazil entered the war with enthusiasm, and Vargas could rejoice in the increased popularity of his government without thinking of the ultimate consequences for himself. The Brazilians furnished strategic materials, cooperated in the security of the South Atlantic, and alone among Latin American countries sent a small army (some 22,000 men) to fight in the European war. One may surmise that Vargas's love for democracy was less important in the decision to furnish troops than was his desire to play a part in history; but the Brazilian Expeditionary Force (FEB) gave a good accounting of itself in Italy. After overcoming problems of supply and training, it added a glorious chapter to Brazilian military annals.

The wartime alliance was of profound importance to U.S.-Brazilian relations for 25 years, or until the participants had passed from the scene; to some extent, it has conditioned the association of the two countries to this day. The Brazilian soldiers got along well with the Americans and generally received a good impression of the United States and its values. Veterans of the FEB were always a pro-U.S. clique in the armed forces. The Brazilian navy likewise learned to operate with the Americans; it was even placed under a U.S. admiral.[4] U.S. air and naval bases were established in the Northeast, and U.S. forces made themselves at home there.

The economies were also meshed. The U.S.-built Volta Redonda steel plant inaugurated the flowering of Brazilian industrialization, while Brazilians and Americans cooperated in the production of strategic materials. Many U.S. businesses entered Brazil, and Pan American replaced the German airlines. Many missions brought Americans to Brazil. There was in all this collaboration remarkably little friction or distrust; and the special relationship came to seem to Brazilians as a fact of nature, to be questioned only years later as the economy fell into difficulties.

COOLING RELATIONS

For five years or so after the war, the warmth of U.S.-Brazilian relations seemed undiminished, perhaps even reaffirmed by the establishment of democratic government in Brazil in 1946. The army in effect demanded that Vargas permit the establishment of a freely elected government like that of the United States, and when he equivocated, it removed him. Vargas's elected successor, Gen. Dutra, who had been pro-Axis as Vargas's minister of war, was very pro-U.S.; friendship with this country he took for granted like love for mother and belief in God.[5] Brazil remained the chief supporter in Latin America and a Cold War ally, especially after the repression of the Communist Party in 1947–48. The United States tried to secure for Brazil a seat in the Security Council of the United Nations.

Vargas's return to power in 1951 as elected president signalled a turn away from the close alignment. Perhaps Vargas blamed the United States for his ouster—in 1945 the U.S. ambassador had greeted the prospect of elections with an enthusiasm embarrassing for the dictator. More important were Vargas's appeal to nationalism and the changing world picture. Nationalistic sentiments were growing among all sectors, including the armed forces, as the wartime experience receded; and it was increasingly necessary for politicians to appeal to the mass constituency for the newly enfranchised. At the same time, the attention of the United States was drawn first to the reconstruction of Europe under the Marshall Plan, then to the war in Korea. There seemed little need to help Latin America, which, far from having had its industries destroyed, had piled up large foreign-exchange balances and which was not visibly threatened by communism. At the same time, the United States tended to put former ally Brazil on the same basis for weapons sales and loans as formerly pro-Axis Argentina.

As the wartime credit balances were rapidly spent and the economy slowed down, the feeling grew that the United States was neglecting its faithful friend. The Eisenhower administration believed that economic development should be the work of private capital, and Brazil received only modest loans to help it over foreign-exchange difficulties. In rising class tensions, discontent with the system was focused on foreign capital, at this time mostly U.S. capital, and several measures were passed to restrict foreign corporations.

A great victory of the nationalists was the establishment in 1953 of Petrobras to slam the door on foreign oil companies. This measure was promoted by the Communists, who were quite vocal although their party was legally banned, along with a sector of the military, and it aroused great enthusiasm as a declaration of Brazilian independence. A few years earlier, Dutra had been perfectly willing to let foreign (mostly U.S.) countries develop any oil they could find, although they were not eager to undertake prospecting.

The military continued to be basically friendly to the United States, however. In 1950, a leftist-nationalist Varguista slate headed by Gen. Newton Estillac Leal (named minister of war in 1951) won Military Club elections, and subsequently some radical officers published a pro-Communist interpretation of the Korean War. But in March 1952 antileftist sentiment in the forces compelled Vargas to dismiss Estillac Leal. Soon afterward, the antileftist faction, organized as the Democratic Crusade, was victorious in Military Club elections. In February 1954, antileftist military pressures led to the resignation of Vargas's minister of labor, João Goulart, who was proposing 100 percent wage increases that would have placed workers' salaries above those of junior officers.

A few months later, the suicide of Vargas sent tremors through U.S.-Brazilian relations. The immediate cause of the generals' determination to oust Vargas was domestic; the involvement of persons close to the president in the murder of an air force officer. But the officer was killed because he was guarding the conservative, pro-U.S., anti-Communist deputy and journalist Carlos Lacerda, and the leading generals wanted to oust Vargas not only because of unsavory characters around him but also because of his populist, left-leaning policies. It was even charged that he planned to join Perón of Argentina in an anti-U.S. bloc. No proof that the United States was involved in the anti-Vargas move has been produced, but it was and is still widely assumed that the CIA and/or U.S. corporations were responsible for an action beneficial to U.S. economic and political interests. Vargas's suicide note dramatically reinforced this belief by blaming sinister domestic and foreign forces for his undoing. Many who heard the note broadcast dashed into the streets to smash the windows of U.S. firms. The United States definitely became the nationalist target.

In the confused maneuvering that followed Vargas's death, the question of nationalism, basically anti-United States, and anticommunism was usually near the foreground. However, at the beginning of 1956, Juscelino Kubitschek was allowed to take office despite misgivings of many in the military. Kubitschek behaved prudently, carried out a big industrialization program, and gladly received abundant loans from Washington. However, he tried to improve relations with Spanish America and Europe, thereby reducing dependence on the United States. He also complained of neglect by the United States and began investigating trade possibilities with the Communist countries—diplomatic relations with the Soviet Union had been broken in 1947. In 1958, he proposed an ambitious scheme for U.S. development aid for Latin America ("Operation Panamerican"), an idea that the Eisenhower administration found of no interest, but that the Kennedy administration appropriated in 1961 for the "Alliance for Progress." As his administration was waning, in June 1959, Kubitschek dramatically broke with the International Monetary Fund and rejected its conditions for a new loan, thus earning plaudits of the nationalists.

Kubitschek left heavy external and domestic debts, from industrialization and the building of Brasília, to his successors, along with a slowing economy and accelerating inflation. Quadros, a politician of thoroughly populist instinct, sought to meet this situation by fiscal stabilization, pleasing the United States, while placating the nationalists and leftists by turning Brazil sharply toward neutralism. Naive about foreign affairs and diplomacy, Quadros during his brief tenure made friendly gestures toward Cuba and moved to normalize relations with Communist countries, including China, the power then most disliked by the United States. He wanted Brazil to be a Third World leader rather than an automatic U.S. ally and to become economically independent of the United States, which was being viewed not as a helper but as an obstacle to development. When the United States offered advice, Quadros resented it. Much of the time he declined to see the U.S. ambassador.[6] But the United States, pleased with his economic policies, hardly got around to reacting to his foreign policy. In his resignation message, Quadros blamed foreign reactionaries, as Vargas had, and the Brazilian Left has credited the United States with engineering his downfall. His foreign policy was cause, in any event, for the failure of the military to come to his support.

During the Goulart administration, the entanglements of economic problems, economic and political nationalism, populism, and relations with the hemispheric big power frustrated the president, brought him down, and ended the democratic system. Before he became president, Goulart was known for pro-Castro, generally pro-Communist, anti-foreign capital views. But Goulart was a practical politician as well as a demagogue, and in the first part of his presidency, he partly backed off from Quadros's left-leaning neutralism. He named strongly pro-U.S. Roberto Campos ambassador to the United States and conferred freely with U.S. Ambassador Lincoln Gordon, who freely gave advice in a manner no longer conceivable.[7]

Goulart went to Washington in April 1962 to confer with President Kennedy, but Kennedy wanted to talk about the dangers of communism while Goulart was much more interested in economic aid. Goulart seems to have hoped that the United States would solve his economic problems, although Brazil had been the champion of Cuba at the Punta del Este meeting that launched the Alliance for Progress. The U.S. administration rather tolerantly undertook to cooperate with Goulart on a modest scale. In December 1962, Robert Kennedy went to Brazil to express his government's concern over the evident growth of radicalism, perhaps to influence Goulart's cabinet choices.[8] But Goulart did not like being warned against supporters considered Communist by people in Washington and was disappointed that more material assistance was not forthcoming. It was typical of Goulart's dilemma that he was caught up in a quarrel over the expropriation of various U.S. utility holdings. The nationalists were opposed to any considerable compensation, while Goulart hoped to avoid damaging his relations with the United States over a minor issue.

After he recovered full powers of the presidency in January 1963, Goulart began taking a more leftist line, although he was inconsistent and often changed his foreign minister. Perhaps because he lost hope of economic rescue by the United States, he turned toward Third World, if not pro-Cuban positions; Brazilian delegates regularly denounced "Western imperialism" in international meetings. Goulart quickly abandoned a stabilization plan that, with U.S. cooperation, might have shored up the free-enterprise economy. In mid-1963, he reorganized his government and turned from the moderate to the radical left.

Thereafter, the United States became increasingly concerned that Goulart, although he was not Communist but wholly opportunistic, was relying more and more on Communists or persons who sounded like Communists and was leading the country into political disorder that might open the door for communism. On the one hand, the leftist nationalists called for more or less ending foreign investment in Brazil and seeking a noncapitalist way of development; on the other hand, the idea that Brazil might become a hostile "nonaligned" power, like various leftist Third World nations (such as Nasser's Egypt), was enough to cause insomnia in the State Department. Hence, in the latter part of 1963, economic aid was cut off except for projects in the Northeast that would benefit anti-Goulart state governments. Goulart's leftist following was only partly composed of the Moscow-faithful Communists, and the radicals were chaotically divided, but it seemed that

Brazil was careening uncontrollably downhill. The worse the economic situation became, the stronger the discontents and the greater the demand for more or less revolutionary change to a new order. Meanwhile, as order seemed to be breaking down and threats to private property became more frightening to possessors, the economy wilted still more.

The U.S. government stood back, encouraged anti-Communist forces as discreetly as possible, and hoped for the intervention of the armed forces to prevent a possible political disaster. It was a remarkable demonstration of a country coming from extremely friendly relations to vocal hostility without important alteration in material conditions or any consequential new conflict of interest. The change, indeed, came largely through the play of democratic politics, which easily became anticapitalist or anti-U.S. in a country of great inequality.

THE UNITED STATES AND
THE MILITARY COUP

The turn of 1964 sharply changed the foreign as well as the domestic outlook of Brazil, and it did so in ways very beneficial to the United States. It has long been widely believed by Brazilian intellectuals, especially but not only by those of leftist persuasion, that the United States was largely responsible for the military takeover. There have been, of course, scores of coups in Latin America for which the United States has not been blamed, of most of which it disapproved. But the United States was clearly guilty of wanting a coup in Brazil in 1964 and of doing something to bring it about. In the common view of the omnipotence of the CIA, multinational corporations, the Pentagon, and such powers, the conclusion of responsiblity was unavoidable. Theoretically, the coup was regarded as confirmation of the dependent condition of Brazil. This accounted for the repressive character of the government and relieved Brazilians of responsibility. Ianni, for example, wrote of "a colonial fascist regime inaugurated in Brazil in 1964" and that "the tendency toward fascism is another characteristic of structural dependency."[9]

That the United States favored and welcomed the coup is no proof of having made it, however. The Brazilian officers did not need foreigners to tell them how to intervene militarily, and nothing to prove such meddling has come to light through much controversy. In the words of one researcher, "There is no evidence that the United States instigated, planned, directed, or participated in the execution of the 1964 coup."[10] The United States did, however, substantially influence the situation and its outcome.

In part, the United States inhibited the action of the armed forces by its support of democracy, constitutionalism, and elected governments, including that of Goulart, with whom the State Department had fairly good relations at least until mid-1963. After the demise of President Kennedy, the Johnson administration seemed less supportive of democracy in this hemisphere. The generals, however, felt it necessary to insist, on March 31, 1964, that they were intervening to save democracy from a threat of Communist dictatorship.

The armed forces were readier to act in ways approved by the United States because of the good relations established during World War II. Cooperation was close; the Brazilians generally got along well with Americans and admired U.S. ways. Personal friendships bound Brazilians and Americans; notably, Castelo Branco shared a tent during the Italian campaign with Vernon Walters, who became U.S. military attaché in Rio in the critical years. Collaboration between Brazilian and U.S. armed forces continued after the war. The United States had a military mission in Rio, and a joint U.S.-Brazilian Military Commission was given permanent status in 1954. Many Brazilian generals received training in the United States. As the Cold War intensified, especially as the triumph of Fidel Castro raised fears of hemispheric subversion, U.S. military doctrine was focused on combatting subversion, and counterinsurgency and antisubversive methods taught in U.S. military schools were carried to Brazil and other countries by U.S. training and advisors.

This meant that the military was to guard against internal as well as external dangers, that it had cause to take a political stand, and that it should undertake a general mission of protecting the health and soundness of the nation. Counterinsurgency thrust the military into domestic politics as soon as extremist agitation seemed to threaten national values. Thus, in 1964, the Brazilian generals became increasingly convinced of a danger of radical violence. This was hardly irrational; the radical leftists, for their part, were growing confident of their ability to make a social revolution.[11]

Both counterinsurgency thinking and pro-U.S. attitudes were fostered by the ESG, founded with the help of a U.S. mission in 1949. Its doctrine of National Security gave the armed forces the missions of looking into the well-being of the nation and of cooperating with the Western world to defeat communism, which profited from the naiveté and ignorance of politicians. Membership in the ESG group was the bond of many anti-Goulart conspirators.

In view of this background, there was obviously ample communication during the Goulart years between the military and the U.S. Embassy under the able Ambassador Lincoln Gordon, assisted by a gifted attaché, Col. Vernon Walters. These two were visited by anti-Goulart generals who apparently desired not that Americans help them directly in their movement against Goulart but that the United States give its general approval. The ambassador and the State Department had become convinced long before the coup that Goulart was dangerous, and they seem to have conveyed this feeling, although Gordon and Walters were careful to avoid involvement in the plotting.

Moreover, the U.S. government, like everyone else, grossly overestimated the strength of the radicals and anticipated civil war if the conservative military should move against them. Consequently, against the advice of Walters,[12] plans were drawn up to assist the anti-Goulart forces in case of conflict. The plans for "Operation Brother Sam" were put together hastily when a coup seemed imminent; they included a shipment of arms by six transport planes and the dispatch of an aircraft carrier, six destroyers, and four oilers (to provide fuel that might be denied by leftist control of Petrobras) from Norfolk, Va., on April 1.[13] The operation was canceled, of course, when the coup proved quickly successful. It might have led to deep, bloody, and potentially disastrous involvement in a Brazilian civil war. It demonstrated how very seriously the Johnson administration viewed developments in Brazil. It does not appear, however, that these preparations, divulged only years later, influenced the course of events on March 31–April 1, when the issue was decided by the way the nonconspiring generals jumped.

The United States has been repeatedly accused of such actions as introducing 4,000 soldiers in the Northeast, ready to join anti-Goulart forces,[14] although it is not clear how this force could have escaped the notice of the Goulart government. Other efforts to influence Brazilian politics are better documented. For example, the CIA tried, with the help of an AFL-CIO organization, the American Institute of Free Labor Development, to promote U.S. ideas of labor organization and to train labor leaders sympathetic to the United States.[15] More than 100 labor organizers were involved, but they obviously had very little success. Some funds were spent in collaboration with Brazilian anti-Communist groups to influence public opinion; $5 million is mentioned as having been spent on the 1962 congressional elections.[16] U.S. and presumably other foreign businesses also contributed to anti-Communist causes, which included helping to organize the Brazilian Institute for Democratic Action (IBAD) and the huge anti-Goulart march in São Paulo that encouraged the generals to believe a coup would be popular.[17]

A substantial effort to stem Brazil's leftward swing was the effort of the U.S. Agency for International Development (USAID) to uplift the Northeast. This began as an Alliance for Progress showpiece in April 1962, not to injure the Goulart government but to undercut the radicalism of the peasant leagues. It was feared that revolutionary flames would break out in that region of misery and inequality, and President Kennedy made development assistance for the area a priority task. Cooperation between USAID and SUDENE, the Brazilian agency for the region, proved difficult, however, and very little was achieved. On one occasion, USAID tried to influence an electoral campaign by building a few elementary schools,[18] but the leftist candidate won nonetheless. Yet when the U.S. government turned away from Goulart to go on helping anti-Goulart state administrations (with the formal consent of the Brazilian federal authorities), it was a clear signal of discontent with Goulart and of the desire to encourage alternatives.

The CIA is sometimes credited with masterminding many schemes, such as the sailors' mutiny, Goulart's handling of which triggered his downfall. The basic reason for crediting the coup to the U.S. administration was the conviction that the Brazilian ruling class supported by foreign capitalist interests, felt threatened by the campaign of Goulart and his radical supporters to give economic justice to the workers and peasants, hence that the United States intervened for selfish economic and political interests. National and foreign capitalists plotted with the imperialists and military leaders to crush democracy and constitutional government. This view is supported by the long record of U.S. intervention in Latin America and by the testimony of two presidents, Vargas and Quadros, whose downfall was allegedly consummated by imperialist forces. The revelation of "Brother Sam" seemed to clinch the case. Finally, for Brazilians, the most convincing evidence of U.S. responsibility was the fact that the government resulting from the coup conformed admirably to U.S. desires and immediately received large transfusions of aid.

THE PRO-UNITED STATES
MILITARY
GOVERNMENT

While the United States was eager to have the Goulart administration removed, military rule was seen as the last resort. The administration did not want Goulart to be succeeded by a permanent military government but hoped for a more moderate constitutional regime. The congratulatory message sent within hours to interim President Ranieri Mazzilli, president of the Chamber of Deputies—not to the military leaders—was viewed by Brazilians as confirmation of U.S. involvement; but it was intended to strengthen the civilian authorities. It was the U.S. position that the coup was intended to forestall illegality and dictatorship and that normal political processes should be restored.

The military authorities decided to remain in power to carry out a reconstruction of the state, however; and the United States did not protest, although there was some concern about the purges. The choice of Castelo Branco as president was gratifying. The most eminent veteran of the FEB, he had close ties to the United States, was reputed to be a democratically inclined moderate, and was the leader of the pro-U.S. ESG group of generals. Castelo Branco turned brusquely away from the neutralist foreign policy of

Goulart and returned to the old special relationship. He regarded Brazil as the United States' ally in the global contest against communism, and saw it as Brazil's duty to cooperate with U.S. military and diplomatic personnel. Brazil became most favorable of all Latin American countries to U.S. international positions, as shown in voting in the Organization of American States (OAS) and the United Nations.

The Castelo Branco government was sympathetic to U.S. intervention in Vietnam; there were negotiations for sending a Brazilian force in the war,[19] although only a medical team was actually sent. Only preoccupation with Vietnam kept President Johnson from a state visit to Brazil. Brazil deemphasized Latin American unity and preferred Pan-Americanism, including the United States. Despite widespread Latin American reprobation of U.S. military intervention in the Dominican Republic in April 1965, Brazil supported the action, sent a small force of about 1,200 men, and supplied a nominal commander for the inter-American forces. This was a means not only of assisting the United States but also of Brazil's asserting itself on the world scene; the decision was announced before discussion with U.S. diplomats so that Brazil would be seen as acting on its own.[20]

Subsequently, Brazil was the chief Latin American proponent of the U.S. idea of a permanent hemispheric peace-keeping force, and Castelo Branco's foreign minister toured most South American capitals in support of his plan. The basic idea of Brazilian foreign policy at this time was that, the United States and Brazil being on the same side on a morally divided world, Brazil's security depended on the United States. Brazil should do its share, mostly by combating subversion and contributing to collective security of the hemisphere.

Renewed harmony was equally apparent in economic affairs, and the Castelo Branco administration was rewarded for its loyalty with the support for which Goulart was found unqualified. Washington moved with exemplary speed to extend help after the coup, and more than $1 billion in loans was furnished in 1964–68.[21] Economic aid from 1964 to 1970 came to $2 billion, more than that to any other country except Vietnam and India.[22] Military sales were also increased, to the relatively modest amount of $12 million in 1966. Technical assistance was furnished in many areas; any important government office responsible for unpopular policies was likely to have a U.S. advisor.[23]

The new government quickly satisfied the previously negotiated settlement of claims for expropriated U.S. utilities, to nationalist shouts of "sellout," rightists taking the place of silenced leftists. The profits-remittance law that Goulart put into effect in his last week of power, which would have closed the door to foreign capital, was relaxed, despite strong nationalist resistance. Castelo Branco considered economic nationalism akin to procommunism and welcomed foreign investment perhaps more warmly than any previous Brazilian president. He even authorized a concession for Hanna Mining Co., bête noire of the zealous guardians of Brazilian natural resources. Despite Castelo Branco's hospitality, U.S. capital remained wary for a few years, but it began to pour in after stabilization was achieved around 1967.

In sum, Brazil was an exceptionally friendly neighbor and uncommonly amenable to U.S. policy. Many Brazilians regarded Ambassador Gordon as the real ruler of the country. However, Brazil never really subordinated itself to U.S. policy; for example, it did not sever relations with Communist countries established by Goulart (except with Cuba, banned to this day) but rather sought to expand trade with them. It was typical that the Brazilian commander in the Dominican Republic insisted that Portuguese be used at the headquarters. It seems clear that Castelo Branco and his associates felt themselves acting entirely in the best interests of Brazil. They were sincere anti-Communists who had been alarmed by what they perceived as a danger of Communist-directed disorders if not revolution—there had been an attempted Communist revolution, of course, in 1935. It was thus logical to side unequivocally with the superpower opposing communism in the world. It was also fairly plausible to argue that the fastest way to develop the Brazilian economy was close collaboration with the world's greatest economic power. Neither of these attitudes, however, adequately took into account the sentiments of many Brazilians. In the words of a U.S. embassy cable of January 24, 1967, "The extent of Castelo Branco's all-out support for United States policies has served to increase anti-Americanism rather than to lessen it."[24]

DIVERGENCE

Uncritical admiration and adherence to U.S. positions began to ebb along with the euphoria of the new state. Critics who had been silenced by the success of the revolution made themselves heard again, denouncing "denationalization" of the Brazilian economy, and as the excesses of the Goulart period receded, anticommunism came to seem more an excuse for repression than cause for a crusade. Nationalism reemerged also in the inherently nationalistic armed forces.

Although close collaboration continued through the Castelo Branco presidency, the rudder was turned when Costa e Silva became president on March 15, 1967. The group around Castelo, former members of the FEB and affiliates of the ESG, was a minority in the armed forces; Costa e Silva did not belong to this group and had no special attachment to the United States. Less of an intellectual than his predecessor, he almost completely excluded the FEB veterans and brought in a new corps of advisors, whom U.S. officials found less competent and less congenial.

Another change of personalities cut down the ties between the United States and Brazil: shortly after the departure of Castelo Branco, his good friend Lincoln Gordon turned the embassy over to John Tuthill, who had no special attachment to Brazil and who developed no intimacy with its leaders. For a long time, Costa e Silva refused to see Tuthill after the latter had met Carlos Lacerda, who had become almost as bitterly critical of the military regime as he had been of the previous presidents. Tuthill's chief contribution was to prune the inflated embassy staff and to phase out superfluous programs. Despite bureaucratic resistance, he managed to relieve about a third of the employees, and he set the course toward disengagement.

There were more basic reasons for the two countries moving apart. The discomfiture of the United States in Vietnam was growing, and after 1968, the United States was set on withdrawal, which eventually meant defeat. Sympathetic as the Brazilian government might be, it could not ignore the fact that U.S. leadership in the global struggle was faltering. At the same time, the climate of anti-U.S. opinion around the world made it more difficult for Brazil to stand up on the "imperialist" side.

The United States for its part undertook in the Nixon presidency to lower its profile and to reduce involvement in Brazil as elsewhere. The U.S. military mission was cut from 200 in 1968 to 60 in 1971,[25] and arms deliveries were curtailed. Economic aid was also phased out, partly because Brazil was recovering and developing well, partly because of the decreased U.S. commitment worldwide. By 1969, it was insignificant.

U.S.-Brazilian friendship also suffered from the hardening authoritarianism of Brazil. The 1964 coup established military government, not military dictatorship, but the regime was stiffened step by step against the wishes of Castelo Branco in response to what hardliners perceived as threats to their revolution. The succession of Castelo Branco by another officer selected by the generals indicated democracy was far away; and in December 1968, Costa e Silva, by AI-5 and related measures, inaugurated dictatorship limited only by the armed forces themselves. Ambassador Tuthill wanted to issue a strong protest. U.S. Secretary of State Dean Rusk declined, but loans were held up for a few months. Normal relations were resumed, but the repressiveness of the dictatorship, especially 1969–72, precluded cordiality.

Costa e Silva did not turn to economic nationalism, as many had feared, and the climate remained generally favorable to foreign investment. But his government was more inclined to self-reliance and less eager for foreign capital. He asserted Brazilian independence in many ways. He withdrew support for the inter-American peace-keeping force (a lost cause) and demanded tariff concessions from the United States. He declined to subscribe to the Nuclear Non-Proliferation Treaty and tried to organize a Latin American nuclear community. He downgraded the moribund Alliance for Progress. Brazil took a leadership role in organizing the nonaligned Group of 77. It tried to increase Soviet-Brazilian trade. It also engaged in a sometimes acrimonious controversy with the United States over U.S. efforts to restrict imports of Brazilian instant coffee. Although there was little appeal to nationalism and an amicable settlement was reached eventually, this was the first significant economic controversy between the two governments since 1964.

The Brazilian government was not hostile, however. In 1967, Costa e Silva paid a state visit to Washington, and in 1969 Brazil came to the aid of the United States in the dispute with Peru over nationalization of oil properties.[26] Brazilians generally were not aware of the cooling of the friendship.

Following the brief presidency of Costa e Silva, Presidents Médici and Geisel held to the same course of increasingly independent policies combined with basically friendly relations with the United States. The very rapid growth of the economy encouraged the old dream of great-power status for Brazil in the foreseeable future. In 1970, the official goal was proclaimed of raising Brazil to the level of the most advanced states by the end of the century, thanks to a yearly GNP growth of about 10 percent. It became and remained Brazil's policy to resist any freezing of the world order to the benefit of the superpowers. The Brazilians sought frankly to pursue their own advantage pragmatically in the world. Hence they left open their nuclear option, greatly expanded trade with the Soviet Union and eastern Europe, recognized the Beijing government four years before the United States and normalized relations with mainland China, and asserted a 200-mile maritime zone contrary to U.S. policy and fishing interests.

As the United States began talking of détente, Brazil gave less attention to the East-West conflict and more to North-South issues. Brazil stood in the lead in efforts to organize cartels of coffee, cocoa, sugar, and so forth. The Médici government also took general Third World positions on population and control of pollution. In the early 1970s, Brazil also adopted the pro-Arab, pro-Palestinian positions of a large majority of Third World states. In part, this was based on material interests; the Arabs expected Brazilian support in return for oil. It was easy because Brazil has more than 10 times as many persons of Arab as of Jewish background; moreover, Brazil was eager for an influx of petrodollar investments; and Brazilian companies were bidding on large construction contracts in Arab countries. In 1975, Brazil voted for the U.N. resolution equating Zionism with racism; Geisel reportedly was going to change the Brazilian vote in the final tally but decided not to do so because he resented pressure from the State Department.[28] Geisel named a nationalist, Antônio Azeredo da Silveira, as foreign minister, and the latter enjoyed criticizing the United States. The Geisel government irritated the

United States by recognizing the Soviet- and Cuban-backed government of Angola when few non-Communist powers had done so.

Yet the Nixon administration remained basically sympathetic to Brazilian hopes for growth and world standing; and Brazil, despite its shift, continued to be one of the Third World nations most sympathetic to the United States—opposed to socialism and Castroism and hospitable to U.S. economic interests. Médici was welcomed to Washington in December 1971, and Nixon stated his view of the importance of Brazil: "As Brazil goes, so will go the rest of the Latin American continent." In 1973, U.S. Secretary of State Rogers said, "We don't have any problems, really, at the moment at all between the United States and Brazil."[29]

In February 1976, deference to Brazil climaxed when Secretary of State Kissinger and Foreign Minister da Silveira signed a "memorandum of understanding" that the two powers would consult on all issues of mutual concern and would hold semiannual meetings of foreign ministers. Brazil had in 1975 reached similar understandings with Britain, France, and Italy for regular ministerial consultations, and the agreement with the United States seemed to recognize the special position of Brazil. Brazil and Saudi Arabia were the only nations, aside from major Western allies, with which the United States had such an agreement. It had no great practical consequences, but it indicated a turnover of relations; the United States was now wooing Brazil, as in Kissinger's words, "a people taking their place in the front rank of nations."[30]

QUALIFIED FRIENDSHIP

During his campaign for the U.S. presidency, Jimmy Carter attacked the singling out of authoritarian Brazil and the Kissinger-da Silveira memorandum as an example of the misguidedness of the Ford-Kissinger approach to world affairs. The Carter administration found Brazil less congenial; and two of its major policies, opposition to nuclear proliferation and stress on human rights, led to a confrontation with Brazil and pushed relations between the two countries to the lowest point since 1964. Finding that it had no effective weapons, the Carter administration retreated on the nuclear front, and the rights issue receded, so relations were normalized. The old cordiality was not to be restored, however, and the traditional special relationship belongs to the past.

With his idealistic bent, Carter took the need to halt the spread of nuclear weaponry very seriously, stressed it in the campaign, and applied it to the United States by stopping a project for reprocessing spent nuclear fuel to produce plutonium. He tried to make Brazil a test case of the nonproliferation policy, because Brazil in 1975 had entered a mammoth agreement with West Germany for the construction not only of nuclear-power plants but also of uranium-enrichment and fuel-reprocessing facilities.

Having little fossil fuel, Brazil had long proposed to acquire major nuclear-power capabilities and had carried on negotiations with several countries to that end since the early 1950s. In 1967, the National Security Council set nuclear capacity as a permanent national objective, and in that year a contract was made with Westinghouse for a plant to be built at Angra dos Reis, on the coast near Rio, to be completed with a capacity of 626 megawatts by 1977. Even then, however, Brazil was disinclined to rely entirely on the United States. Finding U.S. conditions too stringent and designed to keep Brazil nuclear dependent, the government began working toward nuclear independence.

In 1974, the question became acute because of the sudden rise in the cost of petroleum, making nuclear energy essential for economic growth. Moreover, India exploded a nuclear device, and an Argentine nuclear plant had already become operational. More important, the U.S. Atomic Energy Commission renounced its guarantee of delivery of enriched uranium, casting doubts on the value of nuclear cooperation with the United States. Earlier, the U.S. government had prohibited Westinghouse from construction of enrichment and reprocessing plants in Brazil.

The Brazilian government, desirous of controlling the full cycle from ore to kilowatts and reclaimed fuel, pressed negotiations that had been long proceeding with West Germany; and in June 1975, a contract was announced whereby Germany would furnish technology and equipment for eight power reactors, plus enrichment and reprocessing facilities. The announcement was sensational not only because of its magnitude, but also because it promised Brazil the means, despite safeguard provisions, to proceed rather easily to the construction of nuclear weapons if desired. The U.S. press and Congress expressed indignation that Germany was making good business thanks to U.S. self-denial.

The Ford administration reacted only mildly, however. The U.S. ambassador in Bonn had been briefed during the negotiations, and the administration had urged the Germans to desist; but after safeguards against misuse of uranium had been included, there was no further protest. The question was not raised with the Brazilians. When alarm was expressed in Congress after the publication of the contract, the administration seemed mostly concerned with defending its record.

Jimmy Carter in 1976 blamed the Ford administration for having failed to prevent the deal. From his first day in office, he began pressing the Germans to withdraw from the agreement, then 18 months old, even threatening withdrawal of troops from West Berlin.[31] The Germans remained unmoved, and the U.S. State Department turned to the Brazilians, over whom it had even less leverage. In March 1977, U.S. Deputy Secretary Warren Christopher went to Brasília to urge modification of the accord, but the Brazilians flatly rejected enrichment facilities in the United States or under international control, and Christopher stayed only one day.

Although Carter continued his general drive against the spread of the potential for nuclear weapons, he conceded in June that he had no means to compel Germany and Brazil. However, Secretary of State Vance, making a Latin American tour in place of Carter, returned to the attack in Brazil. His arguments went unheeded as he was unable either to offer the Brazilians an attractive alternative or to make it clear that they would suffer from proceeding with their program. The nuclear question came up again, however, on the occasion of Carter's state visit to Brazil in March 1978. The president then urged his own views on nonproliferation in a diplomatic way, and he and Geisel in effect agreed to drop the matter.

The U.S. action was thus never very forceful, and the Brazilians had little cause for complaint except about Carter's exerting pressure on Germany without consulting them as provided by the 1976 memorandum. But the Brazilian reaction was strongly negative. The U.S. demand seemed belated, capricious, and hostile to Brazil's political and economic independence. Whereas there had previously been many doubts, "to support the accord became a national honor, the accord became untouchable," and the government enjoyed a surge of national unity.[32]

For Brazil, nuclear technology was symbolic of modernization, a mark of power of industrialized countries, the lack of which amounted to obvious permanent inferiority. Moreover, the Brazilians felt their striving for nuclear equality to represent, like that of India, the moral right of the less-developed nations. Behind the talk of checking nuclear proliferation, they saw the commercial interest of the nuclear industry, particularly Westinghouse, in keeping them dependent on enriched uranium from the United States. They also felt the United States should accept their assurances of disinterest in atomic weapons—although there have been various statements to the effect that Brazil should have the capability of making an atomic bomb if it should become necessary.

Nonetheless, as the Carter administration dropped its opposition, many Brazilians raised theirs; an antinuclear movement arose like that in the United States and Europe. There were the expectable delays and cost overruns, the economics of the program were questioned in light of Brazil's abundant hydroelectric potential, and the shortage of foreign exchange forced curtailment of nonurgent imports. It became doubtful that the enrichment and reprocessing plants to which the United States had objected would ever be constructed. The campaign that the Carter administration briefly waged against the Brazil-German deal seemed a remarkable exercise in diplomatic futility, which if successful only would have embittered U.S.-Brazilian relations.

Concurrently with its jousting against nuclear proliferation, the Carter administration took up the banner of human rights. In this connection, however, Brazil was not a primary but a secondary or tertiary target. The issue was largely settled by Geisel's moves toward democratization and by the ending or near-ending of arbitrary treatment of political prisoners before Carter took office; and the U.S. intervention, so far as it went, aroused much less indignation than that caused by the nuclear issue. Indeed, many Brazilians expressed approval.

The Nixon and Ford administrations did not consider it their affair to condemn the Brazilian government for the thousands of arrests of alleged subversives after April 1, 1964, or for the torture and murders of political opponents. The repressions continued on a large scale through the Médici administration, ending in March 1974, but Kissinger was not moved even by the maltreatment of a few U.S. citizens. The Congress, however, kept pushing the executive to take action. In 1976, Jimmy Carter made human rights a campaign theme, and he turned attention to it immediately upon becoming president.

The prime targets of the Carter human rights campaign were the Soviet Union and its satellites in Eastern Europe. But if a human-rights policy was to represent not merely anti-Communist politics but a general ideal, it had to apply everywhere. Brazil was not prominent among the transgressors, but it could not be excluded. It would not seem that the Carter administration particularly desired to challenge Brazil on the issue, but controversy arose because of the general report mandated by Congress in 1975 on human-rights observance by recipients of U.S. military assistance.

The report was delivered to the Senate Committee on Foreign Relations in March 1977. The section dealing with Brazil noted liberalization under Geisel despite conservative opposition, cited charges and corrective actions, and dealt with infractions about as gently as reality permitted.[33] It might have largely escaped notice if prior to submission to Congress the U.S. Embassy had not thrust a copy of the report into the hands of the Foreign Office without previous consultation. This was intended as a courtesy, but it was interpreted as "intolerable interference." Within hours, the Brazilians denounced the military-aid agreement in effect since 1952, and it is said that some hotheads in the military talked of breaking diplomatic relations.[34] Irritation was increased by the fact that the report was presented at the very time Warren Christopher was trying to brake the nuclear program.

The Geisel government claimed it needed no prodding from the United States on the subject of human rights, and Foreign Minister da Silveira said that the United States would do well to pay more attention to economic and social rights. But there was no Brazilian retaliation beyond the termination of military-aid agreements that Brazil wanted to liquidate in any case. Some members of the Carter administration criticized the Brazilian record; and Rosalynn Carter, in Brazil in June 1977, took up the rights question while visiting two U.S. priests who had been maltreated by police in Recife. But there was little acrimony. President Carter, in Brazil in March 1978, met with several oppositionists and spoke of the desirability of international scrutiny of the record, but he avoided interventionism and put an end to the asperities surrounding the issue.

Many Brazilians seem to have regarded any U.S. attention to violations of rights in their country as intolerable meddling, and it put opposition groups in an awkward position. However, Carter was cheered publicly when he spoke of human rights, and some Brazilians welcomed the Carter approach as helping to moderate official policy and to push toward liberalization. There has been no admission, of course, that the U.S. policies had any effect. In any case, the maltreatment of political prisoners—and political imprisonment—was gradually eliminated during the Geisel and Figueiredo administrations, although the police reserved the authority to deal more ruthlessly with nonpolitical prisoners. Unlike the case of Argentina and of many other countries, the United States did not propose to apply material penalties to Brazil (aside from ending military aid, in which the Brazilians took the initiative). The episode may have been an overall plus for the standing of the United States in Brazil.

There remained, however, some residue of irritation over the issues of nuclear power and human rights. Despite the visits of Rosalynn and Jimmy Carter and of Vice President Walter Mondale to Brazil, neither Geisel nor Figueiredo returned the courtesy, although Geisel traveled to various European capitals and to Japan, and Figueiredo in his first two years visited many countries of Latin America and Europe. Relations remained amicable but not close; the 1976 memorandum was shelved by the Carter administration precisely because it gave special status to Brazil. When Carter looked around for Latin American support on the issue of a Soviet combat division in Cuba, Ambassador (formerly Foreign Minister) da Silveira took no notice.[35] When Carter chastised the Soviet Union for the invasion of Afghanistan, Brazil remained aloof from both the Olympic boycott and the grain embargo and increased its food exports to the Soviet Union.

The rapprochement of Brazil with Argentina—war with which was mooted as late as the 1970s—removed a long-standing reason for Brazil to lean toward the United States. Brazil also reduced its dependence on the United States by improving relations with its other Spanish American neighbors, extending influence to such countries as Bolivia and Paraguay and particularly cultivating the friendship of Chile and Venezuela. Figueiredo's summit diplomacy raised Brazil's standing without generating apprehensions of Brazilian expansionism, and Brazil generally acted as a moderating force in South American politics. Brazil's trade with other Latin American countries has grown to surpass that with the United States (the European Economic Community holding first place). Brazilian hostility to Castroism remained, however, a link with U.S. policy. In October 1980, the twenty-first U.S.-Brazilian naval maneuvers were held on the regular schedule.

It was anticipated that the Reagan administration would restore cordial understanding with the basically conservative Brazilian government. The latter, however, did not seem eager to rush into any new embrace. As Foreign Minister Ramiro Saraiva Guerreiro said, "We think the United States will decide what to do by itself. We have our own methods on foreign affairs, and we will be willing to talk at the official level about relations within the hemisphere as we would with any of our neighbors."[36]

In February 1981, when Vernon Walters came to Brasília to explain the administration's concern over the Cuban-supported guerrilla movement in El Salvador, the Brazilian authorities listened politely but offered to do nothing;[37] and Brazil declined to join Argentina, Uruguay, and Chile in supporting the Salvadoran government. Subsequently, Brazil made an effort to·develop trade with leftist Nicaragua.[38] Brazil opposed the United States position in the law-of-the-sea negotiations and found the presence of Cuban troops in Angola justified by the aggressive actions of South Africa. There are perennial irritations over U.S. duties or quotas on such Brazilian products, as steel, shoes, and textiles. Brazil entered several large trade agreements with the Soviet Union, providing for exchange of soybeans for oil, for Soviet assistance with the Brazilian fuel-alcohol program, for collaboration in hydroelectric projects, and for large, low-interest Soviet credits. Trade with the Soviet Union was disappointing, however, because it remained hugely unbalanced. In 1981 Brazil sold $621 million on credit, while buying only $31 million, and no progress was made in developing imports of Soviet goods.[39]

Vice President George Bush was cordially received in Brasília in October 1981. He removed an irritant by easing the ban on Brazilian purchase of enriched uranium for the Angra nuclear plant, and he invited President Figueiredo to Washington, an invitation that was cordially accepted. Contacts between U.S. and Brazilian militaries were resumed.[40] In the Falklands conflict between Britain and Argentina, Brazil successfully walked a tightrope between Argentina and the United States, supporting the Argentinian claim in principle but disapproving of Argentina's use of force.[41] In the shadow of the Falklands war, Figueiredo made a brief and barely noticed visit to Washington on May 12, 1982. Anti-U.S. nationalism was notably absent in the lively electoral campaign of 1982.

In December, President Reagan made Brasília the first and most important stop on his Latin American tour, in tribute both to its importance and its progress toward electoral democracy. Warmly received, he set the stage for increased cooperation in various practical areas, and he announced a (previously granted and spent) short term loan of $1.2 billion to help Brazil through its debt crisis.

The chief topics discussed were trade and financial questions; it is perhaps a sign of maturity that U.S.-Brazilian relations revolve principally around economic problems. Of prime concern is the Brazilian foreign debt, approaching $90 billion at the beginning of 1983, a large portion owed directly or indirectly to U.S. banks. Fear of possible default is interlocked with growing commercial rivalry and resentment of Brazilian penetration of U.S. markets. Washington has repeatedly raised the question of Brazilian export subsidization through tax relief, and Brasília has repeatedly promised to end it. Many U.S. producers have demanded countervailing duties against Brazilian products, such as steel, orange juice, small aircraft, vodka, and chickens, as well as ones that have long been in question, such as shoes and sundry textiles. The United States wants to remove semideveloped Brazil from the lists of the developing nations entitled to concessional loans and special tariff preferences, and duties have been raised on a few Brazilian exports.[42] The United States has held up renewal of the International Coffee Accord, reduced the Brazilian sugar quota in favor of the Caribbean region, and asked for reduction of some Brazilian import barriers, as on computers. There are unfortunate contradictions in the U.S. position. The United States appears a dubious friend, unwilling not only to give economic aid but also to buy Brazilian products. Worse, U.S. trade policy ignores the urgent necessity that Brazil export enough to meet its financial obligations to American banks.

Despite the controversies and Brazilian diversification, the United States still looms large in the Brazilian economy, with about $8 billion in investments. Brazil, however, has come a long road from the days of Kubitschek, when a U.S. loan was a major policy consideration, or of Goulart, when first the U.S. ambassador was to be consulted about cabinet nominations and later the United States was blamed for almost all of Brazil's misfortunes, or from the time of Castelo Branco, when U.S. advisors swarmed through the Brazilian government. Its tone is agreement on essentials despite friendly disagreement in minor matters.

BRAZILIAN FOREIGN POLICY

For many reasons, Brazil is no longer much inclined to align itself with the United States unless there is a clear-cut reason for doing so. Several may be mentioned: the effects of Vietnam, the decline of U.S. prestige, the slackening of the Cold War, the preoccupation of the United States with affairs outside the hemisphere, the relative shrinkage of the U.S. economy in the world, the decrease in the U.S. share in Brazilian foreign trade (from 34.3 percent of Brazilian imports in 1967 to 18.3 percent in 1979), the relative growth of the Brazilian economy, the increasing competitiveness of Brazilian manufactures, and the confidence generated by the booming Brazilian armaments industry. The injuries of the Carter administration are not forgotten. Moreover, the Brazilian economic model—under which state enterprises control basic industries, the state is responsible for more than half of fixed investment, and technocratic planners more or less direct all aspects of the economy—is decidedly alien to the United States. Brazilian military authoritarianism, so far as it is not undone by *abertura*, it also uncongenial to U.S. political ideals. There are, moreover, sectors of Brazilian opinion negatively disposed to the United States: various leftists and others opposed to foreign ownership in the Brazilian economy, military and political nationalists, and ideological rightists.

Brazilian foreign policy is pragmatic, frankly self-interested, and resolutely nonideological, identifying neither with the West nor the Third World. Brazil has its special relations with Africa (especially with Angola), Latin America, the Third World group (as a producer of raw materials) and with the advanced industrial countries, (especially as an importer of capital and technology). Foreign policy reflects the fact that the Third World, which took only 5 percent of Brazil's exports in 1960, took 25 percent in 1980; Brazil does not desire any return of bipolarity. Brazil is concerned with world stability, but does not take much responsibility for it. Brazil avoids passing judgment on other countries, and the bulk of its foreign relations are economic. It has largely given up the euphoric "future great power" ambitions of the early 1970s.

The Brazilian diplomatic service, often called the *Itamaraty* after its headquarters, is strictly professional, highly trained, and somewhat legalistic. It maintains much more continuity of policy than is possible in the United States. Not particularly friendly toward the United States, it quietly promotes Brazilian interests and tries to keep on good terms with nearly everyone. It participates actively in multilateral forums and seeks to project an image of Brazil as a major power in the concert of nations, doubtless looking to the ultimate fulfillment of the dream of Brazilian *grandeza*.

Yet Brazil is fundamentally a friendly power. The long history of good relations has not been forgotten, and there are no deep or emotional issues between the two countries. The fact that the United States has been less dominant, especially over the economy, diminishes a basic cause of irritation; if Brazilians object to foreign interests marring their landscapes, they may think first of German or Japanese corporations, which are often more conspicuous than American. The friendship is less burdened by gross inequality.

But Brazilians know that their furture remains closely linked to that of their counterpart in North America.

NOTES

1. See Stanley E. Hilton, *Brazil and the Great Powers, 1930-1939: The Politics of Trade Rivalry* (Austin: University of Texas Press, 1975).

2. John W. Dulles, *Vargas of Brazil: A Political Biography* (Austin: University of Texas Press, 1970), p. 210.

3. C. Neale Ronning, "The Military and Brazilian Policy Formulation," in *Perspectives on Armed Politics in Brazil*, ed. Henry H. Keith and Robert A. Hayes (Tempe: Arizona State University Press, 1976), pp. 208, 211.

4. Frank D. McCann, *The Brazilian-American Alliance: 1937-1945* (Princeton, N.J.: Princeton University Press, 1973), p. 295.

5. Donald E. Worcester, *Brazil: From Colony to World Power* (New York: Charles Scribner's, 1973), p. 197.

6. Jan K. Black, *United States Penetration of Brazil* (Philadelphia: University of Pennsylvania Press, 1977), pp. 39-40.

7. Ibid., p. 40.

8. Phyllis R. Parker, *Brazil and the Quiet Intervention* (Austin: University of Texas Press, 1979), p. 30.

9. Octavio Ianni, *Crisis in Brazil* (New York: Columbia University Press, 1970), pp. 203-04.

10. Parker, *Brazil and the Quiet Intervention*, pp. 102-03.

11. Joseph A. Page, *The Revolution that Never Was: Northeast Brazil 1955-1964* (New York: Grossman, 1972), p. 19.

12. Vernon Walters, *Silent Missions* (Garden City, N.Y.: Doubleday, 1978), pp. 388.

13. Parker, *Brazil and the Quiet Intervention*, pp. 68-69.

14. Eliézer R. de Oliveira, *As Forças Armadas: Política e Ideologia no Brasil (1964-1969)* (Petrópolis: Ed. Vozes, 1976), p. 52.

15. Winslow Peck, "The AFL-CIO," in *Uncloaking the CIA*, ed. Howard Frazer (New York: Free Press, 1978), p. 264.

16. Parker, *Brazil and the Quiet Intervention*, p. 27.

17. A theme elaborated by René Armand Dreifuss, *1964: A conquista do estado: ação política, poder, e golpe de classe* (Petrópolis: Ed. Vozes, 1981).

18. Black, *United States Penetration of Brazil*, p. 67.

19. *Isto É*, December 14, 1977, pp. 42-45.

20. Alvaro Valle, *As novas estructuras políticas brasileiras* (Rio de Janeiro: Nordica, 1977), p. 139.

21. Peter D. Bell, "Brazilian-American Relations," in *Brazil in the Sixties*, ed. Riordan Roett (Nashville, Tenn.: Vanderbilt University Press, 1972), p. 95.

22. Thomas E. Weil, et al., *Area Handbook for Brazil* (Washington, D.C.: Government Printing Office, 1975), p. 295.

23. John W. Tuthill, "Operation Topsy," *Foreign Policy* 8 (Fall 1972): pp. 65-66.

24. John W. Dulles, *President Castelo Branco: Brazilian Reformer* (College Station, Texas: Texas A. & M. University Press, 1980), p. 442.

25. Black, *United States Penetration of Brazil*, p. 165.

26. *New York Times*, March 2, 1969, p. 1.

27. Carlos E. Martins, "Brazil and the United States," in *Latin America and the United States*, ed. Julio Cotler and Richard Fagen (Stanford, Calif.: Stanford University Press, 1974), p. 299.

28. Walder de Goés, *O Brasil de General Geisel: Estudo do processo de tomada de decisão no regime militar-burocrático* (Rio de Janeiro: Nova Frontiera, 1978), p. 30.

29. Albert Fishlow, "Flying down to Rio: Perspectives on U.S.-Brazil Relations," *Foreign Affairs* 57 (Winter 1978): 396.

30. *Newsweek*, March 1, 1976, p. 48.

31. *Visão*, November 14, 1977, p. 19.

32. Ibid., February 21, 1977, p. 14; *Isto É*, March 16, 1977, pp. 5, 23.

33. U.S. Senate Committee on Foreign Relations, Subcommittee on Foreign Assistance, *Human Rights Reports Prepared by the Department of State* (Washington, D.C.: Government Printing Office, 1977), pp. 111-12.

34. *Visão*, November 14, 1977, p. 20.

35. *Veja*, October 3, 1979, p. 38.

36. *New York Times*, January 4, 1981, p. 7.

37. *Isto É*, March 4, 1981, pp. 32-33.

38. *Latin America Weekly Report*, May 14, 1982, p. 10.

39. *Latin America Weekly Report*, July 23, 1982, p. 9.

40. Joint Publication Research Service, *Latin America Report*, April 30, 1982, pp. 45-46.

41. *Latin America Weekly Report*, August 27, 1982, p. 6.

42. *Isto É*, August 25, 1982, pp. 74-75.

7

Conclusion: The Brazilian Condition

THE MIXED ECONOMY

The economy of Brazil, approximately equal to that of Canada, with a GNP of around $250 billion in 1980, is the tenth largest in the world. With a per capita product of $1,800 in 1981, it is relatively much closer to the advanced industrial nations than to most nations of Asia and Africa. Brazil's is also one of the more rapidly growing economies, having increased agricultural production by 4 percent yearly and industrial production by 8.3 percent a year, 1970–80, despite troubled times after the petroleum price crunch of 1973–74. Brazilian output is comparable to or greater than that of India or China, with six to eight times the population. Brazil produces, for example, 16 million tons of steel per year and over 2 million vehicles; and it is the home of most of the 500 largest corporations of Latin America. It has raised its share of world production.

Brazilians are planning super-fast trains, but they have also done much to modernize agriculture. They have been successful in pushing exports of soybeans (the largest single earner of foreign exchange), citrus products, sugar, and other crops. Brazil is the world's second largest agricultural exporter, following the United States. But coffee exports, which were once well over half of total exports, have fallen behind and recently have been less than 10 percent. Manufactures (including machine tools and heavy equipment), which in 1973 were only 30 percent of Brazil's exports,[1] have accounted for most of the recent rapid increase of exports, were 20 percent in 1979, 31 percent in 1980, 21 percent in 1981—amounting to quadrupling since 1973.

Brazil sells large numbers of small (20-seater) airplanes to the United States, as well as engine parts for U.S. automobiles. It exports more cars and parts than coffee. It is one of the 10 leading arms exporters, selling perhaps $1.2 billion in 1981 and $2 billion in 1982 to nearly 50 countries.[2] This is the biggest Brazilian growth industry. The military government began to build up arms manufacture soon after taking power, but it surged after the controversies with the Carter administration over nuclear plans and human rights, which made the United States seem an unreliable supplier. Brazilian specialties include light planes, simple but advanced machine guns, small rocket missiles, and above all, light armored vehicles, of which Brazil is the world's second producer (after the Soviet Union). Sales are mostly but not entirely to Third World countries.

Another aspect of Brazilian progress is that it has moved away from being a supplier of raw materials to industrial countries. Forty percent of Brazil's exports go to less developed countries; the rise of trade with Latin America has been especially strong. Brazilian manufactures are tropicalized and likely to be suited to the simpler needs of less affluent countries, while Brazilian engineers are accustomed to working under tropical conditions.

Brazilians, needing credit, dispute the U.S. contention that Brazil should be scratched from the list of developing countries qualified for concessionary loans. But the country has come very far since Vargas, having deposed the rural-based oligarchy of the Old Republic in 1930 and setting out on a policy of industrialization. The primary aim was import substitution, which received a boost in World War II but was continued after it. It was official policy in the 1950s to protect any Brazilian manufacturer that could make a product similar to a foreign one, and pressure was put on foreign corporations to produce in Brazil if they wanted to sell there. Efforts were made to plan investments for growth. This led to problems of exchange controls, currency devaluation, inflation, disincentive for exports, and uneconomic production; however, it was successful in generating a growth rate of 6 percent per annum, 1947–62.[3]

After the downturn of 1962–64, the military regime tried to stabilize and solidify the economy by cutting government expenditures, collecting taxes, curtailing credit, stabilizing the currency, opening up competition, and holding down wages. Thanks to such conventionally approved policies, to substantial foreign aid (some $2.5 billion in 1964–71),[4] to political stability, and to favorable world markets, from 1968 Brazil began growing rapidly, 11 percent yearly to 1974, a rate as high as any in the world. Emphasis was shifted from protected, hence possibly uneconomic, industrial development to export-oriented production competitive on the world market and hence economically sound. This required increased reliance on foreign technology and capital in order to keep up with world leaders. By corollary, state control was necessary to prevent major strategic items, such as petroleum and mining, from coming under foreign control. Brazilian national capital came in third place, mostly filling in the gaps. However, good performance of the economy (although the lower sectors of the population benefited less) effectively legitimized the military government through its most repressive and potentially most unpopular years.

Although growth slowed after 1974, it continued to be good by world standards, at 4–7 percent yearly. However, the success of the military government was one-sided, and inequality, already excessive, increased through the period. The poorer half of the population received 17.4 percent of income in 1960, 13.5 percent in 1976, and 12.6 percent in 1980. The bottom 20 percent received only 3.4 percent of income in 1970, and were down to 2.8 percent in 1980, while the top 1 percent raised its share from 14 percent to 17 percent. In the rural sector, the change during the decade was sharper: the lower half sank from 22.4 percent to 14.9 percent, while the top 1 percent rose from 10.5 percent to 29.3 percent. Under the modernization and mechanization policies of the military government, landholding became ever more concentrated. Half of the agricultural land in 1982 was in estates over 2500 acres, owned by 1 percent of landholders. Meanwhile, the agricultural sector declined from 44 percent to 30 percent of the population.[5]

It was a measure both of remaining poverty and of maldistribution that 88 percent of the working population earned from $40 to $400 equivalent monthly, while 1.6 percent earned more than $1,600.[6] In the latter half of the 1960s, the real minimum wage declined, rising thereafter but more slowly than productivity, so it was about the same in 1976 as in 1966.[7] This was a by-product of policies designed to encourage industrialization; some gained impressively and the national product grew several times over, but many were left behind. Although incentive programs have brought spots of affluence, the Northeast continued to be the national poorhouse, with GNP per capita about one-third of the national average, while São Paulo boomed; much of the inequality in Brazil is regional. Inequality is also a product of urbanization; earnings in the cities are more than double those in the countryside. Economic class in Brazil is not strongly hereditary, however; nearly two-thirds of the elite are of middle-class origin.[8] Brazilian inequality is offset, at least for a few, by opportunities to get rich.

Inflation was another ill that the military government failed to cure. This was a chronic problem since World War II, generally increasing from 1958 (24 percent) to 1963 (81 percent).[9] It reached 100 percent early in 1964 because of wage pressures, subsidization of essentials, and excessive government costs. A chief purpose of the military government in 1964 was to bring it down; and the austerity program reduced it to 40 percent in 1966 and below 20 percent in the early 1970s, thanks basically to ending currency emissions. Indexation made it possible to finance the shrinking deficits by bonds and also to encourage savings. But pressures grew with the oil price increase of

1974, plus rising costs of imported wheat. These combined with climbing interest rates to bring an economic slowdown. Fears of recession and unemployment plus the desire to maintain a high rate of growth called for ever bigger expenditures, and inflation crept back up, heading toward 100 percent late in 1980 and peaking at 110 percent in April 1981. The financial guide of the government, Minister of Planning Delfin Neto, who took office in January 1980 with a bold expansionist program, was compelled to inaugurate an austerity program. This slightly checked the inflation rate in 1981; but in 1982 it surged back up to 100 percent.

The federal budget is officially balanced, but it includes less than 20 percent of government expenditures.[10] Enormous extrabudgetary outlays require the government to borrow or to print money. The deficit, largely caused by state enterprises and loans, came to 6.52 percent of GNP in 1982.[11] Another major source of inflation is the making of loans, mainly to agriculture but also for industrial development, at interest rates far below the inflation rate. Borrowers repay less in real terms than they borrowed, and the state makes up the difference. There is also a strong temptation to use concessionary loans for speculative purposes, thus adding to inflationary pressures. A further factor in inflation has been the more liberal wage policy of the government, allowing wages up to three times the minimum to rise at 110 percent of the inflation rate. Inflation compounds itself by raising costs to the government and squeezing its receipts as taxpayers postpone payment.

Along with inflation has come the ballooning of Brazil's foreign debt. Borrowing has always been a necessity for Brazil, to get over balance-of-payments deficits and to provide capital for growth, the national capital market being very limited. Foreign aid, moreover, was phased out in the early 1970s. The military government tried to reduce foreign borrowing along with inflation, but both mushroomed in the more difficult times after 1973. The debt was up to $25 billion by the end of 1976, and it continued to grow from negative trade balances and public and private borrowing.

In 1982 the debt question came to a crisis because of the worldwide recession and consequent difficulty of continuing the rapid growth of Brazilian exports. In 1981 Brazil chalked up a modest favorable balance of trade for the first time since 1977,[12] but in 1982 the balance slipped back. The continued expansion of the debt in monetary terms had been partly compensated by the decline of the value of the dollar in real terms, but in 1981–82 inflation in the United States slowed and prices for many Brazilian exports, especially raw materials, declined; the debt then suddenly became much more burdensome.

In response, Minister of Planning Delfim Neto undertook an austerity program, including reduction of loans and an effort to hold down borrowing by state enterprises, restrictions on imports, a stiff tax on foreign-exchange transactions, freezing of interest rates, and controls on most prices. The result was a halt to growth and an upsurge of unemployment to nearly 9 percent,[13] high by Brazilian, although not by Latin American, standards. Worst hit were the electronic and automotive industries. Having learned to take continual expansion for granted, they found themselves forced to lay off thousands of workers.

This stiff economic medicine may have helped, but it produced no cure, and the burden of debt continued to grow heavier. The Mexican financial crisis coming on in mid-1982 shook international lenders and made them seek to reduce their exposure generally in Latin America. As a result, Brazil, in December 1982, found itself on the edge of bankruptcy, owing approximately $90 billion. In January it was forced to suspend payments and the situation was salvaged only by securing large additional credits from the International Monetary Fund, at a price of still more austerity. The heady visions of spiralling growth evaporated.

The painful condition of the economy generated criticism of the government and strengthened the call for *abertura*. It also reinforced the demand that the government divest itself of many or most of the 554 state enterprises. The Brazilian government has played a direct role in the economy since colonial times, when commerce and industry were closely regulated. From the beginning of the century, the state helped coffee growers, took over railroads, and managed banks.[14] Vargas much enlarged the state sector, especially steel and petroleum. Enterprises in trouble were nationalized to keep them running, utilities because rates could not be raised enough to make them profitable. Despite theoretical dedication to the market economy and to private enterprise, the military government after 1964 made Brazil semisocialist to counter foreign control, to keep resources in Brazilian hands, and to promote rapid industrialization by undertaking costly and risky infrastructural developments.

State banks provide over 70 percent of investment loans, and it is asserted that the state controls more than 60 percent of business.[15] Of the 200 largest enterprises in 1981, state firms accounted for 78 percent of capital, 47 percent of sales, 48 percent of work force, and 67 percent of profits.[16] Of the 6,945 largest firms, the state accounted for 50.8 percent of capital (38.6 percent being Brazilian private capital and 10.5 percent belonging to multinational corporations).[17]

Some state firms, especially the giants of steel, mining, electricity, and petroleum, show high indexes of profitability, production per worker, and export sales,[18] and there is no thought of divesting them. However, criticism of the state role in the economy as an aspect of military government has been rising since the beginning of *abertura*, and Presidents Geisel and Figueiredo indicated opposition to it in principle. The practical impetus for denationalization is financial, however. Many state enterprises lose money, and their debts fall to the state; they also contract foreign loans on their own, which account for 70 percent of the foreign debt. Central control is difficult; the government finds itself responsible for practically autonomous enterprises, from which it cannot secure adequate information.[19]

The technobureaucrats who run state enterprises somewhat as their property, including many military and former military, naturally resist denationalization. In 1981, however, a commission of three ministers was set up to reach, by summary procedures, a decision for either privatization, transfer, or deactivation of state enterprises; foreign capital was invited to participate in minority status. There remained some doubt, however, whether much could change. In some opinions, state enterprise is a natural expression of the military power.

The real question is much broader than state ownership. Aside from formal ownership of much of the economy, the Brazilian government has broad powers of capricious taxation, price fixing, control of investments, and licensing of almost anything. This is an essentially political problem, the outcome of which depends on the futures of *abertura*, constitutionalism, and pluralism.

Another open question of the economic structure is the role of foreign corporations, which have provided most of the leading edge of modernization. Brazilian opinion has always been ambivalent toward them; they are desired for practical reasons and disliked for political reasons. The attack came to a climax in the days of João Goulart; the embrace was warmest in the government of Castelo Branco. Then, and to some extent ever since, nationalistic Brazilians of both Left and Right have seen the military regime acting too much on the behalf of foreign capitalists, holding down wages for their benefit and surrendering Brazilian resources to them. It has always been good rhetoric to assail foreign corporations and the CIA.

With the coming of *abertura*, criticisms have tended to increase, as politics return to normal. Labor peace is no longer secure, and wages tend to rise, perhaps faster than inflation. It is significant that Daniel Ludwig was virtually compelled by the uncooperativeness of the government to sell the gigantic Amazonian estate of Jari to a Brazilian consortium for about a quarter of its $1 billion cost. The foreign sector, in which the U.S. share has shrunk to less than 30 percent, will probably have to learn new ways, dealing more with the Brazilian public and less with military bureaucrats.[20]

On the other hand, Brazil continues to need foreign investment, and large amounts of it flow into the country. The state may favor multinationals in practice, even while theoretically disliking them, because they are seen as modernizers and because they pay taxes religiously. Brazil has never been xenophobic as have various Spanish-American nations, and those most in contact with multinationals do not seem to be hostile. A poll of 232 union members showed 66 percent holding the government responsible for economic woes, only 10 percent the multinationals.[21]

The outcome of these issues rests on political trends, while politics rest on economic developments. A substantial downturn would divide the supporters of the government and encourage criticism and clamor for relief. If difficulties lead to union unrest, the military authorities might conceivably give up their effort to administer the country, as the Peruvian generals did in 1978–79, or they might decide to use force to keep order and reassert unqualified dictatorship.

Brazil has big problems and big resources. Population growth is still rapid, about 2.4 percent per year, especially in the poorer areas that least need more people, and the economy is called upon to provide jobs for 1.6 million entrants into the labor force yearly to keep unemployment from growing. This means continued rapid growth, difficult to assure and probably inflationary, simply to keep from falling further behind. Poverty and inequality seem inevitable—prosperous modern Brazil has millions of abandoned children. Even by comparison with other countries of similar GNP per capita, Brazil has high rates of infant mortality, parasitic diseases, and malnutrition—about 40 percent of Brazilian children are undernourished.[22]

Yet Brazil is blessed among nations in its potential. Its serious weakness is shortage of petroleum. Long exploration has failed to turn up major oil fields, and 70 percent of oil must be imported—oil is almost half the total import bill. This has stimulated the production of fuel alcohol, in which Brazil leads the world. Brazil may be the first nation to rely on renewable fuel resources, although the alcohol program weakened when oil prices moderated in 1981–82. Brazil is also fortunate in hydroelectric power potential, estimated at well over 200 million kilowatts. The world's largest hydroelectric project by a wide margin will be Itaipú, on the Paraná River, which is to produce 12.6 million kilowatts in 1988.

Despite this abundant power source—Brazil by 1983 had a surplus of electricity—the government insisted on nuclear development. The extremely ambitious program contracted with West Germany in 1975 has come into difficulties, however. The first commercial reactor, built by Westinghouse, was to come on stream in 1977; but it managed only trial runs by 1983. Its successors suffered similar delays and cost overruns until the government finally bowed to fiscal necessity in January 1983 and cancelled or postponed further construction. This also meant surrendering aspirations for a bomb-making potential.[23]

The nuclear program seemed mandatory, despite high costs, for "Brazil as a great power." Modern technology should be joined with natural resources to put Brazil in the forefront of nations. On the one hand, Brazil pushes the manufacture of computers; on the other, it plans to invest $61 billion, including many billions in foreign loans, in the fabulous mineral deposits of the Serra dos Carajás in the northeast Amazon region, with 18 billion tons of high-grade iron ore and large amounts of manganese, nickel, copper, bauxite, and gold (19 tons in 1982), all to be exploited by strictly Brazilian enterprise. It is only to be hoped that this project will not grind down, like the grand projects of the Médici era for the exploitation of Amazonia, in mismanagement and corruption.

Brazil has been reaching for its destiny ever since colonial days, and confidence that greatness may be at hand rises and falls. The answer lies in politics, whether the Brazilians can find ways to govern themselves that make energies creative instead of self-destructive.

THE POLITICAL CRUX

There are many Brazils, many faces of that immense and diverse land. But there are two basic sides of Brazilian society: the indigenous, often exotic, and the modern cosmopolitan. On the one hand are the huts of the Northeast, the endless back country, and tropical villages, on the other are the big factories and smart shops of the cities, especially in the South. Brazil is a land of voodoo, with its possessive rituals and African pantheon, worshipped at perhaps 300,000 temples, of family vendettas, and of the "animal game" (jogo do bicho). A gambling syndicate could put pressure on the police, who were accused of improper raids, by threatening to halt its essential operations. Brazil is a country in which only 5 percent of the population ever sees a private dentist, dental care by the social security system is limited to extraction, and cosmetic surgeons make fabulous incomes. Brazil lost the equivalent of at least $3 billion of production by taking time out to follow the World Cup Soccer Tournament in Spain in 1982, and the country went into mourning when the Brazilian team lost.[24]

Only 40 percent of children went beyond first grade in 1980, the same fraction as in 1948, and only 17 percent finished sixth grade.[25] Secondary schools, educating not for productivity but for status, prepare for a university education that only a tenth of their entrants receive. Yet Brazil has excellent technical schools with tens of thousands of eager students, perhaps 40 percent of them children of the working classes,[26] and probably the best scientific facilities of Latin America.

Despite campaigns, a quarter of the population over age 10 is still illiterate, and nearly as many are destitute; 67 percent of the population is counted as living in poverty.[27] For a population of about 125 million, there are printed about 2 million newspapers daily, but the Brazilian press is the most informative in Latin America and one of the best of the Third World. Manaus, the capital of Amazonia, is backward in the production of fruit; it is almost typical of Brazilian reality, or unreality, that the government proposes to make it a center of electrical manufacturing.

Broadly speaking, the poorer, the more backward Brazil is authoritarian; the richer and modernized Brazil is more democratic, or at least would like to be. Correspondingly, the former, which has been neglected by the military technobureaucratic regime, has supported it, while the more advanced sectors, which have greatly prospered, have been restive and critical and have clamored for rights for the people. A basic reason for the call for *abertura* and for Figueiredo's staking his moral authority on it is that economic growth under the military regime since 1964 has greatly strengthened the modern sector.

Pressures to democratize are manifold. The political model of the modern world is electoral democracy, fascism is discredited, communism hardly seems a viable alternative, and sundry authoritarianisms lack a convincing rationale. Brazilian conservatives and radicals alike admire U.S. democracy, although for different and partly contradictory reasons. To be democratic means to belong to the advanced nations. Brazilians see no reason that they should have an inferior form of government. The democratic order is advantageous in dealing with the world commercial community, and it is good for trade. Opening of the system to permit more inputs and freer interaction seems necessary to continued economic growth. The government, too, needs the kind of information elections give it. Only by relaxing controls can the military rulers keep in touch with people. Censorship chokes, and a population without means of making itself systematically heard becomes apathetic and uncooperative. The years of *abertura* have seen a renaissance of Brazilian art, especially of the cinema, after dead years of repression.

Abertura also represents a political calculation that a slackening of the reins will permit the opposition to divide and hence weaken itself, as the natural divisions in the country, repressed by dictatorship, come to the fore in relaxation. But probably the strongest drive for democratization comes from the classes that find it advantageous or practical. This means most obviously, the old political class—the many persons, articulate and influential almost by definition, who worked with and lived by the democratic process: legislators, political managers, and their aides and dependents. For many of the upper classes, politics is an avocation and fulfillment, and they resent exclusion from the process of government.

Among others particularly fond of the democratic order and in a position to press for it are journalists, for whom democracy means not only freedom but also share of power. Brazilian journalists battled steadily to make censorship unsustainable, and when censorship is removed they continually ask questions that can be answered only by political freedom. They are joined by lawyers, whose vocation lies in legality; the Brazilian bar forcefully challenged arbitrary powers and denial of rights. Artists, writers, and educators also want the latitude of action a free society can give them. Businessmen, too, generally prefer a democratic order in which their rights are assured against arbitrary action and in which they expect their demands to be heard (but not necessarily those of the workers). Only a constitutional order gives security, stability, and guaranteed access of outsiders to the political process. Labor leaders similarly, unless engaged by the state, desire the freedom of action that only a democratic society can give.

For such reasons, as the initial moral impetus of the revolution has worn out and special powers can no longer be justified by pointing to the anarchic horror of Goulart days, *abertura* has come to seem to most people a virtual necessity. There are, however, strong impediments to any far-reaching slackening of control or to surrender of power by its military holders. Brazil is fairly accustomed to military power. It required about 10 years to become habituated, but military rule has long since changed from the exceptional to the routine. There seems to be general cynicism; a poll found that 87.1 percent regarded the new parties as based only on immediate political or personal interests.[28] Much of the middle class is employed by the state and presumably not eager to see any disruption of it. As much as two-thirds of the population may be in one way or another dependent on the public sector. A substantial majority of the population has no clear recollection of the democratic republic, and the younger people have been taught very little about it in school. The leadership that would present itself as an alternative government is either aging or has had little practical experience with political power.

The majority of active officers likewise know the armed forces only as governing power, and they may see no reason to withdraw unless there should be much more serious splits in the military than have recently been visible or unless they should become convinced that civilians could run the country better. The thousands of military in administrative positions not only have their vested interest but have come to consider themselves relatively competent because they have devoted a much greater amount of time to education than have their civilian counterparts. It must be recognized, in fact, that the soldiers have given Brazil a fairly competent government by the standards of the past. The successive military presidents, although not conspicuously brilliant, have been sane and judicious. They have come to office without political obligations, able to choose staff; and the administration has been normally competent.

On the other hand, the military leaders hardly see a practicable alternative to themselves. The parties in Brazil have never done their job well, and there is little reason to believe they are more capable now. The military retained power in 1964 due, in large part, to the lack of trustworthy civilian politicians; and they have not seen politicians subsequently rising to their expectations, that there should be not a return to the old politics but rather a construction of new politics.[29]

The political class has generally clung to the old values and methods.[30] Figueiredo, disappointed by the lack of gratitude on the part of civilian leaders for the gifts of amnesty, freedom to organize, and the promise of elections, is said to have been disgusted by their narrowness and selfishness.[31] There is also a question whether a democratic regime could adequately manage the economy—in which the recent record of the military government has not been brilliant. If austerity is necessary, it is not to be imposed by a democratic regime.

The Brazilian system has always been hierarchic and unequal, and since 1964 it has only become more so and correspondingly less favorable for democracy. The military and technobureaucrats have taken their place alongside or above the old elite of landowners and the new elite of industrialists. The military, public officials, and employees of state enterprises were exempted from severe restrictions on the purchase of foreign exchange for travel; *Jornal do Brasil* asked whether they did not form a new ruling class.[32]

Brazilians take for granted government intervention in almost all aspects of life, from business to sports; and the vast growth of state enterprise and state employment makes a system of transfer of power by the ballot more problematic. Too much is at stake to expose it all to the hazards of truly free elections. It has not, in any case, been the Brazilian way to bring the masses into the political equation except as manipulated; the military government has not even tried to propagandize the people very much or to mobilize them as a following. The faith is rather in technology, for which the masses are inconsequential.

The armed forces are, and will doubtless continue to be, residual holders of power in the Brazilian system, as they are in almost all Latin American countries. They are basically autonomous, with control over their own promotions, under ministers who are active-duty officers. It would be very hard for any president—civilian or military— to deprive them of their ability to take command by coup if they should strongly desire to do so. The SNI also holds enormous power, which has only been strengthened during the *abertura*[33] and which could not easily be wrested from it. It is not to be expected that the army should be democratic in an undemocratic society. The *abertura* is consequently subject to military concurrence; in the words of Carlos Castelo Branco, perhaps the outstanding Brazilian commentator, this is "the imperative reality of the regime under which we live."[34]

It is hence the purpose of *abertura* to engineer adequate safety valves and a sense of participation without real surrender of authority. Should there be disorder or damaging conflicts, the military power could always decree a reversal. It is intended that the executive should remain capable of directing the country without much interference from without. It should get away from dictatorship without opening doors to anarchy, seeking legitimation with minimal sacrifice of power. An elected Congress should not try to set programs or even really to judge them but to give its sanction and aid in carrying them out. This implies a sort of manipulated democracy, which is made easier by the exclusion of illiterates from the franchise, by the continued existence of extensive backward areas, and by the general knowledge that if the parties overstep their limits they are likely to lose their modest gains of the past decade. The advisors of the president have thus far been sophisticated and inventive in the engineering of limited or "relative" democracy.

Ultimately, however, the success of *abertura* requires the bringing of wider circles into the political arena, the conciliation of labor, and the reduction of class differences. Democracy creates a demand for more democracy, and the development of Brazil ultimately requires genuine responsibility of and to the people of Brazil. It remains to be seen whether Brazil can escape the pendulum swing of much of Latin American politics between unbearable dictatorship and unworkable democracy. If the political architects in Brasília can devise a system whereby authority remains competent and stable yet is adequately reponsible to popular opinion, this will be not only slightly miraculous but also momentous for Latin America and beyond. The example of the successful Brazilian military government was extremely influential; the example of successful *abertura* may be even more so.

NOTES

1. *Business Week*, November 2, 1981, p. 37.
2. *Foreign Broadcast Information Service, Latin America*, January 19, 1982; *Christian Science Monitor*, November 12, 1982, p. 15.
3. Werner Baer, *The Brazilian Economy: Its Growth and Development* (Columbus, Ohio: Grid, 1979), p. 78.
4. Riordan Roett, ed., *Brazil: Politics in a Patrimonial Society* (New York: Praeger, 1978), p. 160.
5. *Isto É*, September 30, 1981, p. 73; ibid., January 20, 1982, p. 60.
6. Joint Publications Research Service, *Latin America Report*, October 20, "1980 Census Statistics," 1981, p. 20.
7. Baer, *The Brazilian Economy*, p. 102.
8. Peter McDonough, *Power and Ideology in Brazil* (Princeton, N.J.: Princeton University Press, 1981), p. 58.
9. Donald E. Syvrud, *Foundations of Brazilian Economic Growth* (Stanford, Calif.: Hoover Institution Press, 1974), pp. 18–19.
10. *Veja*, September 9, 1981, p. 94.
11. *Veja*, December 15, 1982, p. 139.
12. *O Estado de São Paulo*, January 12, 1982, p. 28.
13. *Veja*, October 21, 1981, p. 116.
14. Baer, *The Brazilian Economy*, pp. 136–37.

15. Alexandre de Souza Costa Barros, *Jornal do Brasil*, August 2, 1981, p. 2.

16. *Visão*, July 27, 1981, p. 61.

17. *Veja*, July 15, 1981, p. 93.

18. Baer, *The Brazilian Economy*, p. 152.

19. Ibid., p. 159; *Latin American Regional Report, Brazil*, September 17, 1982, p. 1.

20. *Veja*, July 15, 1981, p. 93; *Isto É*, January 27, 1982, pp. 66–68.

21. *Isto É*, September 2, 1981, p. 25.

22. Peter T. Knight and Ricardo Moran, *Brazil: Poverty and Basic Needs Series* (Washington, D.C.: World Bank, 1981), pp. 21–28.

23. *O Estado de São Paulo*, November 13, 1981, p. 7, June 11, 1982, p. 23; *Foreign Broadcast Information Service, Latin America*, November 24, 1981, p. D3; ibid., March 26, 1982, p. D1, May 10, 1982, p. D2; *Latin American Regional Report, Brazil*, February 5, 1982, p. 5; *Isto É*, January 19, 1983, pp. 16–23.

24. *New York Times*, November 8, 1981, p. 3; *New York Times*, July 8, 1982, p. 4.

25. *Veja*, February 18, 1981, p. 52; *Jornal do Brasil*, May 3, 1981, p. 18.

26. *Time*, December 1, 1975, p. 42.

27. *Jornal do Brasil*, April 26, 1981, p. E2.

28. *Visão*, April 6, 1981, pp. 46–47.

29. Alexandre de Souza Costa Barros, "The Brazilian Military: Professional Socialization, Political Performance, and State Building" (Ph.D. dissertation: University of Chicago Press, 1978), p. 168; Edmundo Campos Coelho, *Em busca de identidade: O exército e a política na sociedade brasileira* (Rio de Janeiro: Forense-Universitária, 1976), pp. 178–79.

30. Jerald A. Johnson, "Brazilian Bureaucracy and Politics: The Rise of a New Professional Class" (Ph.D. dissertation, University of Texas, Austin, 1977), p. 321.

31. *Veja*, March 11, 1981, p. 26.

32. *Jornal do Brasil*, September 17, 1982, p. 10.

33. Carlos Chagas, "The System, Even More Rigid," *O Estado de São Paulo*, February 7, 1982, p. 4; Joint Publication Research Service, *Latin America Report*, March 8, 1982, p. 22.

34. *Jornal do Brasil*, May 15, 1981, p. 2.

Bibliography

Aguiar, Neuma. *The Structure of Brazilian Development*. New Brunswick, N.J.: Transaction Books, 1979.

Baer, Werner. *The Brazilian Economy: Its Growth and Development*. Columbus, Ohio: Grid, 1979.

Bandeira, Moniz. *O Governo João Goulart: As Lutas Sociais no Brasil*. Rio de Janeiro: Civilização Brasileira, 1978.

Barros, Alexandre de Souza Costa. *The Brazilian ·Military: Professional Socialization, Political Performance, and State Building*. Dissertation, University of Chicago, 1978.

Bello, José Maria. *A History of Modern Brazil, 1889–1964*. Stanford, Calif.: Stanford University Press, 1964.

Benevides, Maria V. M. *O Governo Kubitschek—Desenvolvimento Econômico e Estabilidade Política, 1956–1961*. Rio de Janeiro: Paz e Terra, 1976.

Bruneau, Thomas. *The Church in Brazil*. Austin: University of Texas Press, 1982.

Bruneau, Thomas. *The Political Transformation of the Brazilian Catholic Church*. London: Cambridge University Press, 1974.

Burns, E. Bradford, ed. *A Documentary History: Brazil*. New York: Alfred A Knopf, 1966.

_____ . *A History of Brazil*, 2nd ed. New York: Columbia University Press, 1980.

_____ . *Nationalism in Brazil*. New York: Praeger, 1968.

Cardoso, Fernando H., and Bolivar Lamounier, eds. *Os Partidos e as Eleições no Brasil*. Rio de Janeiro: Paz e Terra, 1975.

Castelo, Branco Carlos. *Or Militarer no Poder.* Vol. 1: *Castelo Branco*. Vol. 2: *O A to 5*. Rio de Janeiro: Editora Nova Fronteira, 1978.

Chelsky, Marta. *Land Reform Bill in Brazil: The Management of Social Change*. Boulder, Colo.: Westview Press, 1979.

Chilcote, Ronald H. *The Brazilian Communist Party: Conflict and Integration, 1922-1972*. New York: Oxford University Press, 1974.

Coelho, Edmundo Campos. *Em Busca de Identidade: O Exército e a política na Sociedade Brasileira*. Rio de Janeiro: Forense-Universitária, 1976.

Cohen, Youssef. *Popular Support for Authoritarian Governments: Brazil under Médici*. Ann Arbor: University of Michigan Press, 1979.

Daland, Robert T. *Exploring Brazilian Bureaucracy: Performance and Pathology*. Washington, D. C.: University Press of America, 1981.

Dreifuss, René Armand. 1964: A conquista do estado: ação política, poder e golpe de classe. Petrópolis: Ed. Vozes, 1981.

Dulles, John W. *Anarchists and Communists in Brazil, 1900-1935*. Austin: University of Texas Press, 1974.

_____ . *Castelo Branco: The Making of a Brazilian President*. College Station, Texas: Texas A. & M. University Press, 1978.

_____ . *President Castelo Branco: Brazilian Reformer*. College Station, Texas: Texas A. & M. University Press, 1980.

_____ . *Unrest in Brazil: Political-Military Crisis, 1955-1964*. Austin: University of Texas Press, 1970.

_____ . *Vargas of Brazil: A Political Biography*. Austin: University of Texas Press, 1967.

Erickson, Kenneth P. *The Brazilian Corporative State and Working Class Politics*. Berkeley: University of California Press, 1978.

Escola Superior de Guerra. *Doutrina Básica*. Rio de Janeiro, 1979.

Evans, Peter B. *Dependent Development: The Alliance of Multinational, State and Local Capital in Brazil*. Princeton, N.J.: Princeton University Press, 1979.

Faucher, Philippe. *Le Brésil des militaires*. Montreal: University of Montreal Press, 1981.

Fernandes, Florestan. *Reflections on the Brazilian Counter Revolution*. Armand. N.Y.: M. E. Sharpe, 1981.

Fiechter, Georges-André. *Brazil Since 1964: Modernization under a Military Regime*. New York: Halsted Press, 1975.

Fleischer, David V., ed. *Os Partidos Políticos no Brasil*. Brasília: Editora Universidade de Brasília, 1981.

Fleischer, David V. "Parties, Elections and 'Abertura' in Brazil," in *The New Political Militarism in Latin America*, ed. Robert Wesson. New York: Praeger, 1982.

Flynn, Peter. *Brazil: A Political Analysis*. Boulder, Colo.: Westview Press, 1978.

Fontaine, Roger W. *Brazil and the United States*. Washington, D. C.: American Enterprise Institute, 1975.

Furtado, Celso. *Diagnosis of the Brazilian Crisis*. Berkeley: University of California Press, 1965.

Goés, Walder de. *O Brasil de General Geisel: Estudo do processo de tomada de decisão no regime militar-burocrático*. Rio de Janeiro: Nova Fronteira, 1978.

Hiil, Lawrence F. *Diplomatic Relations between the United States and Brazil*. Durham, N.C.: Duke University Press, 1932.

Hilton, Stanley E. *Brazil and the Great Powers, 1930-1939: The Politics of Trade Rivalry*. Austin: University of Texas Press, 1975.

Jaguaribe, Hélio. *Economic and Political Development: A Theoretical Approach and a Brazilian Case Study*. Cambridge, Mass.: Harvard University Press, 1968.

Jenks, Carl Major. *The Structure of Diplomacy: An Analysis of Brazilian Foreign Relations in the Twentieth Century*. Durham, N.C.: Ph.D. dissertation, Duke University, 1979.

Jenks, Margaret S. *Political Parties in Authoritarian Brazil*. Durham, N.C.: Ph.D. dissertation, Duke University, 1979.

Johnson, Jerald A. "Brazilian Bureaucracy and Politics: The Rise of a New Professional Class." Ph.D. dissertation, University of Texas, Austin, 1977.

Jurema, Abelardo. *Sexta-Feira 13 de Março: os últimos días do Governo João Goulart*. Rio de Janeiro: Edições O Cruzeiro, 1964.

Keith, Henry H., and Robert A. Hayes, eds. *Perspective on Armed Politics in Brazil*. Tempe: Arizona State University Press, 1976.

Knight, Peter T., and Ricardo Moran. *Brazil: Poverty and Basic Needs Series*. Washington, D.C.: World Bank, 1981.

Lamounier, Bolivar, ed. *Voto de Desconfiança: Eleições e Mundança Política no Brasil, 1970-1979*. Petrópolis: Ed. Vozes, 1980.

Leal, Victor Nunes. *Coronelismo*. New York: Cambridge University Press, 1977.

Macaulay, Neill. *The Prestes Column: A Revolution in Brazil*. New York: New Viewpoints, 1974.

Malloy, James M. *The Politics of Social Security in Brazil*. Pittsburgh, Pa.: University of Pittsburgh Press, 1979.

Marshall, Andrew. *Brazil*. London: Thames and Hudson, 1966.

McCann, Frank D. The Brazilian-American Alliance: 1937–1945. Princeton University Press, 1973.

McDonough, Peter. *Power and Ideology in Brazil*. Princeton, N.J.: Princeton University Press, 1981.

McDonough, Peter, and Amaury de Souza. *The Politics of Population in Brazil: Elite Ambivalence and Public Demand*. Austin: University of Texas Press, 1981.

Morris, Michael A. *International Politics and the Sea: The Case of Brazil*. Boulder, Colo.: Westview Press, 1979.

Oliveira, Eliézer R. de. *As Forças Armada: Política e Ideologia no Brasil* (1964–1969). Petrópolis: Ed. Vozes, 1976.

Overholt, William H., et al. *The Future of Brazil*. Boulder, Colo.: Westview Press, 1978.

Page, Joseph A. *The Revolution that Never Was: Northeast Brazil 1955–1964*. New York: Grossman, 1972.

Parker, Phyllis R. *Brazil and the Quiet Intervention*. Austin: University of Texas Press, 1979.

Pedreira, Fernando. *Brasil Político 1964–1975*. São Paulo: Difel, 1975.

Perry, William. *Contemporary Brazilian Foreign Policy: International Strategy of an Emerging Power*. Beverly Hills, Calif.: Sage, 1976.

Poppino, Rollie E. *Brazil: The Land and People*. 2nd ed. New York: Oxford University Press, 1973.

Reis, Fábio, ed. *Os Partidos e o Regime*. São Paulo: Ed. Símbolo, 1978.

Rodrigues, José Honório. *The Brazilians: Their Character and Aspirations*. Austin: University of Texas Press, 1967.

Roett, Riordan, ed. *Brazil in the Seventies*. Washington, D.C.: American Enterprise Institute, 1976.

———, ed. *Brazil in the Sixties*. Nashville, Tenn.: Vanderbilt University Press, 1972.

———. *Politics in Foreign Aid in the Brazilian Northeast*. Nashville, Tenn.: Vanderbilt University Press, 1972.

———. *Brazil: Politics in a Patrimonial Society*. New York: Praeger, 1978.

Rosenbaum, H. John, and William G. Tyler, eds. *Contemporary Brazil: Issues in Economic and Political Development*. New York: Praeger, 1972.

Santos, Wanderley Guillerme dos. *Poder e política: cronica do autoritarismo brasileiro*. Rio de Janeiro: Forense Universitária, 1978.

Schmitter, Philippe C. *Interest Conflict and Political Change in Brazil*. Stanford: Stanford University Press, 1971.

Schneider, Ronald M. *Brazil: Foreign Relations of a Future World Power*. Boulder, Colo.: Westview Press, 1977.

———. "The Brazilian Military in Politics," in *New Military Politics in Latin America*, ed. Robert Wesson. New York: Praeger, 1982.

———. *The Political System of Brazil*. New York: Columbia University Press, 1971.

Selcher, Wayne A. *Brazil in the International System: The Rise of a Middle Power*. Boulder, Colo.: Westview Press, 1981.

———, ed. *Brazil's Multilateral Relations between First and Third Worlds*. Boulder, Colo.: Westview Press, 1978.

Skidmore, Thomas E. *Politics in Brazil*. New York: Oxford University Press, 1966.

Soares, Glaúcio. *Sociedade e Política no Brasil*. São Paulo: Difel, 1973.

Stepan, Alfred, ed. *Authoritarian Brazil: Origins, Policies, and Future*. New Haven, Conn.: Yale University Press, 1973.

———. *The Military in Politics: Changing Patterns in Brazil*. Princeton, N.J.: Princeton University Press, 1974.

Syvrud, Donald E. *Foundations of Brazilian Economic Growth*. Stanford, Calif.: Hoover Institution Press, 1974.

Valle, Arturo. *Estruturas políticas brasileiras*. Rio de Janeiro: Editora Laudes, 1970.

Viana, Luiz. *O governo Castelo Branco*. Rio de Janeiro: Biblioteca do Exército, 1975.

Wagley, Charles. *Introduction to Brazil*. New York: Columbia University Press, 1971.

Weffort, Francisco C. *O populismo na política Brasileira*. Rio de Janeiro: Paz e Terra, 1978.

Weil, Thomas E., et al. *Area Handbook of Brazil*. Washington, D.C.: Government Printing Office, 1975.

Wesson, Robert. *The United States and Brazil: Limits of Influence*. New York: Praeger, 1981.

Wirth, John D. *The Politics of Brazilian Development, 1930–1954*. Stanford: Stanford University Press, 1970.

Worcester, Donald E. *Brazil: From Colony to World Power*. New York: Charles Scribner's, 1973.

Young, Jordan M. *Brazil 1954–64: End of a Civilian Cycle*. New York: Facts on File, 1972.

Index

Abertura, 37, 39, 42–43, 51–52, 59, 68–69, 83, 115–16, 171–72, 175–78; progress of, 40–42
Acão Integralista Brasileira. See AIB
Abi Ackel, Ibrahim, 75
Abreu, General Hugo de, 70
Abreu, Leitão de, 41
"Additional Act" (1945), 92
ADP (Democratic Parliamentary Action), 101, 103
ADESG (Association of Graduates of the Superior War College), 55; course offerings, 134; as political elite, 133
Affonso, Almino, 113
AFL-CIO, 151
Agrarian reform, 28–29
Agriculture: based on slavery, 6; predominant vocation, 8
AI-1. See Institutional Act 1
AI-2. See Institutional Act 2
AI-5. See Institutional Act 5
AIB (Acão Integralista Brasileira), 98
Airplanes, export of, 168
Aleixo, Pedro, 35, 105
Aliança Liberal, 100
Allende Gossens, Salvador, 36
Alliance for Progress, 147, 151, 156
Alvares Cabral, Pedro, 1
Alves, Márcio Moreira, 34
Amazon: development of, 37
American Institute of Free Labor Development, 151
American Revolution: influence of, 3
Andrade, Doutel de, 110; family, 49
Angola: recognition of, 2, 71, 157
Angra dos Reis nuclear plant, 158
ANL (National Liberation Alliance), 96, 98

Anti-communism: sentiments of, 28
Anti-Goulart forces, 151–52
Appointments, political, 55
"April Package" (1977), 38, 75, 107
Aragão, Admiral Cândido, 24
Aranha, Oswaldo, 144
ARENA (National Renovating Alliance), 30–36 passim, 38–39, 51, 55, 65, 82–83, 103, 105–6, 108, 110, 114, 117–18
Argentina, 142
Arms: export of, 168
Arms Production Public Corporation (EMBEL), 77
Army, dissension in, 124
Arns, Evaristo Cardinal, 36
Arraes, Miguel, 30, 113
ASCB. See Brazilian Association of Civil Servants
Association of Graduates of the Superior War College. See ADESG
Automobiles: exports of, 167–68

Bahia, 86–87
Bandeirantes, 2
Bankers, 63
Barbosa, Rui, 9
Barros, Ademar de, 17, 20, 23, 29, 31, 49–50, 92–93, 95–96, 102; populist politician, 50
"Basic Reforms" (Goulart), 81, 101
"Basic Doctrine," 134–35
Beltrão, Hélio, 79
Bernardes, Artur da Silva, President, 9–10, 92, 100, 129
Bias Fortes family, 49
Bittar, Jacó, 111

Bloco Parlamentario Revolucionário (BPR), 103
Boia frias, 48
Bossa nova group, 100
BPR. See *Bloco Parlamentario Revolucionário*
Brandt, Willy, 111
Brasília, 17
Brazil: and Germany, 143–44; as constitutional monarchy, 4; as empire, 1, 4–7; as federal republic, 7; as political unit, 4; change in U.S. relationship, 145–46, 154–55; early history, 1–2, fascist/Nazi tendencies in, 143–44; first constitution of, 4; in World War I, 142; in World War II, 14, 144; independence of, 4; leftist tendencies in, 11
Brazilian Association of Civil Servants (ASCP), 78
Brazilian Communist Party. See PCB
Brazilian Democratic Movement. See MDB
Brazilian Enterprise for Agricultural Research (EMBRAPA), 76
Brazilian Expeditionary Forces (FEB), 32, 92, 132, 144, 154–55
Brazilian Institute for Democratic Action (IBAD), 58, 101, 151
Brazilian Labor Party. See PTB
Brazilian Rural Federation, 65
Brazilian School of Public Administration (EBAP), 78
Britain, investment of, 9
Brizola, Leonel, 19, 22, 85–86, 95, 101, 110–11, 116–17
"Broad front," 34
Bureaucracy, admission to, 77
Bush, George, U.S. Vice President, 162

Cabinet, imperial, 5
Cabos eletorais, 47
Cacao Institute, 56
Cacique, 47
Café Filho, João, 17, 81, 99
Câmara, Dom Helder, 36

Campos, Francisco, 12, 26
Campos, Milton, 27
Campos, Roberto, 28–29, 35, 55, 89, 99, 148
Campos Sales, Manuel, President, 8
Cardoso, Fernando H., 100
Carlos, Antônio, 56
Carter, Jimmy, U.S. President, 157–61
Carter, Rosalynn, 161
Cassation, 27, 31, 34–35
Castello Branco, Carlos, commentator, 177
Castelo Branco, General Humberto, President, 23–27 passim, 30–35 passim, 38, 55, 58, 69, 74–75, 84, 88–89, 95, 126–27, 131, 134, 152, 155; death of, 33; one-term presidency, 32; pro-U.S. action of, 150, 154; stabilization policy of, 29; sympathy for U.S. Vietnam involvement, of, 153
Castro, Fidel, 18, 150
Censorship: of broadcast media, 40, 116; decrease of, 38; defiance of, 14; of political dialog, 36; of press, 9–10, 34, 36; ended, 40
Center for Internal Defense Operations (CODI), 127
Central Intelligence Agency, U.S. (CIA), 151–52, 172
CGT. See Labor Confederation
Chaves, Aureliano, President, 35, 42, 75
China, People's Republic of, 156
Christian Democratic Party. See PDC
Christopher, Warren, U.S. Secretary of State, 159
Church: opposition to government of, 33–34, 36, 38, 42; leftist terms of, 68
"Church base communities," 41, 67
CIA. See Central Intelligence Agency
CIP. See Inter-Ministerial Price Commission
Civil liberties, 4
Civilian politics, fragmentation of, 25
Civilians, colonial regulations for, 2

Clergy, European, 67
Clientelism, 48–49, 62
CLT. See Consolidation of Labor
    Legislation
COBRASMA, 63
CODI. See Center for Internal Defense
    Operations
Coffee: as basis of economy, 8; as new
    source of wealth, 5; price supports
    for, 13
Coffee barons, 8
Coffee growers, organization of, 58
Coffee Institute, 56
Coffee, instant, controversy, 156
"Cohen Plan," 12
"Colonels," 8
Commissão Parlamentar de Inquérito
    (CPI), 82
Command and General Staff School,
    126
Commercial groups, 63
Communism: dangers of, 57; fear of,
    24; sympathies to, 27
Communist countries, normalized
    relations with, 147
Communist insurrection (1935), 12
Communist Party, Brazilian. See PCB.
Communists, 16, 67, 143; at mass rally
    (1964), 22; in opposition to foreign
    industry, 146; purged from official
    positions, 15; in unions, 23
Comte, August, positivist philosophy
    of, 6, 130
Confederation of Agricultural Workers
    (CONTAG), 62
Conference of the Producing Classes, 63
Congress: dismissal of, by Vargas, 143;
    forcible closure of (1937), 12; of
    1945, 15; dissolution of (1968), 34;
    recall of, by Médici, 35; relations
    with presidents, 74; role of, 60;
    under military regime, 74–75
CONLAP. See Conference of the
    Producing Classes
Conservative party: under empire, 5–6;
    slavery, abolition of, 6
Consolidation of Labor Legislation

(CGT), 77–78
Constitution: first (1823), 4; of 1891, 7,
    87, 129; of 1934, 11; 0f 1937, 12;
    of 1946, 15, 73, 80, 87, 93
CONTAG. See Confederation of
    Agricultural Workers
Cordeiro de Farias, General Oswaldo,
    132
Coronéis, 47–49, 87
Coronelismo, 47–48, 62: decrease of, 48
Corporatism, 56–58, 65
Corruption, political, 55
Costa e Silva, Marshal Artur da,
    President, 23, 25–26, 30, 34, 37,
    47, 75, 79, 106, 131, 154–56;
    ARENA candidate (1966), 6;
    election of (1966), 32–33; paralysis
    of, 35; refusal to see U.S.
    ambassador, 155
Council of Bishops, 67
Council of Industrial Development, 76
Coup, U.S. involvement in, 151–52
Court of Justice (Tribunal de justiça),
    84
Covas, Mário, 113
CPI. See Comissão Parlamentar de
    Inquérito
Cuba, 18

Daland, Robert T., 59, 79
DASP. See Department of the
    Administration of Public Service
De Nigris, Theoboldo, 63–64
Debt question, 163, 170
Debts, domestic and foreign, 147; of
    Kubitschek government, 17
Decurso de prazo, 41, 81, 115–16
Deficit, 170
Delfim Neto, Antônio, 33, 60–61, 71,
    170
Democracy, in Brazil, 27–18; limited
    restoration of, 39; promises of, 14
Democratic Crusade, 146
Democratic Parliamentary Action. See
    ADP
Democratic Social Party. See PDS
Democratization: drive for, 175;

pressures to, 175; reversal of, 31, 38

Demonstrations, 59

Department of the Administration of Public Service (DASP), 76–77

Department of Internal Security (DSI), 76–77

Dependence on U.S.: reduction of, 161

Detachment of Operation and Information (DOI), 127

Diamonds: discovery of, 2

Dias, Giocondo, 115

Dictatorship: establishment of, 34

DIESSE. See Inter-Syndicate Group of Socioeconomic and Statistical Indicators

Distensão, 52

Divorce statute, and Church, 68

DNPEA. See National Department of Agricultural Research

Dominican Republic, U.S. intervention in, 153

DOI. See Detachment of Operation and Information

DOPS. See State Department of Political and Social Order

Doutrina Básica. See Basic Doctrtine

DSI. See Department of Internal Security

Dutra, Eurico, President, 15, 26, 74, 92, 96, 99, 145–46; encouragement of foreign investment, 16

Dutra, Olivio, 111

EBAP. See Brazilian School of Public Administration

EMBEL, 77. See also Arms export

EMBRAPA. See Brazilian Enterprise for Agricultural Research

Economic aid, U.S.; discontinued, 148

Economic growth, 167

Economy: balanced budget of, 32; British investment in, 9; decline of, 19; foreign dominance in, 5; improvement of, 37

Education: elementary, 174; higher, expansion of, 38; political, 54–55

El Salvador government: support of, 162

Elbrick, C. Burke, U.S. Ambassador, 36

Elections: during empire, 5; manipulation of, 58; of 1945, 14; of 1955, 17; of 1966, 32; of 1982, 41–43, 89, 117–18; turnout, 52

Elections: rural, 48

Electoral college, 76

Electricity: production of, 173

Electrobras, 28, 71, 74, 101

Emperor: overthrow of (1889), 7; powers of, 4

Empire: cabinets of, 5; civil liberties of, 5; Conservative party of, 5; elections under, 5; Liberal party of, 5; social order, under, 5

ESG. See Superior War College

Estado Novo, 12–13, 26, 51, 56, 68, 73, 80, 87, 92, 98–100, 118, 126, 129, 135, 143–44

Estatizacão, 64

Estillac Leal, General Newton, 146

Etelvino Lins Law, 48

European influence, 3, 5

Exiles, political, 39

Export policy: airplanes, 168; arms, 168; automobiles, 167–68

Falklands conflict, 162

Family influence, 53

"Father of the Poor" (Vargas), 16

FEB. See Brazilian Expeditionary Forces

Federal bureaucracy: education for, 78; hiring freeze of, 78

Federal Court of Appeals (Tribunal Federal de Recursos), 84

Federal Tribunal of Accounts, 82

Federation of Industry of the State of São Paulo (FIESP), 63–64

FGTS. See Guarantee Fund for Length of Service

FIESP. See Federation of Industry of the State of São Paulo

Fiel, Filho, 38

Figueiredo, General Edson do, 30
Figuereido, João Baptista, President, 39–42, 55, 64, 70, 75, 78, 88, 108, 116–17, 126–27, 161, 175, 177; visit to U.S., 162
Figuereido Ferraz, Ester do, 76
First Republic, 56, 80, 87, 93
FMP. See Popular Mobilization Front
Fonseca, Marshal Deodoro da, President, 7
Fonseca, Marshal Hermes de, President, 8–9
Força Publica, São Paolo, 124
Ford administration, 158, 160
Foreign business, 64: role of, 172; capital, dependence on, 31; domination of economy by, 5
Foreign debt, 163. See also Debt question
Foreign industry: restriction on, 146
Foreign investment, 28
"Foreigners' Law" (1981), 68
FPN (Nationalist Parliamentary Front), 100–1
Franchise, 11, 51
Freedmen, 6
Freemasonry, 6
Freire, Paulo, 53
Freitas, Chagas, 49
French Revolution, influence of, 3
Frota, General Sílvio, 39, 70, 131
Fuel, fossil: scarcity of, 158
FUNRURAL (social agency), 53, 62
Furtado, Celso, 19

Geisel, Ernesto, President, 29, 37–39, 55, 59, 67, 75, 84, 106–7, 127, 131, 156, 159–61
Geisel, Orlando, 37
General Staff, 126
Germany: and Brazil, 143–44; nuclear agreement with, 158
Gold, discovery of, 2
Golbery. See Silva, Golbery do Couto e
Gomes, Brig. Eduardo, 92
González, Felipe, 111
Good Neighbor Policy, 143

Gordon, Lincoln, U.S. Ambassador, 148, 150–51, 154
Goulart, João, President, 17–19, 25, 27–29, 34, 51, 74, 81, 95, 99–102 passim, 124, 127, 150–53 passim, 172: appeal to masses, 21–22; "basic reforms," of, 21; desire for U.S. economic aid, 148; manipulation of military advancement by, 22–23; Minister of Labor, 16; opposition to, 88; overthrow of, 24; practical politics of, 148; pro-communist sentiments of, 96–97, 147–48; resignation of, 146
Great Depression (1929), 10
Guanabara, 88
Guarani language, 2
Guarantee Fund for Length of Service (FGTS), 61, 77
Guerreiro, Ramiro Saraira, 162
Guttsman, W. L., 60

Hard-liners, 131. See also "Linha dura"
Herzog, Vladimir, 38: widow of, 86
Hitler, Adolf, 143
High Command, military, 126
Human rights controversy, 160–61

IBAD. See Brazilian Institute for Democratic Action
IBM, 64
IMF. See International Monetary Fund
Immigration, to southern states, 8
Impeachment of presidents, 81
Independence, Brazilian, 4
Indians, slavery of, 1–2
Industrial development, 145
Industrialists, 63: organization of, 56
Industry, growth of, 8, 17
Inequality, economic, 168
Inflation, 5, 13, 169–70
Institute for Economic and Social Research (IPES), 58, 101, 127
Institutional Acts, 12
Institutional Act 1 (AI-1), 26, 32

Institutional Act 2 (AI-2), 30, 84, 100–3
Institutional Act 3 (AI-3), 31
Institutional Act 5 (AI-5), 34, 69, 75,
84, 155: revocation, 39
Integralistas, 12, 98, 143
Inter-Ministerial Price Commission
(CIP), 63
International Monetary Fund (IMF),
17, 147: credits from, 171
Inter-Syndicate Group of
Socioeconomic and Statistical
Indicators (DIESSE), 61
"Interventors," 11, 69
IPES. See Institute for Economic and
Social Research
IPI. See Tax on Industrial Products
Itamarty, 164

Janistas, 99
Jari, sale of, 172
João IV (king), 4
Johnson administration, 150–51, 153
Joint Services General Staff, 132
Judiciary, Brazilian, 15
Junior Officers' School, 125
Jurema, Abelardo, 22

Kennedy, John F., 148
Kennedy, Robert, 148
Kissinger, Henry A., 157
Kruel, General Amaury, 24
Kubitschek, Juscelino, President, 17,
20, 26–27, 34, 50, 74, 81, 98, 102,
135, 147
Labor: demands of, 57; discontent and
strikes of, 34, 61
Labor Confederation (CGT), 69
Labor laws, 13
Labor negotiations, 61
Labor Party, 61
Labor unions, 20: increased demands
of, 61; increased independence of,
60; solidarity of German workers
to, 61
Labor, urban, demonstration by, 59
Lacerda, Carlos, 16, 18, 22–23, 28–29,
31, 33–34, 79, 98–100, 146, 155;

followers of, 34–35
Land reform, 19
Landed gentry, 8
Law of Foreign Nationals (1980), 40,
42, 68
League of Nations, Brazil in, 142
Leftist tendencies, Brazil, 11
Lei Falcão Law), 116
Leitão de Abreu, General João, 41
"Liberal Alliance," 10–11
Liberal party, during empire, 5
Liberator Party. See PL
Liberal professions, 66
"Liberation theology," 67
Lima, General Affonso Augusto de
Albuquerque, 30–31
"Linha dura," 4
Literacy, 5, 174: as voting requirement,
51; campaigns, MOBRAL and
MEB, 53
Lott, Marshall Henrique Texeira, 17,
85, 97
LSN. See National Security Law
Ludwig, Daniel, 172
Ludwig, General Rubem, 71, 75
"Lula." See Silva, Luis Inácio da
Luz, Carlos, 17, 81

Magalhães, Juraci, 99
Magalhães, Sergio, 101
Maluf, Paulo, 88
Mandado de segurança, 83
Manifesto dos Mineiros, 92
Manaus, 174
Mangabeira, João, 97
"March of the Family with God for
Liberty," 23
Marchesan, Nelson, 42
Marighela, Carlos, 36
Marines, mutiny of, 22
Marshall Plan, 145
Mazzili, Ranieri, 25–26, 81, 152
McDonough, Peter, 59, 79
MDB (Brazilian Democratic
Movement), 30–32, 38–39, 49, 52,
82–83, 103, 105–10 passim, 113,
117

MEB. See Literacy campaign
Medeiros, General Octavio, 62, 75, 127
Médici, General Emílio Garrastazu,
    President, 35–39 passim, 75, 82,
    84, 127, 156–57; popular support
    of, 37
"Memorandum of understanding," 157
Military: alienation of, by Quadros, 18;
    control of Brazil, 7;
    democratization of, 130;
    dominance of army in, 123'
    entrenchment of, 176–77;
    equalizing force, 137–38; fear of
    communism; ideology, 130,
    134–35; interest group of, 70;
    internal division in, 124, 131; lack
    of vote of, 51; political activity,
    128–29; opportunities in public
    service, 130; in politics, 54–55;
    professionalization of, 125; purge
    of old regime by, 25–27; unlimited
    dictatorship of, 25
Military assistance, 160
Military authority, curtailed in 1982,
    117
Military-civilian conflict, 9, 25, 34
Military Club, 128
Military Command, flux of, 126
Military establishment, in conflict with
    emperor, 7
Military Household (Casa Militar), 126
Military officers, education of, 124–26
Military police, 88
Militia, state, 124
Mills, C. Wright, 60
Minas Gerais, 2, 19, 86, 88, 93: protest
    of (1789), 3; strength of, 8
Ministry of Debureaucratization, 79
Ministry of Education and Culture
    (MEC), 69
Ministry of Labor, 56, 62
Ministry of Land Tenure Affairs
    (1982), 62
Ministry of Planning (SEPLA), 60, 74
Miscegenation, acceptance of, 6
Mitterand, François, 111
MOBRAL. See Literary campaign

Mondale, Walter, U.S. Vice President,
    161
Monopolies, legality of, 2
Monroe Doctrine, 141
Monteiro, General Euler Bentes, 39,
    131
Monteiro, General Goes, 130
Morais, Prudente de, President, 8
Moreira, Neiva, 110
Motta, Paulo R., 59
Mourão Filho, General Olímpio, 12,
    24, 26
Multinational Corporations, 64
Municipal Participation Fund, 55
Municipios, 49, 65, 69, 88–89: rural, 48
Mussolini, Benito, 143
Mutiny of naval forces (1893–95), 7

Napoleon, 3–4
National Alcohol program, 71
National City Bank, branches in Brazil,
    9
National Democratic Union, See UDN
National Department of Agricultural
    Research (DNPEA), 76
National Directorate of Students, 69
National Information Service (SNI),
    29, 35, 39, 59, 62, 76–77, 116,
    127–28, 177: establishment of, 74
National Intelligence School, 127
National Labor Party. See PTN
National Liberation Alliance. See ANL
National Motor Vehicle Manufacturers
    Association (ANFAVEA), 64
Nationalist Parliamentary Front. See
    FPN
National Petroleum Council, 13
National Renovating Alliance. See
    ARENA
National Security Council, 62, 76,
    126–27, 132, 158
National Security Law, 40–41, 60,
    84–86, 111
National Student Union (UNE), 68–69:
    abolishment of, 27; clandestine
    congress of, 31, 33; legality of, 39
Nationalism, 3, 9

Nationalist, victory of, 146
Naval forces: mutiny of, 7, 23
Navy, Brazil, 9
Nazi support of *Integralistas,* 12
Negrão de Lima, Francisco, 30
Neutralism, Brazil, 145, 147
Neves, Tancredo, 105, 112
New States. See *Estado Novo*
Nixon administration, 155, 157, 160
Nonaligned group of, 77, 156
"November Package" (1982), 42, 115
Nuclear development, 173-74
Nuclear industry, 159
Nuclear proliferation controversy,
157-60
Nuclear Non-Proliferation Treaty,
155-56
Nuclebras, 71

OAS. See Organization of American
States
"Old Boy" network, 60, 64, 78
Old Republic, 73, 129
OPEC. See Petroleum Exporting
Countries
Opening. See *Abertura*
"Operation Brother Sam," 151-52
"Operation Panamerican," 147
Organization of American States
(OAS), 153

Pará, 86
Paraguayan War (1865-70), 6-7, 129
Paraná, 98
Partido Comunista Brasileiro. See PCB
Partido Comunista do Brasil. See PC
do B
Partido dos Trabalhadores. See PT
Partido Federalista. See PF
Partido Libertador. See PL
Partido Popular Democrático e
Socialista. See PPDS
Partido Republicano. See PR
Partido Social Democratico. See PSD
Partido Social Progressista. See PSP
Partido Socialista Brasileiro. See PSB
Partido Trabalhista Brasileiro. See PTB

Party discipline, lack of, 101
Party of the Brazilian Democratic
Movement. See PMDB
Party of the Workers. See PT
Party system, reform of, 88
Passarinho, Jarbas, 34
Partrão, 47, 49
Paulista rebellion (1932), 73
PC do B (Communist Party of Brazil),
97, 112
PCB (Brazilian Communist Party),
10-11, 15, 18, 20, 35, 92-93,
95-97, 103, 112, 114-15, 119:
illegality of, 12, 15, 96; repression
of, 145; Soviet influence on, 15;
sympathetic to Vargas, 16
PDC (Christian Democratic Party),
17-18, 97-99, 119
PDS (Democratic Social Party), 42, 51,
65, 83, 114-17 passim
PDT (Partido Democratico
Trabalhista), 110-11, 117
"Peasant Leagues," 20, 27
Pedro I, 4, 86: abdication of, 5
Pedro II, 5-6, 86, 129: in conflict with
Catholic hierarchy, 6; with
military, 7; victim of republican
sentiments, 6
Peixoto, Marshal Floriano, 7
Pelego politicians, 50, 64, 94
Pereira, Augusto, 92, 128
Pernambuco, 86
Perón, Juan, 20
Pessoa, João, 11
Peterson, Phyllis, 91
Petrobras, 13, 16, 37, 70, 74, 101, 146:
establishment of, 16, 146; leftist
control of, 151
Petroleum Exporting Countries
(OPEC), 37
PF (Partido Federalista), 100
Pilla, Raul, 92, 100
Pinheiro, Israel, 30
Pinochet administration, 127
Pinto, José de Magalhães, 23, 29, 112
PL (Liberator Party), 92, 100, 119
PM (Military Police), 88

PMDB (Party of the Brazilian Democratic Movement), 53, 70, 85, 110, 112–118 passim
Police tortures, 67
Political: appointments, 77; education, 53; consciousness, 52–53; loyalty, 49; opposition, gradual emergence of, 42
Popular Party. See PP
Popular Mobilization Front (FMP), 69
Popular Representation Party. See PRP
Population: diversity of, 174; early expansion of, 2
Populism, 49, 57
Populist parties, 93
Portela, Eduardo, 69
Portela, Petrônio, 62, 112
Portugal, 1–2, 98
Portuguese aristocracy, 3–4
Positivism, 130, 135
Power elite, concept of, 60
PP (Popular Party), 59, 85, 112, 114–15
PPDS (Partido Popular Democrático e Socialista), 111
PR (Republican Party), 92, 100, 105
Presidency: election procedures for, 73–74; liberalization of, 75; power of, 12, 73, 75
Press: censorship of, 9, 59, 143; freedom of, 5; informativeness of, 174
Prestes, Júlio, President, 10–11
Prestes, Luis Carlos, 9, 12, 15, 96–97, 115
"Prestes Column," 9–10
Profit remittance law, 21, 28, 153
Progressive Social Party. See PSP
PRP (Popular Representation Party), 92, 98, 105, 119
PRT (Rural Labor Party), 93
Protective tariff, 13
PSB (Partido Socialista Brasileiro), 97, 105
PSD (Social Democratic Party), 14–15, 17, 21, 92–93, 98–102 passim, 118
PSP (Progressive Social Party), 93, 95, 102, 105
PST (Socialist Labor Party), 93, 95, 105
PT (Party of the Workers), 53, 70, 111–12, 117–18
PTB (Brasilian Labor Party), 14–15, 17, 21, 26, 50, 85, 92–97 passim, 101–2, 105, 110–11, 118
PTN (National Labor Party), 93, 95, 105
Public service: employees, 64; promotions in, 77–78; salaries of, 77

Quadros, Jânio, 17, 26, 29, 74, 81, 93, 95, 97, 99–100, 147–49, 152: resignation of, 18; as populist politician, 50
"Queremistas", 14

Reagan, Ronald, 162
Regional Labor Courts (TRT), 85
Renovating Labor Movement (MTR), 93
Representation: according to population, 80; in chamber of deputies, 80; proportional, 81
Republican Club (1870), 6
Revolution of 1930, 87, 129
Revolution, military, of 1964, 88
Revolutionary efforts, in Colonial Brazil, 3
Ribeiro, Jair Dantas, 21, 24
Ribeiro, Darcy, 110
Rio Branco, Baron of, 142
Rio de Janeiro, 88: as capital 1, 4
Rio Grande do Sul, 7–8, 87, 98
Riocentro incident, 41, 70, 86
Roman Catholicism, 67
Rogers, William P., U.S. Secretary of State, 157
Roosevelt, Franklin D., 143
Root, Elihu, U.S. Secretary of State, 142
Rubber boom, 8
Rural Labor Party. See PRT
Rural workers: demands of, 62;

dependence of, 47; political loyalty of, 47
Rusk, Dean, U.S. Secretary of State, 155

Sales tax revenues, 88
Salgado, Plínio, 12, 98
Salvador, as capital, 2
Santa Catarina, 8
São Paulo, 80, 86–88: affluence of, 9; insurrection of, 11; strength of, 8; strikes of, 111
Schmidt, Helmut, 61
Schwartzman, Simon, 102
SEAP, 77
S and D. See Security and Development
Second Republic, 74
Security and Development (S and D), 130, 135–37, 150
SEPLAN. See Ministry of Planning.
Sergeants' revolt (1963), 20, 51: politicization of, 22
SESC, 66
Shipping, control of, 2–3
Silva, Golbery do Couto e, 29, 75, 101, 127, 135
Silva, Luis Inácio da (Lula), 43, 61, 111–12, 117; trial of, 86
Silveira, Antônio Azeredo da, 156–57, 160–61
Sinimbu, Visconde de, 84
Slavery, 6–7
SNI. See National Information Service
Soares, Mario, 111
Social Democratic Party. See PSD
Social: inequality, 3; order, under the empire, 5; revolution, danger of, 56–57; services, political bartering of, 49
Socialist Labor Party. See PST
Souza, Washington Luis Pereira de, President, 10–11
Soviet Union: influence on Brazilian Communist Party, 15; overtures to Kubitschek, 147
Spain, 1
Stabilization plan, economic, 19

State Department of Political and Social Order (DOPS), 88
State enterprises, 171–72: reduction of, 79; Vale do Rio Doce, mining, 14; Volta Redonda, steel plant, 14
Stepan, Alfred, 125
STM. See Superior Military Court
STF. See Supreme Court
Strikes, prohibition of, 36, 61
Students, political activity of, 33–34, 52, 54, 69–70
Sublegenda, 42, 105, 115
SUDAM, 78
SUDENE, 78, 151
Sugar and Alcohol Institute, 56
Superior Electoral Court (TSE), 84–85, 110–11
Superior Labor Court (TST), 85
Superior Military Court (STM), 85–86, 111
Superior War College (ESG), 27, 30, 32, 35, 55, 126–27, 130, 136, 154: alumni groups of, 55; basic text of, 134; command of, 132; concept of elite, 132; establishment of, 132; membership diversity of, 133; national security curriculum of, 133; political training of, 134; pro-U.S. attitudes of, 150, 152; traditions of, 133
Supreme Court (STF), 75, 84, 96

Tarso, Paulo de, 69
Távora, Juarez, 17, 99
Tax on Industrial Products (IPI), 88
Taxation: modernized, 28; prerogatives of, 87
TCU. See Tribunal de Contas da União
"Technobureaucratic elite," 77–78
"technocrats," 55
Television, as campaign tool, 50–51
Tenentes, 11, 32, 87, 99, 124, 129: leadership of, 9; rebellion of, 9
Tenentismo, 27
Terrorism, leftist, 35–36
Third World, alignment with, 156
Tiradentes, 3, 141

Torture, 38, 86
Trade: controversies on, 163; freedom of, 4; with Nicaragua, 162; with U.S., 142–43; with U.S.S.R., 162
"Trade Union Republic," threat of, 22
Trade unions, dissolution of, 27
Tribunal de Contas da União Contas (TCU), 82
TRT. See Regional Labor Courts
TSE. See Superior Electoral Court
TST. See Superior Labor Court
Tupi language, 2
Tuthill, John, U.S. Ambassador, 155

UDN (União Democrática Nacional), 14–18 passim, 27, 31, 35, 49, 92, 93, 98–102 passim, 105
UNE. See National Students Union
União Democrática Nacional. See UDN
USAID. See United States Agency for International Development
United States: accusation of coup involvement, 149; and Brazil, 141–42; Brazilian policy toward, 20; economic aid to Brazil, 14, 153; decline of global leadership of, 155, 163; decline in friendship with, 155; influence of, after World War I, 9; influence on Brazilian constitution, 7; on political parties, 30; minor conflicts with, 141–42; trade with Brazil, 142–43; wartime alliance with Brazil, 144
United States Aid for International Development (USAID), 31, 69, 151
United States War College, as model for ESG, 132
Universities, in colonial South America, 5
Upper class, indolence of, 3

Urban guerrilla war, 35–36
Uruguay, 4, 24

Vale do Rio Doce, 14
Valladares, Benito, 68
Vance, Cyrus, U.S. Secretary of State, 159
Vargas, Getúlio, President, 5, 10–11, 17, 20, 27, 50, 56, 73–74, 80, 82, 87, 89, 91–92, 98, 117–18, 129–30, 143–45, 152; attempted assassination of, 12; economic program of, 14; exclusion of Integralistas, 12; "Father of the Poor," 16; ouster of, 13, 15; policies of, 11, 13; political style of, 14; state capitalism of, 57; suicide of, 16, 74, 81, 146–47
Vargas, Ivette, 85, 110
Venturini, General Danilo, 62
Vidigal Filho, Luíz Eulálio Bueno, 63–64
Vila Militar, 30, 34
Viscount of Cabo Frio Foundation, 76
Volkswagen, labor negotiations, 61, 64
Volta Redonda Steel Plant, 14, 144–45
Voters: appeal to, 50; rural registration of, 47
Voting: practices of, 93; strength, 10
Voto vinculado, 42

Walesa, Lech, 111
Walters, Vernon, U.S. military attache, 150–51, 162
Washington Luíz. See Souza, Washington Luíz Pereira de
Westinghouse, 158–59
White collar employees, 66
World War I, Brazil in, 9, 142
World War II, Brazil in, 144
Writ of security, 83

About the Authors

Robert Wesson is a senior research fellow at the Hoover Institution of Stanford University and a professor of political science at the University of California, Santa Barbara. He received an M.A. from the Fletcher School of Law and Diplomacy, and a Ph.D. from Columbia University. His books include *Foreign Policy for a New Age*; *State Systems*; *Modern Government: Three Worlds of Politics*; *The United States and Brazil: Limits of Influence*; *Democracy in Latin America: Promise and Problems*; *U.S. Influence in Latin America in the 1880s* (ed.); and *The New Military Politics in Latin America* (ed.).

David V. Fleischer is an associate professor of political science at the University of Brasília. He received his B.A. from Antioch College and an M.A. and Ph.D. from the University of Florida. He worked in Brazil as a Peace Corpsman and served with the Department of State on the Brazilian desk. He has been visiting professor at the Federal University of Minas Gerais in Belo Horizonte, the University of Florida, and SUNY-Albany. He has published numerous studies of Brazilian politics, especially on elites, electoral systems, parties and legislatures. In 1982, he was named to the select Ministry of Justice Commission to draft legislation for the new mixed electoral system to be put into effect in 1986.